Caste Re-Configurations and U.P. ELECTIONS

Caste Re-Configurations and U.P. ELECTIONS

SUNIT SINGH

KANISHKA PUBLISHERS, DISTRIBUTORS
NEW DELHI-110 002

in Association with

G.B. Pant Social Science Institute, Allahabad

KANISHKA PUBLISHERS, DISTRIBUTORS
4697/5-21A, Ansari Road, Daryaganj
New Delhi-110 002.
Phones : 327 0497, 328 8285
Fax : 011-328 8285

First Published 2002

ISBN 81-7391-499-0

PRINTED IN INDIA

Published by Madan Sachdeva for Kanishka Publishers, Distributors, 4697/5-21A, Ansari Road, Daryaganj, New Delhi-110 002; Typeset by Arora Computer Point, Delhi, and Printed at Nice Printing Press, Delhi.

Foreword

The socio-political environment in Uttar Pradesh during the preceding decade was volatile in nature. The state did not enjoy the privilege of a stable government formed by one party running through the full term of five years. It witnessed the rise and fall of many coalition governments. The alliances between the political parties did not last long. Barring the Bhartiya Janata Party and the Samajwadi Party, all other political parties in the state suffered splits. The chief ministership of the state changed hands seven times. The state experienced four Lok Sabha and three State Assembly elections. It was the decade of unstable governments, splits in parties and frequent mid-term polls.

All the more significant was the fact that whereas before 1996 the alliances were formed to check the ascendancy of the BJP, there was no hesitation among parties, barring the SP, in forming alliances with the BJP in the post-1996 period. Under these circumstances it was felt pertinent to study the attitude and behaviour of the electorate and patterns of their electoral participation.

The present volume is an outcome of the studies conducted during the Lok Sabha elections of 1996, 1998 and 1999 and the State Assembly election of 1996. Thus, it provides an insight into the behaviour of the electorate in the post-1996 period.

All the studies included in the volume were conducted by Dr. Sunit Singh, a Research Associate in the Institute and were funded as internal projects by the G.B. Pant Social Science Institute, Allahabad.

By introducing an Achievement Status Index based on the empirical data collected through an extensive survey. Dr. Singh has been able to demonstrate the existence and size of the stratification among different caste groups. He has classified the electorate into three strata—high, medium and low. It has been presented that all the caste groups have representation in the higher strata of the society and similar is the case of medium and lower strata also. The proportion of the electorate in different strata differs in the caste groups. The sample covered was representative to the universe and therefore the patterns of stratification emerging from the study are realistic.

He has maintained that all the castes have social networks within them, which consist of a nucleus surrounded by numerous orbits. The prosperous dominant sections of the caste constitute the nuclei while others are situated on outer orbits in accordance with their economic strength. The aggregate size of all the nuclei is about 12 percent of the total electorate. These nuclei control the entire caste-based social network and are dominant in social, economic and political spheres. The nineties have seen the state power being captured by them, which they have used to promote their economic interests. He has compared his findings with the results of the NSS regarding assets ownership. The NSS data reveals that 13.5 percent households own more than half of the total assets in the rural areas. Thus, there is not much of a difference with regard to the 12 percent dominant sections found out as nuclei by Dr. Singh through his Achievement Status Index and the 13.5 percent through the NSS data on the basis of average value of asset ownership per household.

The study brings out another significant feature of the electorate behaviour. It emerged that the electorate denounced the political parties and their leaders. At the time of elections, however, they were found enthusiastically voting for one party or the other and running after the leaders. The social networks played a decisive role here. The electorate situated on different orbits of the social network follows the nuclei. This bond is determined by the expectation of the continuance of the current gains or the likelihood of the future gains. Thus the role of personal gains accruing to the electorate is the key factor in the enhancement of the capability among the nuclei to mobilise the electorate in its favour.

In the study it has been maintained that the identities of political parties are no more based upon ideologies, policies and programmes. The parties are identified with different caste combinations. These caste combinations are utilised to capture the state power.

It has been established in the study that the four caste-based formations — the upper castes, the OBCs, the SCs and the Muslims — effective in the pre-1996 period of the decade had reached its plateau in 1996. After the 1996 elections, the State got a hung assembly, which necessitated a new configuration of social forces. The earlier caste combinations disintegrated and new combinations consisting of erstwhile antagonistic castes appeared. The parties are continuously engaged in the process of such reconfigurations one after the other.

I hope that the study will attract attention of the social scientists and will inspire further research in this direction.

January 15, 2002

Janak Pandey
Director
GB Pant Social Science Institute, Allahabad

Acknowledgements

The present book is a longitudinal study to examine the dynamics of voting behaviour during the general elections in Uttar Pradesh. It covers three Lok Sabha elections of 1996, 1998 and 1999 and the State Assembly elections of 1996. During each election the studies were organised independently. Yet there was continuity in the sense that the studies attempted to analyze the determinants of the electorate's attitude and behaviour as individuals as well as members of the group. The methodology and the location of all the studies were the same.

All the four studies were funded entirely by the G.B. Pant Social Science Institute, Allahabad. I owe a special debt to the Institute for supporting the studies as internal research projects.

I acknowledge my profound gratitude to Professor Janak Pandey, the Director of the Institute who enriched the studies through his comments and suggestions. But for his inspiring guidance and ungrudging support and insistence the book would not have been completed. I am also thankful to the former director of the Institute Professor S.P. Nagendra who encouraged us to take up the study of 1996 Lok Sabha elections and generously sanctioned the necessary support for the purpose.

I express my sincere gratitude to the faculty of the Institute who offered many valuable suggestions in course of discussions held from time to time on the findings presented during the internal seminars of the Institute. Mr. R. N. Goel undertook enormous pains in going through the manuscript and getting it ready for publication but formal words can hardly express the depth of my feelings for his help.

A team of experienced and sincere investigators who collected the field data under adverse circumstances performed the hardest part of the job. The team included Mohd. Israel, Anwar Naeem Siddiqui, Madan Gopal Gupta, Gyan Nath Jha, Brijesh Kumar Singh and Hari Kant Upadhyaya. I sincerely thank all of them.

Mr. Anjesh Kumar, the Computer Programmer in the Institute worked tirelessly and with a sense of urgency in providing statistical support in the shortest possible time. I owe special thanks to him and also to Mr. Pramod Kumar Agarwal, Mr. B.J. Bose and Mr. Sandeep Kumar Jaiswal of the computer centre who took enormous amount of pains in typing the manuscripts. I am also thankful to Mr. Shree Shanker Tewari, Dy. Librarian and the staff of the library of the Institute who provided all support in supplying the material whenever required.

For the forthcoming and willing cooperation by the District Election Office and its staff in providing full access to the official records, I thank them.

The respondents selected for various surveys are particularly to be thanked for they allowed themselves to be interviewed despite inconveniences. Their freely expressed views have been the real strength of the present endeavour.

I am aware of the limitation in acknowledging the help and support from quarters not mentioned here but I acknowledge my sincere gratitude to all those colleagues and friends who encouraged me in completing this study.

Sunit Singh

Contents

Foreword *v*

Acknowledgements *ix*

List of Abbreviations *xiii*

List of Tables *xiv*

1. Introduction 1

2 The Context and The Caste 15

3. Stratification Among Caste Groups 43

4. Electorate's Attitude Towards Electoral Processes 61

5. Experimenting with Caste Re-Configurations 78

6. Shift in Party Preferences 123

7. Conclusions 177

Appendices 195

Bibliography 231

Index 237

List of Abbreviations

ASI	Achievement Status Index
AVA	Average Value of Assets
BJP	Bhartiya Janata Party
BSP	Bahujan Samaj Party
CAG	Comptroller and Auditor General
Cong	Indian National Congress (I)
HDI	Human Development Index
JD	Janata Dal
MBC	Most Backward Castes
MLA	Member of the Legislative Assembly
MP	Member of the Parliament
NSS	National Sample Survey
OBC	Other Backward Castes
PWD	Public Works Department
SC	Scheduled Castes
SP	Samajwadi Party
ST	Scheduled Tribes
UCH	Upper Caste Hindus
UF	United Front
UP	Uttar Pradesh

List of Tables

Table 2.1 Basic Demographic Data of U.P. and India 17
Table 2.2 Average Annual Growth Rate of UP and India, 1951-56 to 1992-96 18
Table 2.3 Gap between Per Capita State and National Income 1950-51 to 1995-96 19
Table 2.4 State-wise Human Development Index (HDI) in India 19
Table 2.5 Sectoral Composition of State Income (Current Prices) 20
Table 2.6 Sectoral Distribution of Main Workers 1981 and 1991 21
Table 2.7 Percentage Distribution of Workers by Category of Employment in UP 23
Table 2.8 Estimates of Poverty for U. P. 23
Table 2.9 Population Below the Poverty Line in U.P. as Percentage of All-India 24
Table 2.10 Unemployment Rates in UP as Percent of Labour Force 25
Table 2.11 Statewise Productivity of Male Agricultural Worker (1992-95) 25
Table 2.12 Employment in Organized Sector in Uttar Pradesh 26
Table 2.13 Estimated Number and Percentage Distribution of Rural Households by Household Types 27
Table 2.14 Distribution of Rural Households by Broad Size-Classes of Land Owned and Land Operated in U.P. 28
Table 2.15 Distribution of Operational Holdings In U.P. by Size-Categories 29

Table 2.16	Average Value of Assets Per Household by Size-Classes of Land Owned in Rural Uttar Pradesh	31
Table 2.17	Distribution of Households and Corresponding Average Value of Assets per Household by Asset Holding Groups	32
Table 2.18	Distribution of Assets in Value Terms (Rs.) between Different Asset Holding Groups	33
Table 2.19	Number of Tractor and Tractor Trollies Owned by Households of Different Size of Operational Land Holdings	35
Table 2.20	Pattern of Sharecropping among Rural Households by Size Category of Land Owned	38
Table 2.21	Area and Demographic Statistics of Allahabad and U.P.	40
Table 2.22	Occupational Distribution of Main Workers in Allahabad and U.P.	41
Table 2.23	Percentage Distribution of Operational Land Holdings by Size-Category in Allahabad and U.P.	41
Table 2.24	Number of Electors by Lok Sabha and Vidhan Sabha Constituencies during 1996 Parliament Election	42
Table 3.1	Distribution of Effective Sample and Sample Loss	46
Table 3.2	Rural-Urban Distribution of Voters	49
Table 3.3	Caste-wise Distribution of Voters	51
Table 3.4	Occupational Distribution of Voters	52
Table 3.5	Classification of Voters by Educational Levels	53
Table 3.6	Age-wise Distribution of Voters	53
Table 3.7	Weights to Various Occupations	57
Table 3.8	Weights to Different Educational Standards	57
Table 3.9	Distribution of Voters in Different Caste Groups by Achievement Status Index	58
Table 4.1	Sample Size and its Classification by Coverage	63
Table 4.2	Mean Values of Voters' Attitude Towards Electoral Processes	69
Table 4.3	Means (Scale Range 1-5) of Items Related to Voters' Political Affiliation and Identity	73
Table 4.4	Means (Scale Range 1-3) of Determinants of Voting Decisions	74
Table 5.1	Factors Responsible for Sample Loss	90
Table 5.2	Distribution of Sample Respondents by Caste, Domicile and Gender	93

Table 5.3	Mean Value of Various Forms of Political Participation	96
Table 5.4	Mean Value of the Determinants of Vote	99
Table 5.5	Mean Value of the Perception about the Campaign Strategies for Wooing the Voters	100
Table 5.6	Caste-wise Distribution of Electorates by Party of their Choice	113
Table 6.1	Factors Responsible for Sample Losses	139
Table 6.2	Caste-wise Distribution of Respondent by Domicile and Gender	140
Table 6.3	Occupation-wise Distribution of Respondents	141
Table 6.4	Mean Values of Items of Political Participation and Party Affiliation in 1998 &1999	143
Table 6.5	Mean Values of Determinants of Voting Decisions in 1998 and 1999	145
Table 6.6	Mean Values of the Perception about the Campaign Strategies of Different Parties for Wooing the Voters	147
Table 6.7	Partisanship and Shift in Preferences by Castes and Caste-Groups during 1998 &1999	150
Table 6.8	Party Candidates and their Caste in Allahabad and Phulpur Parliament Constituencies	160
Table 6.9	Comparative Chart of Caste-wise Composition of Support Bases of Different Parties: 1998 & 1999	170

1

Introduction

The present chapter has been divided into three sections. In the first section the relevance of popular participation in governance through elections has been highlighted. The second section has dealt with a contemporary phenomenon of the emergence of caste as a political entity and its effects on the Indian democracy. In the last section the objective of the present book and its plan have been introduced.

Democracy and Elections

The formation of popular government by the means of elections has been under debate for a long time. No better alternative has emerged as yet. Elections are an acceptable platform for communication between state power and the people. The rulers obtain legal and moral validity periodically for their authority to rule through elections. Looked at from the point of view of the people, the elections are means of their active intervention in the power play. It is the central institution for popular participation in government. Without elections the mass of the population has no means to influence the choice of the nation's governors (Rose 1980; 1). Therefore participation of voters in the general elections is an important indication of maturity of a democratic order. Electoral exercises are the basic ingredient of the democratic process. One widely and rightly used index of democratization in a political system is the proportion of the potential electorate that actually votes (Burnham 1980; 35). It is only at the time of elections that the voter finds opportunity to express himself on the development, character and direction of democracy, while the new generation brings forth it's rising aspirations. The suppressed dissatisfaction and disillusionment of others is also raised peacefully through the elections. Elections are a serious affair, a vital part of the democratic process by which people exercise their political choice and their right as citizen (Seminar 1996; 12). The results of general elections mirror the individual ideas in totality. As such, during general elections various institutions use nearly all available means of communication in one form or the other at a competitive level. Elections are very important and clear test of the rise and fall of various ideologies and organisations and institutions linked with them.

Elections are held periodically in most of the countries of the world. Adult citizens obtain the right to vote in elections. There are countries where the right to vote is automatically conferred upon an individual with the attainment of the prescribed age. In others, it is the duty of the individual to get himself registered as a voter. Likewise, the utilization of right to vote is voluntary in some countries while, in others there is provision for punishment for non-participation. In some countries the governments are elected directly by the voters, in others, it is indirectly in two or more stages. Be it as it may, the right to vote was—and still is—supposed to be the key to share in the political process (Ganguly & Ganguly, 1982). Today the conferment of the right to vote on the attainment of the adulthood may seem so normal but history would testify that people in general, who were out of the orbit of the state power had to undergo through hard struggle in order to attain this right. Some social scientists have seen the conferment of the right to vote contemptuously as a reductive event (Singh 1996; 41), for they say the political right of the citizen is reduced to casting of vote only. There is no opportunity for an electorate, in their opinion, to assert his political rights before and after the elections. In spite of all this, the right to vote has been treated as entirely personal decision of an individual and at the same time voting occupies a central place in democratic politics (Powell 1980; 5).

In the background stated above it is expected from a state to make large-scale arrangements which include security and law and order during each election. Along with it, all the political parties and candidates plan out for campaign to obtain maximum number of votes in their favour which includes selection of candidates, their nomination, publication of manifestos, campaigning in constituencies through public meetings, rallies, mass contacts etc. Various pressure groups also insist on different parties and candidates to campaign in their favour. Also, greed of power attracts ruling and opposition parties to indulge in election violence and terror. Sometimes the ruling party involves state terror towards the fulfillment of this objective.

Elections are the time when public behaviour finds an unfettered expression. The major facets of a citizen's personality as a candidate, as a sympathizer, as an ideological comrade or an adversary; as an idealist or an opportunist; as a man of settled belief or a power of vacillating emotions; and as a common man, publicly airing his grievances against the system or its specific organs, are brought into sharp focus (Tewari 1993; 56). Thus, general elections are a good occasion for social scientists to review the state of their discipline. This is because no other normal political event has as extensive a reach and as multi-layered an impact on the political system as a general election (Desouza 1996; 36). It has rightly been pointed out that every election is a potential turning point in history and deserves a full study as a contemporary event, an opportunity to observe politicians and party organisations at full stretch, to examine the influence of press and broadcasting, to assess the involvement of ordinary citizens. (Butler, Lahiri & Roy 1989; 5). It is a very challenging task. The best scholarly attempts to understand political processes come in the form of voting behaviour studies. Even if the level of political development may not be as high as one would like it to be, elections in an open polity are more than mere periodical rehearsals for the endorsement of thc assumed structural needs of the system. Voters do learn to act politically and imbibe political elements into their universe of perceptions and evaluations (Sheth 1975; 3).

As pointed out, for each individual there is a point in the multidimensional policy space where he would most prefer the collective decision to be. The farther away a collective choice is from his optimum, the more dissatisfied he is with it. There is thus a direct relationship between distance and dissatisfaction and this is the main determinant of the nature of voting. In the policy space it is dependent on numerous inter-related components of the environment surrounding the behaviour set. Voting behaviour study thus necessitates the observation of the process in its entirety (Ganguly & Ganguly 1982).

As an institution, democracy is not valuable for its own sake; never mind that it has become so popular today that there is no longer any dispute about its being the best form of government. The danger however is that if democracy fails to promote 'communicative competence' despite its popularity, it is bound to degenerate into an oligarchy where a handful of self-serving elite will exercise power in the name of the people (Nagendra 1991; 11).

In the post-green revolution phase a good number of rural leadership came up on the political scene not only at the local or regional level but at the national level also. This leadership was intensely involved in the institutions and processes in the rural areas. They were benefited most with the rural development programmes. Now their attitude and behaviour have taken an assertive form.

Democracy and Caste

After Independence, it was believed that with a liberal democratic constitutional system and universal suffrage, the Indian political system would gradually develop its own processes of democratic decision making, rational administration and modern citizenship. Features such as patronage relations based on caste and religious loyalties and solidarity based on ethnicity were regarded as vestiges of underdevelopment that would go away with greater participation of people in democratic institutions. It was assumed that as the project of nation building gets under way and democratic rights are extended to the people, as the development process also gets under way and more and more people and communities benefit from it all and the sources of poverty, unemployment and human misery are eliminated, and as productive forces unfold and dialectics of history gets working, there will be no need for 'parochial' structures of caste, community, tribe and various feudal vestiges and people will enter into new relationship of a more secular and political kind. These assumptions have since been belied. (Kothari 1997; 440).

For quite a long time the phenomenon of caste based mobilisations was concealed, particularly during the one party dominance system of the Congress party. The fourth general elections (1967) provided overt indications of strengthening of the caste identities during electoral mobilization. It was under the impact of 'anti-manuvad' mobilisations, 'anti and pro-mandal' movements and 'rath yatra' that the general elections in 1991 witnessed the process of polarisation and antagonistic associations of caste and communities in electoral politics. Its climax was visible during the State Assembly elections held in 1993. Thus, electoral mobilization based on castes and other parochial considerations could be categorised into three phases. First, the period of the one party dominance during which dissent was neutralized by compromises and adjustments within the party (1952-1967); second, the phase of overt caste based mobilizations (1967-1985) and third, the period of polarisation of castes in the form of antagonistic associations and their leaders emerging as the principal source of identification (1985 onwards).

Rajni Kothari pointed out that the process of politics is one of identifying and manipulating existing structures in order to mobilize support and consolidate positions. Where the caste structure provides one of the most important organisational clusters in which the population is found to live, politics must strive to organise through such a structure. The alleged casteism in politics is thus no more and no less than politicization of caste. Kothari found an interactive role between caste and politics and concluded that in the process both remain the real actors when he observed that by drawing the caste system into its web of organisation, politics finds material for its articulation and moulds it into its own design. In making politics their sphere of activity, caste and kin groups, on the other hand, get a chance to assert their identity and to strive for positions (Kothari 1970; 442). Rudolph and Rudolph (1987) have observed that the caste associations have brought about fusion and have taught the illiterates to participate in democratic politics. They have enabled disadvantaged groups to find advantage in their numbers. This, according to them, is the democratic reincarnation of caste in modern India. This view has been criticized as a neat generalization imposed on a complex reality. (Kothari 1970; 227).

The group theory of politics regards electorate as a large number of groups and associations who vote in groups. Voting is essentially a group experience. People who work or live or play together are likely to vote for the same candidate (Lazarsfeld, Berelson

& Gaudet 1944; 6-7). About the nature of castes in India in the form of group it was said that these groups were exhaustive, exclusive and discrete; that every person was a member of such a group and of only one; he was clearly recognised by others as a member of his separate group. Membership of his group influences most of his roles and activity; there was high degree of 'role-summation'. No one should try to change his inherited membership and any attempts by individuals to stuff themselves to a higher group were strongly disapproved. It was pointed out that the classical consumption of vote as a rational individual choice is a myth and untrue even in mature democracies. In the western liberal parliamentary democracy the voter has expressly rejected the assumption of that conception, such as rational debate on issues, rational individual choice on vote etc. and has adopted that conception to a situation in which debate is substituted by negotiation, the individual decision by collective group decision. (Kini 1974; 178). In India an individual belonging to a caste joins his group with a view to improve the value position of the whole group. According to this school of thought voting on caste basis is a conscious effort by the group of electorate. Identification with a caste implies a subjective psychological reality influencing the behaviour of the individual. In this sense caste becomes a political category concerned more with the redistribution of power in society and polity (Kini 1974; 166). This school views that the caste has transformed from merely a traditional stratum into a modern type pressure group.

The caste system may have lost some of its ritualistic and traditional functions as the regulator of social behaviour but now it had assumed the new role of regulating political behaviour (Siriskar, 1977; 75). In this sense caste itself became a political category. With a transformed and politicized entity the caste had performed a democratic function in India. Identification with a caste while aspiring for a share in power had in itself been termed as a democratic instinct. It was also democratic in the sense, that having become conscious of the political power of vote, the castes today demand or bargain for opportunities that bring them on par with more advanced sections of the society. It is even probable that caste associations have linked the mass of electorate to the new democratic process, making them comprehensible to people who have politically illiterate and are thus made a success of representative democracy (Kini 1974; 166).

Spatial expansion of caste has also been emphasised. Increasingly, caste is not a local consideration, which works in favour of a candidate of one's own caste. Now caste identities and affiliations are imagined at the level of state, even at the level of the whole country.

It has also been pointed out that the politicization of caste among poorer people has happened due to their disappointment with the Indian state on which they had relied too much for ending their condition of oppression and discrimination. As a result of this disappointment the poorer and socially marginalised sections, including the ethnic and religious minorities, have started seeking out their own futures on the basis of their own identities and numbers. This has led to a mobilization based on caste, sub-caste (including religious minorities), tribe, ethno-regional and such other identities (Kothari 1998; 442).

Sriniwas maintains that the introduction of adult franchise has made caste important. Numerically dominant castes tend to operate as "important pressure groups in politics at the district and state level". At the same time it has been emphasised that although the caste did resurface as a result of democratic processes itself, in its resurfacing it got transformed. The institution of caste has been strengthened by the excessive mobilization of caste sentiments by the politicians in their competition for power and influence. The parties utilise social groups for strengthening their own electoral base, while the latter have tried to utilize parties for gaining a share in the resources being made available through state agencies.

During the late eighties, particularly after Mandal movement, the assertive role of castes in Indian politics was highlighted. Castes have been projected as a modern institution with emancipatory functions for deprived sections (Alam 1999). From politicization to accelerated participation and now the empowerment of historically disadvantaged and marginalised groups was characterized as the revolutionary role of caste in India. This phenomenon has been termed as 'great secular upsurge' (Kothari 1990) as well as 'second democratic upsurge' (Yadav 1998) in Indian politics. Taking a different position Sriniwas and others (1990) maintained that in every caste there are rich and poor people and the rich are oppressors and exploiters of the poor, not only of other disadvantaged castes but of their own caste also. The two positions, so different from each other, would necessitate an in-depth analysis of the ground reality.

Overview of Previous Studies based on Sample Survey Methods

In India the study relating to voters' behaviour based on survey method was pioneered by V.M. Siriskar (1966) with the coverage of the electorate of Poona in 1962 general elections. Although, prior to Siriskar, attempts were made during the first general election to study the voters' preferences and consciousness with the help of survey techniques. Being the initial attempts those studies conducted at Bombay, Hyderabad and Bihar were quite elementary in terms of statistical analysis. Siriskar made use of the panel studies organised in America to analyse the voters' behaviour. His study was built around 1457 voters selected through random sampling, who were contacted three times — two times before and once after the election. The sample was drawn from four assembly segments, which were part of the Lok Sabha constituency of Poona. All these constituencies were urban. During the same period S.P. Verma and C.P. Bhambari (1967) also attempted to study voters' behaviour through sample survey. But the number of constituencies was less, size of sample was small and it was a study based on one time (pre-election) survey with the help of structured schedules. However, this study covered urban as well as rural constituencies simultaneously from Jaipur district in Rajasthan.. Aloo J. Dastur and Usha Mehta (1963) also conducted a study in Bombay during the same general election, contested by the two stalwarts Krishna Menon and Acharya Kriplani. Still, all these studies were not able to throw light on socio-cultural and economic factors of voting behaviour.

In 1967, at the time of the fourth general elections, the voting behaviour studies in India took a major step forward in terms of methodology and coverage. The RPC of Planning Commission of India decided to finance the election studies organised by different scholars in different parts of the country with a common theoretical framework and methodology, so that the results could be made comparable and in turn a profile of the Indian voter in general could be developed. Being a nation-wide effort the common methodology was obviously to neglect the local peculiarities but some of the scholars covered the local dimensions additionally. The areas covered in this venture were Rajasthan (S.P. Verma and Iqbal Narain), Gujrat (Pathak), Bombay city (Aloo J. Dastur), Madhya Pradesh (B.R. Parohit), Punjab and Haryana (B.S. Khanna and Satya Deva) and Uttar Pradesh (Raj Narain). All these studies were panel studies in two waves.

In addition to the above studies with common design, RPC of the Planning Commission sponsored some other worth mentioning studies. Among them two studies based on panel survey have come out in published form. The first one was directed by Yogesh Atal This study had a focus on behaviours of local communities during elections. Its orientation was different from other RPC sponsored studies. Rather than analysing only the voting behaviour of the sample population, it sought to relate political behaviour with communicational development and other processes of modernisation. The methodology followed in this study may be described as a combination of the quantitative techniques of survey research, traditional anthropological techniques of observation, and the techniques of handling documentary evidence-content analysis. This study was conducted in three waves in Etah district of U.P.

Another major study during the fourth general election was conducted by NGS Kini at Nagpur. This study was also sponsored and financed by the RPC and the work was published in 1974. Statistical relationship among variables have been dexterously worked out. His effort to articulate the concept of two cultures empirically was academically stimulating. It was a panel study in two waves. The first wave was administered before the election and the second wave immediately after the election. The size of sample was 300, which worked out to 0.08 percent of the total electorate in Nagpur. The interview was conducted with the help of structured schedules.

Bangendu Ganguly and Mira Ganguly organised panel surveys during 1972 and 1977 general elections. Both the studies followed a multistage sampling procedure. Sampled voters were interviewed in the post election phase. Authors classified the survey data into three broad groups—*(i)* social variables, *(ii)* attitudinal variables and *(iii)* decisional variables. Along with cross-tables and analysis of variance the study included factor and discriminant analyses. The study was developed on hypothetic-deductive-observational procedures. Both the studies were based on the data collected from three West Bengal Lok Sabha constituencies—Calcutta South, Asansol and Diamond Harbour.

Ramashray Roy (1973) presented a comparative study of voters' behaviours during mid-term elections of 1969. The study was conducted at the Centre for Studies in Developing Societies (CSDS) and was supported by the Indian Council of Social Service Research.

Data relating to the voters' behaviour from four states—U.P., Bihar, Punjab and West Bengal, were included in the study. After comparing the data he tried to identify the features of ongoing political processes and electoral behaviour in different parts of the country. Along with this study Roy also organised a study in 1967 general election in Bihar with an extensive field survey.

During 1980 general elections Usha Mehata, Rosebeh Billnona and Usha Thakkar (1981) conducted a study to gauge the voting behaviour and assessed whether the behaviour coincided with the election verdict. They also gave a comparative picture of the voting behaviour in 1977 and 1980 in the four Lok Sabha constituencies of Bombay. The study intensively examined the status of women voters and the role of different political parties, with special reference to the Janata Party, for the uplift of women. The Bombay University supported the study.

The G.B. Pant Social Science Institute, Allahabad organised studies in four Lok Sabha constituencies of Allahabad, Phulpur, Nainital and Garhwal in Uttar Pradesh during 1991 elections. The reports were published in mimeographed form in 1993 edited by L.R. Singh. These studies were based on primary data collected before elections. Selected voters were interviewed with the help of structured schedules.

In recent years, opinion polls have become popular in our country. Such opinion polls are conducted by various market research organisations, usually in collaboration with some newspaper or magazine. These opinion polls are often involved in pre-election surveys. These polls are intended to analyse electorate's responses on various issues. As such, they are a welcome development. But as soon as such polls become manipulative and start serving any particular political party, the purpose of the science of psephology gets defeated. Therefore during the general elections of 1996 the Election Commission restricted the newspapers and magazines from publishing pre-election opinion polls on the ground that they might influence the decision of the voters. Besides, the problems of limited coverage, significance of the questions phrased and the results interpreted were also pointed out. Then, there were issues of the quality of professionalism and motivation of the investigators, lack of honesty in responses on the part of the electorate and the proportion of undecided voters at the time of the survey but who actually voted during the polls. There was another problem of purely statistical analyses of voting behaviour. It neglected thoughtful and broad-based analyses of voting behaviour and its implications in respect of social changes at the groud level that they reflected.

Plan of the Book

The Objective: The present book is a longitudinal study with a multidisciplinary approach to examine the dynamics of voting behaviour during the general elections. It includes three Lok Sabha elections and one State Assembly election in Uttar Pradesh held between 1996 and 1999. The endeavour has been to analyse the institutions and processes that motivated the electorate to participate in the polls, the determinants that influenced the voters' choice and the features of the prevailing electoral environment in the state. An attempt has also been made to explain the situation in which the voter strikes a balance between his choices as an individual and as a part of an aggregate. Frequent elections provided repeated opportunities to study these issues in a comprehensive manner. However, the present book is not simply a compilation of analyses of electorate's behavior during various elections. Rather, it is an attempt to present a composite picture of the electorate's behavior through the period covered.

The Coverage: The location of all the studies was the district of Allahabad. This gave the advantage of compatibility in terms of location over a period of time. The district of Allahabad is situated at such a point that it borders three planning regions of Uttar Pradesh —Eastern, Central and the Bundelkhand. In addition, Allahabad City has a cosmopolitan nature. All these characteristics make this district fairly representative of the state. After the bifurcation in 1995, the district now consists of two Lok Sabha constituencies-Allahabad and Phulpur. Each constituency has five assembly segments.

The Survey: The studies covered in the book were based on sample survey. The sample for each study was selected from the updated voters' list. It was drawn on stratified basis with the help of systematic sampling method. However the size of sample in each survey was not the same. In the first survey of 1996 Lok Sabha elections the sample of 2500 electorate was drawn from all the ten assembly segments falling in the two Lok Sabha constituencies. After facing a sample loss of about 30 percent the effective sample consisted of 1718 respondents. In the second survey conducted during the 1996 Assembly elections the size of effective sample was 265, drawn from the two assembly segments, one each from the two Lok Sabha constituencies under study. In the third survey at the time of 1998 Lok Sabha elections unlike the first survey, only six assembly segments were covered, three each in Allahabad and Phulpur, instead of all the ten assembly segments. Thus, the size of the sample was naturally reduced to 600 and after having a sample loss of about 30 percent, a total of 425 respondents were covered. In the fourth survey, instead of drawing a fresh sample the sample, of the third survey was repeated. In this survey the sample loss got reduced to about 20 percent and the effective size of the sample consisted of 331 respondents. The data of this survey was utilised for comparative analysis of the electorate's attitude and behaviour during the 1998 and the 1999 elections. The duration of the survey was also the same. Incidentally, the team of investigators was also the same. Thus, it can be assumed that the data of 1998 and 1999 surveys were comparable to a large extent. By repeating the sample with the same team of investigators turned out to be of an added advantage. The acquaintance between the two made the communication straight and the data collected became more realistic. With the help of experienced investigators the primary data were collected. Voters were approached for interview only once during each survey because it was assumed that repeated visits of investigators could distort the responses.

The Questionnaire: The questionnaire for the first survey was different from the questionnaires of the following surveys. In the first survey the respondents were asked to express their opinions in terms of binary options i.e. in agreement or disagreement with a given statement. Besides, there were some projective questions also with a view to enable the respondents to express their view freely on certain aspects of political processes. In subsequent surveys projective questions were not included in the questionnaire. Further, instead of binary options, scales were introduced to make the responses quantifiable. There was another reason for doing so. Often, the respondents preferred to situate themselves somewhere between the two extreme positions. Therefore recording the responses on scales was found a better method. These questionnaires were divided into three parts. The first part was devoted to creating confidence in the respondent by the investigator. The second part consisted of items on opinions and attitudes of respondents on various issues of electoral processes while the third part related to background information of the respondents. By and large the questionnaires were kept unchanged in the last three surveys. The state was experiencing unprecedented volatile political changes at a fast pace. In this situation a few questions had to be added in the questionnaires with every new election to elicit the responses to the new situation. The questionnaires were improved and standardized after going through pilot surveys at each time. The questionnaires were prepared in Hindi language, which is the mother tongue of the people of the region covered. Hence, in case any respondent or his family member or any one in the field desired to go through the questionnaire he could understand the purpose of the survey. It was helpful in providing a foundation for confidence building between the investigator and the respondent.

The Chapters: The book is divided into seven chapters. In the introductory chapter the relevance of popular participation in governance through elections for a democratic system has been discussed. A brief description of the contemporary phenomenon of caste-based voting has also been presented. Besides, the chapter includes an overview of the voting behaviour studies based on sample surveys. The second chapter has been divided into two sections. In the first section the prevailing socio-economic conditions of UP vis-a-vis India have been discussed. It provides a contextual background, which influences the political mobilisation and electoral behaviour in the State. In the second section the socio-economic features and a brief electoral history of Allahabad have been outlined. The third chapter is based on the survey conducted during the Lok Sabha elections of 1996. In this chapter an endeavour has been made to capture the prevailing stratification among the different caste groups on the basis of an Achievement Status Index (ASI). The fourth chapter is based on the findings of the study conducted during the State Assembly elections held in 1996. In this chapter the attitude and behaviour of the electorate towards the electoral processes and the determinants of their voting choices have been presented. The analysis presented in the fifth chapter goes beyond the caste group level. It includes the study of the attitude and behaviour of the electorate in terms of their castes instead of caste groups. The process of caste reconfiguration in the state politics experimented during the Lok Sabha elections of 1998 has been outlined in this chapter. The sixth chapter is based on the findings of the election study of the 1999 Lok Sabha elections. The analysis on political participation, determinants of voting, electoral environment, shift in party preferences and the losses and gains to parties due to the changing caste alliances have been presented in this chapter. In the concluding chapter, some emerging trends in the socio-economic and political environment of the state have been analysed. The dynamics of certain institutions and processes, which determined the nature of the governance and development in the State during the nineties has been presented in this chapter.

2

The Context and The Caste

The present chapter has been divided into two sections. In the first section the prevailing socio-economic conditions of UP vis-a-vis India have been discussed. It provides a contextual background that influences the political mobilisation and electoral behaviour in the State.

In the second section the socio-economic features of Allahabad have been outlined. The similarities regarding these features between the State and the district of Allahabad have also been delineated.

I

The Context—Uttar Pradesh[1]

Uttar Pradesh, being the most populous state in India has the highest share of 16.4 percent in country's population and homes about 140 million people. In terms of population size it would be the seventh largest nation in the world. The state is situated in the northern parts of India. It has international boundaries with Nepal and China in the north. At the same time it has common boundary with six

1. The Hill region of Uttar Pradesh comprising 13 districts was constituted as a separate state named—Uttaranchal in November 2000. In the present study Uttar Pradesh denotes the state as it stood before the bifurcation.

Indian states namely Himachal Pradesh, Haryana, Delhi, Rajasthan, Madhya Pradesh and Bihar. It is also the fourth largest state in India in terms of area, encompassing 294 thousand square kms., which is about 9.0 percent of the country's area.

Uttar Pradesh has been divided into five planning zones—Hill, Western, Central, Eastern and Bundelkhand. For administrative purposes the 83 districts of the state have been grouped into 19 commissionaries. The state has 348 sub-divisions, 904 development blocks, 1,12,803 populated villages and 702 cities and urban agglomerations (Statistical Diary, UP, 1999).

The total population of the state was 88.34 million in 1971. It increased to 110.86 million in 1981 and further to 139.11 million in 1991. The increase in population in these two decades, 1971-81 and 1981-91, was almost the same, at 25.49 percent and 25.48 percent respectively. As against these trends, the increase in the country's population shows a declining trend, from 24.66 percent between 1971-81 to 23.85 percent between1981-91 (Table 2.1).

A lower share in the country's area with higher share in its population has led to a higher density of population. The density of population in the state was 473 persons per square km. in 1991 against 274 for the country.

The population of the scheduled castes, the weakest and most disadvantaged section of the society, is 29.28 million, about 21.0 percent of the state's population, against a lower share of their population in the country, at 16.5 percent only.

Uttar Pradesh has the highest birth rate among all Indian states. At the same time the death rate is not much different from the national average (Table 2.1). This has caused an extremely worrisome demographic situation in the state (GOUP 1999; 25) More so, the survival chances in the state are very low. Female life expectancy, for instance, is still below 55 years, and the under-five mortality rate is as high as 141 per thousand. Among all major Indian states, Uttar Pradesh has the highest under-five mortality rate, the second highest crude death rate, and third lowest life expectancy figure. The number of maternal deaths per 100,000 live births in Uttar Pradesh continued to be as high as 931 in mid-eighties. Thus, life in Uttar Pradesh is short and precarious. This has created a social attitude, which has been responsible for higher fertility rates. People take chances with more births in the hope that some of them would survive even if some die. In fact, Uttar Pradesh has made comparatively little

Table 2.3
Gap between Per Capita State and National Income 1950-51 to 1995-96

(in rupees)

Year	*Per Capita Income*		*Absolute Gap*	*Relative Gap %*
	U.P.	*India*		
1950-51	267	259	8	3.0
1960-61	306	252	54	21.4
1970-71	486	633	147	23.2
1980-81	1278	1630	352	21.6
1985-86	1999	2730	731	26.8
1990-91	3590	4983	1393	28.0
1995-96	5983	9321	3338	35.8

Source: Plan Documents of Uttar Pradesh.

Table 2.4
State-wise Human Development Index (HDI) in India

Sl. No.	*Major States*	*Life Expectancy of Birth Projected for 1986-91*	*Life Percentage 1991*	*State Domestic Product Capita at Current Prices 1988-89*	*Human Deve-lopment Index (HDI)*
1.	Andhra Pradesh	60.70	44.09	3211	0.30
2.	Bihar	57.60	38.48	2111	0.11
3.	Gujrat	59.90	61.29	4893	0.53
4.	Haryana	62.70	55.85	5537	0.60
5.	Karnataka	62.70	56.04	3787	0.46
6.	Kerala	68.70	89.79	3146	0.75
7.	Madhya Pradesh	55.50	64.20	2404	0.14
8.	Maharashtra	62.40	64.87	5362	0.64
9.	Orrisa	56.10	49.09	2793	0.21
10.	Punjab	62.50	58.51	6274	0.54
11.	Rajasthan	58.20	38.55	2923	0.19
12.	Tamil Nadu	60.80	62.66	3593	0.45
13.	Uttar Pradesh	51.90	41.60	2764	0.07
14.	West Bengal	59.70	59.70	3542	0.39

Source: Annual Plan, 1995-96, Government of Uttar Pradesh, p. 59.

important indicators i.e. *(i)* State Domestic Product (SDP) per capita, *(ii)* Literacy percentage and *(iii)* Life expectancy. According to this index also Uttar Pradesh is found to be the most backward among the major fourteen states of the country (Table 2.4). The low level of human resource development reflects the substantial under investment in education and health services in the state (GOUP, 1999, 25).

Sectoral Distribution of Income and Workers

The sectoral composition of state income in UP has registered a noticeable change during the period between 1981-91. The share of primary sector that includes agriculture and allied activities, has declined sharply from 52.3 to 42.6 percent. The contribution of the secondary sector comprising manufacturing and construction industry, rose from 15.3 to 20.8 percent whereas the share of the tertiary sector grew from 32.4 to 36.6 percent during this period (Table 2.5).

Table 2.5
Sectoral Composition of State Income (Current Prices)

Period	*Percent Share in State Income*		
	Primary Sector	*Secondary Sector*	*Tertiary Sector*
1980-81	52.3	15.3	32.4
1985-86	45.2	18.5	36.3
1990-91	42.6	20.8	36.6
1995-96	41.6	20.8	37.6

Source: Plan Documents of U.P.

However, the occupational classification of the main workers indicates that there has not been any perceptible change in the sectoral distribution of work force in the state during 1981 to 1991. With a modest decline in the percentage share (from 74.5 percent to 72.2 percent) agriculture and allied activities continue to occupy the dominant position in the state economy. With the exception of only three states—Bihar, Madhya Pradesh and Orissa, all other major states in India have smaller proportion of workers dependent on agriculture and allied activities than U.P. During this period the annual growth rate of cultivators was merely 1.5 percent whereas in case of workers engaged in mining and quarrying, it was as high as

4.8 and for agricultural labourers it was 3.9 percent (Table 2.6). Thus, the growth in the proportion of rural labourers has been substantially higher than in that of cultivators. If we look at distribution of the state income we find that the share of agriculture and allied sector has drastically declined from 52 percent in 1981 to 42 percent in 1991. The implication of this phenomenon is that although agriculture and allied sector still engage the largest work force and generate highest proportion of income but during the decade 1981-91 other sectors have generated relatively higher income than agriculture. It also indicates that the agriculture sector in the state is registering very slow growth. It is in the state of stagnation if not decline. The annual growth rate continued to remain unchanged at a low level of 2.7 percent during the period of VI, VII and VIII Five-Year Plans. This rate was 5.7 percent per annum during the V Plan. The average income per worker in this sector is bound to decline over the years. The continuous erosion in the income of workers in the sector which is employing 70 percent of the work force is obviously harmful to the economic development the state.

Table 2.6
Sectoral Distribution of Main Workers 1981 and 1991

Sl. No.	*Sector*	*Workers (in lakh) 1981*		*Workers (in lakh) 1981*		*Annual Growth Rate During 1981-91*
1.	Cultivators	189.58	(58.52)	220.31	(53.27)	1.51
2.	Agricultural Labourers	51.77	(15.98)	78.33	(18.94)	4.23
3.	Plantation/Forestry/Fisheries Livestock & hunting	1.77	(0.55)	2.96	(0.72)	5.28
4.	Mining & Quarrying	0.20	(0.06)	0.35	(0.08)	5.76
5.	Primary Sector	243.32	(75.11)	301.95	(73.00)	2.20
6.	Manufacturing household	29.22	(9.02)	32.06	(7.75)	0.93
	(a) industry	12.02	(3.71)	9.97	(2.41)	-1.60
	(b) Non-household Industry	17.20	(5.31)	22.08	(5.34)	2.50
7.	Construction	3.30	(1.02)	5.10	(1.23)	4.45
8.	Secondary Sector	32.52	(10.04)	37.62	(9.10)	1.30
9.	Trade & Commerce	14.69	(4.53)	25.51	(6.17)	5.68
10.	Transport Storage and Communication	6.65	(2.05)	7.71	(1.86)	1.51
11.	Other Services	26.79	(8.27)	41.28	(9.98)	4.42
12.	Tertiary Sector	48.13	(14.86)	74.50	(18.01)	4.50

Figures in parentheses represent the percentage share to total workforce.
Source: Figures are of the respective censuses.

The share of work force in the manufacturing sector has declined from 8.8 percent in 1981 to 7.8 percent in 1991 (Table 2.6). This fact taken together with the decline in workforce in agriculture and allied activities implies that the workforce shifted from the latter was not absorbed in the former. The manufacturing sector is the key sector for the development of any economy. It provides stability and strength to the economy. Therefore, the decline of even one percent point in the share of workers in this sector is damaging to the state economy.

Within the manufacturing sector the proportion of workers employed in non-household industries has remained unchanged (5.3 percent) between 1981 and 1991. However, in absolute terms their number has increased from 1.72 million to 2.21 million during this period. The annual growth rate was at par with the growth rate of total work force in the State. On the contrary, the proportion of workers in the household industry sector has declined from 3.7 percent to 2.4 percent during this period which in absolute terms amounts to 1.2 million to 1.0 million, registering a negative growth rate of -1.6 percent per annum. All these figures indicate that most of the growth in this sector was contributed mainly by capital intensive industries with labour intensive industries receding into background (GOUP 1996; 47).

The percentage share of workforce registered an increasing trend only in the tertiary sector that includes trade and commerce, transport, storage and communication and other services. The relative share increased from 14.9 percent in 1981 to 18 percent in 1991 which means the shift of workers from cultivation and household industry has been absorbed mainly by this sector.

Thus, during the period between 1981 and 1991 six major activities-mining and quarrying, plantations and forestry, agricultural labour, construction, trade and commerce and other services have registered higher annual growth rates (Table 2.5). These activities could absorb overwhelmingly a large number of unskilled or semi-skilled workers and their level of income was very low. It may be summarized that the bulk of additional employment has been generated in low-paid activities (Singh 2000; 90). The Table 2.7 reveals another significant feature of changes in the nature of between 1977-78 and 1993-94 workforce in the state. The share of workers engaged in self-employment has decreased by 0.21 percent points and in regular salaried employment the decline was 0.98 percent points whereas the share of casual workers increased by 1.19 percent points. These figures reflect the increasing trend of casualisation of labour in the state.

Table 2.7
Percentage Distribution of Workers by Category of Employment in UP

Category	*1987 43rd round -88*	*1993 50th round -94*
Self employed	71.80	71.59
Regular employed	9.76	8.78
Casual employed	18.44	19.63
Total	100.00	100.00

Source: NSS reports.

Poverty and Unemployment

The state is identified as one of the poorest states in India. The widespread poverty can be visualized in every part of the state in the form of very low standards of living among majority of the population. It is true that in terms of percentage of total population the poverty level has come down over the years. The percentage of population below the poverty line was 49.2 percent in 1977-78, 47.2 percent in 1983, about 42 percent in 1987-88 and 40 percent in 1993-94 (Table 2.8). However, in absolute terms, the actual number of persons below the poverty line increased from 50.60 million in 1977-78 to 60.44 million in 1993-94. (Table 2.8) Thus during the period of last fifteen years (1977-94) nearly 10 million persons were added to the population living below the poverty line. This shows that during this period every year more than six lakh people were being added to the population living below the poverty line.

Table 2.8
Estimates of Poverty for U. P.

Year	*Percentage*			*Number (in Lakh)*		
	Rural	*Urban*	*State*	*Rural*	*Urban*	*State*
1973-74	56.53	59.48	56.98	449.99	84.87	534.86
1977-78	47.60	57.07	49.19	407.41	98.42	505.83
1983	46.45	50.27	47.19	442.76	114.78	557.54
1987-88	41.10	45.22	41.99	412.03	125.02	537.05
1993-94	42.28	35.39	40.85	496.17	108.28	604.46

Source: Report of Expert Group, Planning Commission, Government of India, July 1993 and Draft Ninth Five Year Plan Volume I, Planning Commission, Government of India, p. 48.

The increase in the intensity of poverty in the State also becomes evident from the data on poverty in Uttar Pradesh with respect to that of all-India. It would be observed that the population below poverty line in the State was 16.63% in 1973-74 which increased to 17.17% in 1987-88 (Table 2.9). This is indicative of deterioration in U. P.'s relative poverty position in the country over the years. Uttar Pradesh had not only a substantial proportion of the total poor population of the country but there was also an increase in this proportion.

Table 2.9
Population Below the Poverty Line in U.P. as Percentage of All-India

Percentage

Year	*Rural*	*Urban*	*State*
1973-74	17.22	14.27	16.67
1987-88	17.96	14.99	17.77
1993-94	20.33	14.18	18.87

Source: Draft Ninth Five Year Plan, Planning Commission, Govt. of India.

Prolonged incidence of poverty at mass level has gone hand in hand with the high rate of unemployment. A large number of unemployed persons in rural as well as in urban areas, educated or uneducated, is conspicuous with its presence in the state. But the NSS data presents a contrary picture. According to NSS estimates the rate of unemployment in Uttar Pradesh registered a declining trend during the past fifteen years. It was 4.71 percent in 1983, which declined to 3.73 percent in 1987-88 and further to 3.59 percent in 1993-94. In 1993-94, (Table 2.10) this rate was 3.71 percent for rural areas as against 5.6 percent at national level. Similarly, in urban areas it was 4.6 percent as against 7.4 percent at the national level. Among 15 major states the position of Uttar Pradesh was better than in 12 states where the unemployment rates were comparatively higher (GOUP 1997; 125).

These figures, however, do not present the correct picture of the problem because they show only the extent of open unemployment that hardly touches the magnitude of the disguised unemployment. In case of Uttar Pradesh the phenomenon of

Table 2.10
Unemployment Rates in UP as Percent of Labour Force

Rounds	*Year*	*Rural*	*Urban*	*Total*
27th	1972-73	3.6	4.4	3.75
32nd	1977-78	3.5	—	4.33
38th	1983	3.2	—	4.71
43rd	1987-88	3.0	4.8	3.73
50th	1993-94	3.7	4.6	3.59

Source: NSS Reports.

disguised unemployment or under-employment at mass level is the critical problem rather than open unemployment. As has been pointed out rightly, the open unemployment is increasingly becoming a characteristic of those above the poverty line because the poor can not afford to remain unemployed (Hashim 1999). These under employed are predominantly engaged in agricultural sector. The productivity of male agricultural worker (cultivator + agricultural labour) is at a very low level (0.87). Only Bihar and Orissa were lower than this level in the country (Table 2.11).

Table 2.11
Statewise Productivity of Male Agricultural Worker (1992-95)

State	*Productivity of Male Agricultural Worker (1992-95)*	*Ranking*
Andhra Pradesh	1.04	VIII
Assam	0.90	IX
Bihar	0.33	XIV
Gujrat	1.21	VI
Haryana	2.44	II
Karnataka	1.23	IV
Kerala	1.88	III
Madhya Pradesh	0.96	X
Maharashtra	1.09	VII
Orissa	0.70	XIII
Punjab	3.01	I
Rajasthan	1.01	IX
Tamil Nadu	1.22	V
Uttar Pradesh	0.87	XII
West Bengal	0.87	XII

Source: Draft Ninth Five Year Plan, Vol. I, Planning Commission, Govt. of India, p. 207.

Obviously, the income level of agricultural workers in the state is also very low. Therefore, a large proportion of agricultural workers who had been considered to be employed in terms of NSS definitional standards constituted the large proportion of severely underemployed persons in the state .The draft ninth five year plan of UP has rightly noted, that in fact there is no distinction between unemployed and severely under employed. The Planning Commission of Uttar Pradesh has estimated that there were about 93 lakh persons severely underemployed. In addition to this number there were nearly 18 lakh unemployed also. Thus, by adding both the figures one can safely say that about 111 lakh persons were unemployed in Uttar Pradesh in 1997. Thus, for all practical purposes every fourth person of the work force in the state was unemployed. Mass scale migration of labourers from the state to developed industrial and agricultural regions is indicative of this phenomenon.

Table 2.12
Employment in Organized Sector in Uttar Pradesh

(in '000)

Year	*Public Sector*	*Private Sector*	*Total*
1970-71	1389	542	1931
1975-76	1567	548	2115
1980-81	1791	563	2354
1985	2025	547	2572
1990	2138	528	2666
1994	2134	522	2656

Source: Directorate of Employment and Training, UP.

One major reason for increase in unemployment in the state has been the decline in intake of workers in the organized sector. While the labour force increased by about one million every year, the jobs in the organized sector provided a small quantum of employment. Of the total of 46.1 million employed persons in 1987-88, the employment in organized sector was just 6 per cent of it, whereas in Haryana, Maharashtra, Punjab, Gujarat and West Bengal it was 14-16 percent. Nearly 80 percent employment in organized sector was confined to government sector, opportunities for employment were confined to agriculture and government service. Power, transport, irrigation and industry, which generate employment, are underdeveloped. Despite economic diversification employment in the manufacturing sector has not increased substantially (Hasan 1998). In the last decade, employment in the organized sector has practically stagnated because of a slow-down in public sector employment. Private sector employment in the organized sector has failed to register any increase in UP since 1970-71. The major reasons for declining employment in the organized sector are fiscal constraints of the state budget and continued sickness in public and private enterprises, particularly in the textile units. This decline in employment in the organized sector is a matter of serious concern, as it means that the major burden of providing employment falls on the unorganized sector, already suffering from low productivity and over-crowding (Singh 2000; 92).

Rural Sector

Uttar Pradesh may be identified as a rural state with the overwhelming presence of rural sector across the state. Nearly 80 percent of population resides in rural areas and nearly three-fourth of the workforce depends on agriculture and allied activities for its livelihood. The rural areas of the state are inhabited predominantly by the cultivator households (76.4 percent). Agricultural labourer households constitute nearly 7.6 percent, about 3 percent are artisan households and 13 percent households are engaged in other occupations (Table 2.13).

Table 2.13
Estimated Number and Percentage Distribution of Rural Households by Household Types

as on 30.6.91

Major Household Type	*Estimated Number ('000)*	*Percentage Distribution*
Cultivators	143383	76.35
Agriucltural Labourers	1434	7.61
Artisans	563	3.00
Others	2454	13.94

Source: Sarvekshna, October-December, 1998.

Iniquitous Distribution of Land and Other Assets

On the basis of NSS data on land ownership we find that the pattern of land distribution in the state is extremely inequitous. As shown in the Table 2.14 in the rural areas 4.1 percent households do not possess a piece of land. These are predominantly the agricultural labour households belonging to the scheduled castes. Besides, 9.9 percent households own land holdings of less than 0.002 hectare in size, which works out to less than 20 sq. mts. Another 20.8 percent households have holdings between 0.002 and 0.20 hectares. Further 20.2 percent of the households own land between 0.20 and 0.50 hectares. The households falling in these two landowning categories may be termed as semi-landless. Most of these households also belong to the Scheduled Castes. The households owning land between 0.50 and 1.00 hectares constitute 19.0 percent of the rural households. All these households constituting nearly 70 percent of the total rural households are marginal farmers and a vast majority of them own uneconomic land holdings.

The small farmers owning land between 1.00 and 2.00 hectares constituted 15.3 percent of the rural households and 10.6 percent household were the category of medium farmers possessing 2.00 to 10.00 hectares of land. The big farmers owning land above 10.0 hectares formed only 0.2 percent of the total rural households (Table 2.14).

Table 2.14
Distribution of Rural Households by Broad Size-Classes of Land Owned and Land Operated in U.P.

as on 30.6.91

Size-Class (ha)	*Land Owned*		*Land Operated*	
	Estimated number (00)	*Percentage distribution*	*Estimated number (00)*	*Percentage distribution*
nil	7723	4.1	19185	10.19
<0.002	18648	9.9	2930	1.57
0.002 - 0.20	39179	20.8	39187	20.80
0.21 - 0.50	38049	20.2	35161	18.67
0.51 - 1.00	35788	19.0	37187	19.74
1.01 - 2.00	28819	15.3	31537	16.74
2.01 - 4.00	14880	7.9	16959	9.00
4.01 - 10.00	5086	2.7	5700	3.03
above10.00	377	0.2	492	0.26
All size-classes	188360	100.0	188360	100.00

Source: Sarvekshna July-Sept., 1998, p. 69 and Sarvekshna Oct.-Dec., 1998, p. 109.

If we look at the distribution of the area of operational holdings possessed by different categories of farmers the picture of iniquitous distribution becomes crystal clear. During 1990-91 73.4 percent holdings belonging to the marginal farmers category constituted 31.4 percent, of the total area, that is to say, three-fourth rural households in the state were cultivating only one-third of the cultivable land while about 11 percent, big and medium farmers owning more than 2 hectares of land were controlling about 45 percent of the land (Table 2.15).

Table 2.15
Distribution of Operational Holdings in U.P. by Size-Categories

Farmers' Category	*Size Categories (in hectares)*	*1970-71*		*1990-91*		*% Change Between 1970-71 and 1990-91*	
		Number	*Area*	*Number*	*Area*	*Number*	*Area*
Semi-landless	<0.5	7301.6	1574.9	10461.3	2551.0	43.3	49.6
		(46.7)	(8.7)	(52.1)	(14.2)		
Marginal	0.5-1.0	3142.3	2254.7	4358.0	3097.3	38.7	37.4
		(20.1)	(12.4)	(21.7)	(17.2)		
	< 1.0	10443.9	3829.6	14819.3	5634.3	41.9	
		(66.8)	(21.1)	(73.8)	(31.4)	47.1	
Small	1.0-2.0	2688.9	3775.4	3118.5	4390.7	16.0	
		(17.2)	(20.8)	(15.5)	(24.4)	16.3	
Lower medium	2.0-3.0	1111.4	2685.3	1059.5	2555.9	-4.6	-5.6
		(7.1)	(14.8)	(5.3)	(14.2)		
	3.0-4.0	540.5	1851.8	483.0	1650.0	-10.6	
		(3.5)	(10.2)	(2.4)	(9.2)	-10.9	
	2.0-4.0	1651.9	4537.1	1542.5	4185.9	-6.6	-7.7
		(10.6)	(25.0)	(7.7)	(23.4)		
Upper medium	4.0-5.0	302.7	1343.8	257.7	1141.0	-14.9	-15.1
		(1.9)	(7.4)	(1.3)	(6.3)		
	5.0-10.0	430.0	2867.4	290.8	1901.0	-32.4	-33.7
		(2.7)	(15.8)	(1.5)	(10.6)		
	4.0-10.0	732.7	4211.2	548.5	3042.0	-25.1	-27.8
		(4.6)	(23.2)	(2.8)	(16.9)		
Big	>10.0	112.3	1805.2	45.2	694.0	-59.8	-61.6
		(0.7)	(9.9)	(0.2)	(3.9)		
	All holdings above 2.0	2496.9	10553.5	2136.2	7921.9	-14.4	-24.9
		(16.0)	(58.1)	(10.7)	(44.2)		
	Total	15629.7	18158.5	20074.0	17946.9	28.4	-1.2

In the Table 2.15 given above it will be seen that during the last two decades, from 1970-71 to 1990-91, the number of the marginal farmers has increased sharply. It has been pointed out that this phenomenon has occurred mainly due to growth in the size of family leading to the partition of holdings and also due to the allotments of the Gram Samaj lands to the landless. However, during the last twenty years the number of landholding in the semi-landless category has gone up by 43 percent and that of the marginal category by 39 percent. This is a staggering proportion which has been caused owing to the uneconomic nature of the majority of land holdings in the two categories which leads to the indebtedness and forces the owners to sell a part or the whole of their land reducing these farmers to landlessness or near landlessness. This phenomenon can be termed as the process of marginalisation among the marginal and small farmers.

In the NSS statistics referred in the Table 2.14 about 4.1 percent households have been shown as landless. At the same time in the table it has been indicated that nearly one-third of these households are engaged in sharecropping and therefore have been included in the cultivators category, which means that in fact only two-third of landless households i.e. 2.8 percent of the total households are agricultural labourers. In Table 2.13 it is found that the proportion of households identified as agricultural labourer is 7.8 percent which means, there are nearly 5 percent such households who own land but are not engaged in cultivation. These households mainly belong to the categories of semi-landless or marginal farmers. This phenomenon has surfaced due to *(i)* the land under allotment of the Gram Samaj land being the worst land and it was just unfit for agricultural operation and *(ii)* the land was allotted but the grantee could not obtain possession on the pretext of litigation proceeding launched by erstwhile land holders.

Since Uttar Pradesh is predominantly an agricultural state land ownership is the determining factor for the ownership of other assets. The bigger the size of land holding the larger the ownership of other assets (Table 2.16)

The above table shows that between the different size classes of land owned there is considerable variation in the Average Value of Assets (AVA) per household. The AVA among landless and marginal farmers (owning land less than 1.0 hectares) varies from Rs. 30 thousand to about Rs. 1 lakh 30 thousand whereas small

Table 2.16
Average Value of Assets Per Household by Size-Classes of Land Owned in Rural Uttar Pradesh

Category of Households	*Size-classes of land owned (ha)*	*% Distribution of households*	*Average value of assets per household (Rs.'000)*
Landless	Nil	4.1	34.4
Semi-landless	less than 0.002	9.9	29.4
	0.002 - 0.20	20.8	45.3
	0.20 - 0.50	20.2	75.4
Marginal	0.50 - 1.00	19.0	133.8
Small	1.01 - 2.00	15.3	213.8
Medium	2.01 - 4.00	7.9	384.3
	4.01 - 10.00	2.7	724.0
Big	10.01 & above	0.2	1495.3
	all classes	100.0	139.2

Source: Sarvekshana, Oct.-Dec. 1998, p. 109.

farmers (1.00-2.00 hectares) own assets worth more than Rs. 2 lakhs. The AVA among medium farmers (2.00-10.00 hectares) ranged from Rs. 3.85 lakhs to Rs. 7.25 lakhs while it was around Rs. 15 lakhs among the big farmers (more than 10.00 hectares). The table also reveals that the landless and marginal farmers constituting three fourth of the total rural households were owning assets below the over-all average value of assets per household (Rs. 1.39 lakhs). It proves that in rural areas of Uttar Pradesh socio-economic conditions are such that those households which do not posses land or posses a tiny size of land can not afford do create other forms of assets.

The Table 2.17 shows the distribution of households by the asset holding groups. When we compare this table with the earlier table we find that all the medium and big farmers (owning land more than 2.00 hectares) fall in the top group of asset holding, possessing assets worth more than Rs. 2.50 lakhs. Some households of preceding lower asset holding group of small farmers must also be owning assets worth more than Rs. 2.5 lakhs because the average value of assets per household in this category (Rs. 2.33 lakhs) is quite closed to Rs. 2.50 lakh level. Such small farmers are surely included in the top asset holding group. This group which includes all big and medium farmers and some upcoming small farmers constitutes 13.4 percent of the total rural households, as shown in the Table 2.17.

Table 2.17
Distribution of Households and Corresponding Average Value of Assets Per Household by Asset Holding Groups

as on 30.6.91

Assets holding group (Rs. 100)	*Estimated Number of households*	*Distribution of households (in percent)*	*Average Value of Assets Per household (Rs. 000)*
Less than 5	333	1.77	2.74
5 - 10	730	3.89	7.92
10 - 20	1736	9.22	14.78
20 - 30	1356	7.20	24.49
30 - 50	2764	14.67	39.11
50 - 70	2110	11.20	59.46
70 - 100	2494	13.24	84.51
100 -150	2310	12.26	121.55
150 -250	2480	13.17	194.70
250 & above	2533	13.45	532.74
All Classes	18836	100.00	139.23

Source: Sarvekshna, October-December 1998, p. 173.

The Table 2.17 further reveals that around 13.4 percent of rural households are on an average owning assets worth Rs. 5.32 lakhs which is more than double as compared to the preceding lower group and amazingly 250 times higher than the lowest group. This shows that there is a very high level of disparity among rural households in terms of asset ownership and the assets are concentrated in a handful of households.

The Table 2.18 shows the distribution of different items of assets between various asset holding groups. The total value of all the assets including land and buildings in rural areas of Uttar Pradesh has been estimated at around Rs. 262 thousand crores. Among these assets land alone constituted a share of about 68 percent (Rs. 179 thousand crores) and nearly 20 percent share was created by buildings and hutments. All types of durable household assets constituted 4.08 percent (Rs. 10.7 thousand crores), livestock and poultry 3.12 percent (Rs. 8.2 thousand crores), agricultural machines and equipment 2.58 percent (Rs. 6.8 thousand crores) and all types of transport equipment 1.12 percent (Rs. 2.9 thousand crores).

Table 2.18
Distribution of Assets in Value Terms (Rs.) between Different Asset Holding Groups

Asset holding group	*Land*	*Building*	*Livestock*	*All transport*	*Durable household*	*Agri. mach-inery*
less than 5	167 0.001	343 0.07	49 0.06	35 0.12	285 0.27	7 .01
5-10	1585 0.09	2303 0.44	453 0.55	144 0.48	1045 0.98	40 .05
10-20	9352 0.52	9685 1.86	2586 3.16	392 1.32	3119 2.91	278 .41
20-30	14375 0.80	11567 2.22	2948 3.61	418 1.41	3173 2.96	362 .53
30-50	55402 3.09	33885 6.50	7131 8.73	1240 4.19	7988 7.46	1227 1.81
50-70	68789 3.83	37770 7.25	7174 8.78	1000 3.38	8145 7.60	1561 2.30
70-100	119702 6.62	613347 11.77	9806 12.00	1835 6.19	11668 10.89	4266 6.29
100-150	177261 9.88	68456 13.14	12859 15.74	1944 6.56	13259 12.38	4578 6.75
150-250	324093 18.07	105135 20.18	14981 18.33	5736 19.36	19415 18.12	8451 12.47
250 & above	1023061 57.03	190505 36.56	23734 29.05	16881 56.98	39031 36.43	47016 69.36
all classes	1793737 68.40	520996 19.87	81721 3.12	29625 1.12	107126 4.08	67786 2.58

Source: Sarvekshna, Oct.-Dec., 1998.

It is evident from the Table 2.18 that the 13.4 percent households belonging to the top group of asset holdings controlled nearly 57 percent of land and alongwith the land they possessed about 70 percent of all agricultural machinery and nearly 57 percent of all transport equipment. In case of buildings and durable household goods their share was about 36 percent. The concentration was lowest in the category of livestock and poultry (29 percent).

The above pattern of assets distribution has significant implication. The assets which represent labour intensive occupations i.e. livestock and poultry are not favoured by top group households. On the contrary the assets determining the mechanisation of agriculture are heavily controlled by this group and simultaneously the transport sector which includes trucks, buses and light motor vehicles is also predominantly controlled by them. These assets are income-generating assets and the hiring charges accruing from such assets provide continuous flow of income in favour of this group. The distribution of buildings and durable household goods reveals that the prosperity visible in the rural markets or in the form of 'pucca' houses in countryside is reflective of the economic ascendancy of only a few households.

To make the above phenomenon more explicit the distribution of tractors and tractor trollies can be used as a pragmatic yardstick. The Table 2.19 shows the distribution of tractor and tractor trollies by size category of land holdings. The table reveals that big and medium farmers own about 73 percent tractors. There are some small farmers also who own tractors. These are the small farmers who represent the category of upcoming small farmers (which we have discussed in preceeding paragraphs) which falls in the top group of assets holdings at par with the big and medium farmers. When we include these upcoming small farmers alongwith big and medium farmers they own about 96 percent of tractors and almost all the tractor trollies (Table 2.19).

The ownership of nearly all tractor trollies indicates that lucaritive non-form occupations are fully dominated by this group. These occupations include contract works under various development agencies like road building; irrigation, construction; transportation of forest products, minerals, farm products etc to various markets and running the brick kilns. This section of households can be identified as the dominant section of rural Uttar Pradesh. It constitutes nearly 13.5 percent of the rural households. This section is the major gainer of capitalist farming. This section overwhelmingly dominates non-farm occupations and transport businesses. More than one third of buildings and consumer durables are owned by them and above all, nearly 57 percent land is under their possession. The average value of assets per household of this section is more than Rs. 5 lakhs.

In the preceeding sections the hard facts provide us with insight to understand and explain the socio-political dynamics at the grassroots level in the state. The existing pattern of classifying the

Table 2.19
Number of Tractor and Tractor Trollies Owned by Households of Different Size of Operational Land Holdings

as on 30.6.91

Size-Class of household operational holding (ha)	*Number of Household (00)*	*Number of Tractors*		*Number of Tractor Trollies*	
		Per 100 household	*Estimated number*	*Per 100 household*	*Estimated number**
nil	19185	—	—	—	—
<0.002	2950	—	—	—	—
0.002 - 0.20	39187	—	—	—	—
0.21 - 0.50	36161	0.18	6509 (1.77)	—	—
0.51 - 1.00	37187	0.21	7809 (2.13)	0.06	2231 (0.88)
1.01 - 2.00	31537	2.68	84514 (23.04)	2.11	66543 (26.29)
2.01 - 4.00	16959	6.03	102263 (27.88)	3.99	67666 (26.74)
4.01 - 10.00	5680	24.52	139273 (37.97)	17.42	98946 (39.10)
> 10.00	492	53.74	26440 (7.21)	35.93	17678 (6.99)
All size-classes	188360	1.95	366813 (100.00)	1.35	253066 (100.00)

Figures in pareantheses represent the percentage share in the total.

Source: Data regarding number of households and number of tractors and tractor trollies per 100 households are NSS data published in Sarvekshna, July-September, 1998, p. 165.

*Estimated numbers of tractor and tractor trollies are generated figures based on NSS data.

rural populace on the basis of land holdings into big, medium, small and marginal farmers and the landless would not suffice to encompass the whole of socio-economic ground realties, for it ignores the socio-economic and political conflicts and adjustments which constitute an integral part of day to day life. Keeping in view the relationship between various sections we can distinguish six classes in rural society—

Dominant Section—This section includes big, medium and upcoming small farmers. It constitutes nearly 13.5 percent of the total rural households. Nearly 57 percent land is under their possession. It produces marketable surplus. Their agricultural operation is predominantly mechanized. They earn rent on agricultural machinery. They own big or small non-farm rural business. Most of the highly educated persons in rural areas come from this section and they are employed in government and organized private sector. They also run private schools and colleges in rural areas. They have close links with the government machinery at all levels. They constitute the base of leadership of different political parties and the legislatures and even ministers emerge out of them. They are also in the leadership of their caste organization. In short, this class has become the most important centre of socio-economic, political and even cultural activities in rural areas. Besides all these, this class is now the net employer of rural labourer in farm and non-farm activities in the rural areas.

Agricultural Labour/Rural Labour—Nearly 19 percent of the main workers constitute agricultural labourers in the state (Table 2.6). Apart from such labourers, a substantial number from amongst the marginal farmers is also engaged in agricultural as well as non-agricultural wage employment. As shown in Table 2.16 the landless and semi-landless households constituting about 55 percent of the total households fall in this category. Micro level studies indicate that about 70 percent of labourers participate in the agricultural labour market and only 30 percent participate in the non-agricultural labour market and seasonal migration. (Ravi 1999). Of late, the quantum of employment in non-agricultural sector is rising and better opportunities are leading to the transformation of agricultural labour into rural labour. (Lerche 1999; 193).

Another significant feature of rural labour in the state is the out-migration to nearby or distant destinations. These migrants engage themselves as seasonal labourers in agriculture, petty self-employment in urban areas and even in the menial jobs in the informal sector. It should be noted that able-bodied members of poor households in rural areas prefer to out-migrate at the earliest available opportunity (Singh 2000; 22). The old, infirm and women are left behind. Now able-bodied men are rarely available for agricultural employment throughout the year. Daily labour is now carried out by women and old men (Lerche 1999; 190). This has led to increasing feminisation of the agricultural labourers.

In these circumstances, the agricultural labour is not ready to accept the terms imposed by the landowners. Although the wages in the farm sector are not at par with the wages in the non-farm sector they are enough to subsist. Consequently, there is a widespread poverty in the State but no starvation and there is a hope for betterment. Therefore it is not surprising that this class has become more assertive-socially and politically.

Owner Cultivator—This class broadly represent those households which cultivate their land with the help of faimly labour. The proportion of wage labour in their agricultural operations is very low. They are able to produce small quantity of marketable surplus. The small farmers, alongwith the upper strata of marginal farmers, constitute this section. Their proportion in the total rural households is somewhere around 30-35 percent.

This section is supportive of the dominant section in the struggled for higher prices for foodgrains and lower prices for the agricultural inputs. This section is not supportive of the struggle of agricultural labourers for wage increase.

Share Croppers—The practice of share cropping plays an important role in the attitudes and behaviour of the poor. According to the NSS data as shown in the Table 2.20, nearly one third of the landless households and one sixth of the marginal or semi-landless households are engaged in sharecropping. The two together constitute around 10 percent of the rural households.

Table 2.20
Pattern of Sharecropping among Rural Households by Size Category of Land Owned

Size Category of land owned (in ha)	*Household not engaged in share cropping*	*Household engaged in Sharecroping with leased in land*				*Household who lease out there land*
		less than 0.5	*0.50 to 1.00*	*1.00 to 2.00*	*2.00 & above*	
nil	65.35	27.63	4.53	1.22	1.48	—
<0.002	88.13	7.07	0.93	3.62	0.24	—
0.002 - 0.20	59.69	8.41	5.89	2.04	0.76	23.20
0.21 - 0.50	75.92	—	12.50	4.07	1.06	6.38
0.51 - 1.00	79.80	—	—	11.70	2.65	5.77
1.01 - 2.00	85.70	—	—	—	9.60	5.04
2.01 - 4.00	85.41	—	—	—	4.17	10.42
4.01 - 10.00	89.05	—	—	—	0.60	10.34
10.00 & above	97.27	—	—	—	—	2.73

Source: Sarvekshna, July-Sept. 1998, 62.

Besides, there are a few households among the small farmers which are also engaged in share cropping but unlike the landless and the semi-landless they go for share cropping to maximize the use of the agricultural machinery which they own. Most of them belong to the upper strata of the small farmer category and share cropping helps them in upward mobility. This section is a part and parcel of the dominant section and it forms the section, which is transforming into upcoming small farmers as mentioned in the earlier paragraphs.

The landless and semi-landless sharecroppers must not be clubbed together with the sharecropper of the small or medium farmer households. Here, when we mention the share-croppers class, we mean the sharecroppers of the landless, semi-landless and marginal farmers category.

The share-croppers are primarily cultivators yet they augment their family income through wage employment in agriculture or non-agricultural sector. Therefore there exists a duality in their behavioural pattern. On the question of higher prices for the farm produce and lower prices for agricultural inputs they stand in support of owner cultivators under the leadership of the prosperous farmers. But at the same time they would be sympathetic, even actively supportive, towards the struggle for wage increase.

To sum up, the low growth rate and increasing population pressure have been the significant features of Uttar Pradesh during the nineties. The state has been lagging behind in the development process that is being reflected in the progressively widening gap between the state and national per capita income. It has failed to utilise its abundant natural resources to accelerate the growth process. The condition of human resource has also been very poor, so much so, that in terms of Human Development Index the state has been ranked as the most backward in the country.

The state has perpetually been in the grip of high agrarian density (Singh 2000; 101). A large number of population is dependent on agriculture and more so, around three fourth of the new entrants in work force continue to be absorbed in agriculture or allied activities. Obviously, the rates of urbanisation and industrialisation are very low which makes Uttar Pradesh overwhelmingly a rural agrarian state. The predominance of rural sector can be visualised in all spheres of life in the state. However the rural sector is marked with highly iniquitous distribution of land and other assets. Consequently, the gains of whatever development takes place are being usurped by a few. As a result, on the one hand a small number has emerged as a prosperous section of rural society and on the other a large majority is living under widespread poverty. Yet, this is also true that the conditions of the poor in UP are not so bad as in the case of some other backward regions of the country from where starvation deaths are being reported.

II
The Case: Allahabad

Allahabad district was selected as the case to study the voting behaviour of electorates of Uttar Pradesh. The district is situated between 24°47' N and 25°47' N latitutdes and between 81°19' E and 82°21' E longitudes. It lies in the southern part of the state. The Gangetic plains and adjoining Vindhyan Plateau constitute the topography of the district. Allahabad is surrounded by district Bhadohi and Mirzapur in the east, Kaushambi and Banda in the west, Pratapgarh and Jaunpur in the north and Rewa district of Madhya Pradesh in the South.

Allahabad district covers an area of 5248 sq. kms. which is nearly 1.8 percent of total area of the state. For administration purposes the district is divided into 7 sub-divisions (tehsils), 20 development blocks, 2715 inhabited villages and 11 towns including Allahabad city and Cantonment. (GOUP 1998; 28).

According to the 1991 census the population of the district was 3.75 million (2.00 million males and 1.75 females). The gender ratio was almost similar to the state figures. (874 females per 1000 male). The density of population was 713 per sq. km. which is substantially higher than the state average (473 per sq. km.). About 20.8 percent population resides in urban areas which is slightly higher than the state average (19.84 percent). With 2.7 percent share Allahabad is the most populous district in the state but in terms of population density it ranks 16th out of 83 districts in the state. The decadal growth rate of population during 1981-91 was about 29.6 percent which is higher than the state average (25.48 percent).

The proportion of the Scheduled Caste population in Allahabad was about 21.36 percent, which was nearly at par with the state average (21.05 percent). As regards Muslim population it comprises nearly 13 percent of the total population in the district while the proportion in the state stands at nearly 17 percent. The proportion of Hindu population in the district (86.79%) was higher than the state average (81.7 percent).

The literacy percentage in Allahabad was 46.2 in 1991 that was 5 percent point higher than the state average (41.6 percent). However, the female literacy level in the district (26.7 percent) was quite close to the state level (25.3 percent), which shows that the district is ahead only in case of male literacy.

Table 2.21

Area and Demographic Statistics of Allahabad and U.P.

		Allahabad	*Uttar Pradesh*
Area (in sq. kms)		5246 (1.8)*	294411
Population (1000) 1991		3764 (2.7)*	139112
% of Rural Population to 1991 Total Population		74.6	80.2
Density of Population 1991		713	473
Gender Ratio-1991 (Female per 1000 male)		874	879
Decadal Growth rate of Population (1981-1991)		29.6	25.48
% of SC Population to 1991 total Population		21.4	21.1
% of Muslims to total Population		12.9	17.3
% of Hindus to total Population		86.8	81.7
Literacy Rate(Total)	1991	42.66	41.60
(Male)	1991	60.29	55.73
(Female)	1991	23.45	25.31

*Figures in parenthesis represent the percentage share of Allahabad to U.P.
Source: Statistical Diary, UP, 1999 and Statistical Ballia, Allahabad, 1999.

Similar to the state, the economy of the district is predominantly agrarian in nature as 64 percent main workers are employed in agriculture or allied activities. The proportion was higher for cultivators while it was lower in case of agricultural labourers. The state average is comparatively higher (72 percent). The proportion of workers in other occupations is more or less similar to the state average as shown in the Table 2.22.

The work participation ratio in Allahabad was 30.4 percent which was almost similar to the state average (29.7 percent).

Out of about 5 lakh land holdings, 60.4 percent belonged to semi-landless category and 20.3 percent to marginal farmer category whereas the state average was 52.1 and 21.7 percent respectively. The proportion of small farmers is 11.8 percent in the district which is lower than the state proportion (15.5 percent). The share of medium

Table 2.22
Occupational Distribution of Main Workers in Allahabad and U.P.

Sl. No.		*Allahabad*	*U.P.*
1.	Cultivators	41.3	53.3
2.	Agricultural Labourers	22.1	18.9
3.	Plantation/Forestry/Fisheries/Livestock and Hunting	0.6	0.7
4.	Minning and Quarrying	0.4	0.1
5.	Manufacturing including Household Industry	9.8	7.7
6.	Construction	1.1	1.2
7.	Trade and Commerce	7.9	6.2
8.	Transport, Storage and Communication	2.5	1.9
9.	Other Services	13.8	10.0

Source: Statistical Diary, UP, 1999 and Statistical Bulletin, Allahabad, 1999.

and big farmers is 7.3 and 0.3 percent respectively. All marginal farmers constituted nearly 81 percent and were operating 37.6 percent of land while small farmers owned 21.8 percent of agricultural land. Big and medium farmers comprising 7.6 percent controlled 40.6 percent of land. Thus, the process of marginalization of land holding was faster than the state as a whole.

Table 2.23
Percentage Distribution of Operational Land Holdings by Size-Category in Allahabad and U.P.

Size-Class of operated land holding (ha)	*Corresponding Farmers Category*	*Percentage Distribution of land holdings*			
		Allahabad		*Uttar Pradesh*	
		Number	*Area*	*Number*	*Area*
< 0.5	Semi-landless	60.4	19.6	52.1	14.2
0.5 - 1.00	Marginal	20.3	18.0	21.7	17.2
1.00 - 2.00	Small	11.8	21.8	15.5	24.4
2.00 - 10.00	Medium	7.3	35.0	10.5	40.3
>10.00	Big	0.3	5.5	0.2	3.9

Source: Statistical Diary, Uttar Pradesh, 1999, and Statistical Bulletin, Allahabad,1999.

With the above socio-economic status Allahabad is quite close to the State average. Thus, it will be justified to consider Allahabad as one among the fit cases to represent UP for the study of the State's socio-economic and political processes.

Parliament and Assembly Constituencies

The district of Allahabad has been divided into eleven assembly segments. Among these, three segments—Allahabad City (North), Allahabad City (South), and Allahabad City (West) are comprised predominantly with the urban areas. While other eight segments belong to rural areas. For the Parliament Elections the district has two parliament constituencies—Allahabad and Phulpur. Both these constituencies are made up by clubbing few assembly segments each (Table 2.24)

Table 2.24
Number of Electors by Lok Sabha and Vidhan Sabha Constituencies during 1996 Parliament Election

Lok Sabha Constituency	*Vidhan Sabha Constituency*		*Electors (in low)*		
			Male	*Female*	*Total*
Phulpur (55)	Jhusi	(270)	122	101	223
	Handia	(271)	140	115	255
	Pratappur	(272)	129	106	235
	Soraon	(273)	127	104	231
	Nawabganj	(274)	128	105	233
	Total		**646**	**531**	**1177**
Allahabad(56)	Meja -SC	(267)	145	119	264
	Karchana	(268)	141	116	257
	Bara	(269)	135	110	245
	Allahabad North	(270)	196	160	356
	Allahabad South	(271)	147	121	268
	Total		**764**	**626**	**1390**

Figures in parantheses are the constituency numbers in respective category.

The remaining one assembly segment—Allahabad City (West) is included in the Chail parliament constituency which includes all the these assembly segments of Kaushambi district and one assembly segment of Fatehpur district. The Phulpur constituency is overwhemingly a rural constituency while Allahabad has a sizeable number of urban voters (nearly 40 percent). Taking the two parliament constituencies together nearly three fourth voters (75.69%) belong to rural areas.

3

Stratification Among Caste Groups

The present chapter is based on the survey conducted during the Lok Sabha election of 1996 covering a sample of 1718 respondent voters. The chapter is divided into three sections. In the first section the design of the study have been spelt out. The characteristics of the sampled voters are presented in the second section. In the third section an endeavour has been made to capture the prevailing stratification among different caste groups on the basis of an achievement status index.

I
Design of the Study

In a stratified society like India the political participation of the voter, despite the constitutional provision of universal adult franchise, is dependent upon various socio-cultural determinants on the one hand and their achievement status on the other. For isolating the impact of the socio-cultural determinants the voters have been classified in four caste groups i.e. Upper Castes, Other Backward Castes, Scheduled Castes and Muslims (the Muslims, for the purposes of present study, have been treated as a separate caste group). The achievement status has been explained in the section III of this chapter.

In our society caste groups in themselves are stratified on numerous grounds. They may appear behaving in a homogeneous manner but this can not be denied that all the caste groups have advantaged as well as disadvantaged sections within them. In recent years processes of socio-economic mobility have transformed the relative positions of the privileged within a caste groups. These privileged sections are contesting with each other for better share in power and trying to make their position stronger by consolidating their support on community basis. The present study has endeavoured to analyse the stratification among different caste groups on the basis of primary data collected from the survey conducted at the time of the 1996 Lok Sabha elections.

Data Collection

The two Lok Sabha constituencies falling in the Allahabad district, namely Allahabad and Phulpur were selected for the study. There are five assembly segments in each of the selected constituency. All the assembly segments were taken into consideration for collecting the primary data through field survey. The primary data was collected with the help of structured questionnaire. The survey was conducted during the week immediately before the polling day.

A two-member survey team was assigned the task to collect data for each assembly segment. Thus, a total of twenty investigators were put in for fieldwork. The period for data collection was limited to four days only because the responses might have got affected by the campaign propaganda in case the time gap was larger.

The sampled respondents were interviewed personally. The survey was restricted to single visit only. It was found that some interviewees responded to the questions very enthusiastically, whereas others, especially women, were hesitant and sky. In the earlier election surveys voters were not co-operative in facing interviews but as the number and popularity of the opinion polls increased and their results evinced keen interest in print and electronic media, the voters became familiar with the election surveys and interviews. Such familiarity had helped the interviewers in acquiring data regarding the views and opinions without much resistance from the voters. On an average nearly 15 minutes were required for filling up of a questionnaire. Thus, each investigator was able to conduct interviews on about 18-20 respondent in one day at the rate of eight working hours per day. At this rate each team comprising two investigators was able to complete the survey work within the stipulated period.

The Questionnaire

Taking into account the preceding experiences of the election studies it was decided to keep the questionnaire small as also because the survey was intended to single visit only. The questions were asked in Hindi language. In majority of the questions the respondents were asked to express their opinions in terms of binary options i.e. in agreement or disagreement with a given statement. Besides, there were some projective questions also with a view to enable the respondents to express their view freely on certain aspects of political processes

The questionnaire was pre-tested on 50 respondents representing various age, sex, occupational and educational groups from urban as well as rural areas. The purpose of pre-testing was to check the drafted questionnaire in terms of its field practicability in view of the ambiguity and unnecessary repetition. On the basis of the results of pre-testing the questionnaire was redesigned with certain modifications and inclusions.

Sample Size

A sample of 250 voters was drawn from each of the ten assembly segments. Thus, a total of 2500 voters were selected from the two Lok Sabha constituencies. Expecting nearly 30 percent sample loss, it was hoped that the effective size of the sample would be around 1700 to 1800 voters. Thus, the selected sample constituted about 0.1 percent of the total number of electorate in both the constituencies and its effective size was expected to touch 0.07 percent in real terms.

Sample Selection

For the selection of 250 voters in each assembly segment the stratified sampling method was adopted. In the first instance, five polling booths were selected from each segment with the help of random table. Thus, a total of 50 polling booths were selected. Then by systematic sampling method 50 voters were selected from the updated voters' list of every sampled booth. The first sample was drawn with the help of random table and then every nth unit was included in the sample, 'n' being the quotient of the size of the universe divided by the size of the sample.

Substitution in Sample

It had been observed that in a single visit survey it was not possible to interview every selected voter primarily due to his non-availability at the time of the visit of the investigator. It was decided that if a selected voter was not available at the time of the visit of the interviewer another member from the family be interviewed in his or her place. The interviewers were directed to take care that in such cases a male voter was substituted by a male and a female by a female voter. Another condition for the substitution was that the name of the substituted interviewee must be included in the voters' list. It was assumed that the substituted voter belonging to the same family would display similar views to a large extent.

Effective Sample and the Sample Loss

The size of the sample initially selected for the study was 2500 out of which 2000 were from the eight rural assembly segments and 500 from urban segments. In course of the survey, only 1718 respondents could be interviewed. Thus there was a loss of 31 percent in the sample as shown in Table 3.1. This size of sample loss was approximately at the expected level.

Table 3.1
Distribution of Effective Sample and Sample Loss

		Selected Sample	*Effective Sample*	*Sample Loss*
Rural	Male	1060	878	182 (17.2)
	Female	940	526	414 (44.0)
	Total	2000	1424	576 (28.8)
Urban	Male	315	173	142 (45.1)
	Female	185	121	64 (34.6)
	Total	500	647	206 (41.2)
Total	Male	1375	1071	304 (22.1)
	Female	1125	647	478 (42.5)
	Total	2500	1718	782 (31.3)

Figures in parenthesis show the sample loss as percentage to the total sample.

The sample loss was higher in urban areas (41.2 percent) than in the rural areas (28.8 percent). The loss was nearly double among the female electorate than in the males. The minimum loss was among rural male electorate (17.2 percent) but among the rural women it was very high (44 percent). In urban areas the sample loss was higher among men than women. The reasons responsible for sample losses were non-traceability, non-availability, refusal to respond, migration or death.

The low level of sample loss among the rural male may be explained in many ways. Firstly, the rise in the political consciousness in rural areas had resulted in relatively larger participation in elections. Secondly, the wide publicity given to the results of opinion polls in recent years had also evinced keen interest for the interview among the rural male. Along with these two factors the increased participation in political activities in the recently held panchayat elections was also responsible for active cooperation in the interviews conducted during the survey.

The sample loss among rural women as opposed to men was as high as 44 percent the reason being that women respondents shied away from responding due to social and cultural inhibitions. Secondly, the investigators were not allowed to interview the women by the male members of the family on the ground that they were busy in their domestic chores. Thirdly, the male members of the family argued that the women family members had no different opinions than their own and therefore they themselves would answer for sampled female respondents. Fourthly, the survey was being conducted during the period of the marriage season when large number of women respondents had gone away to their relatives.

In the urban areas, the sample loss among women was caused mainly due to the failure to interview the Muslim women. Although there were instances in which these women were found ready to be interviewed yet because of the resistance by the male members in their family they could not participate in the interview. Even the female investigators were not allowed to interview the Muslim women respondents. The non-availability and untraceability were also the factors for sample loss among them. Due care was taken to avoid the sample loss among working women. The interview time for them was fixed keeping in view their work schedule.

The high level of sample loss among urban male respondents was surprising. The reasons for such loss were shifting of residence of the respondents living in rented premises, transferable jobs, in current house numbers in the electoral lists, going back to their native places after retirement, inclusion of bogus names etc.

At some places the voters were boycotting the elections at the local level because of non-fulfillment of their basic needs like drinking water and roads. Therefore, they refused collectively to be interviewed. It happened in the Soraon block of the Meja assembly segment in Allahabad Lok Sabha constituency.

II
Characteristics of the Sample

The election study based on the interviews of sampled respondents selected from the voters' list, raises a number of questions. It is assumed generally that the electoral list had been carefully prepared and that the selected voter would be available for the interview. However, the effective size of the selected sample gets reduced due to a number of reasons stated earlier. Sometimes the extent of sample loss is so large that there is always a risk of not achieving the right proportion for actual representation of the universe. It is because of this that very often the surveys of voters' opinions are considered unreliable.

In the present survey, 68.7 percent of the sampled voters could actually be contacted. In some studies a 30 percent sample loss had been considered normal (Ganguly & Ganguly 1982; 5). So in many studies the size of the initial sample is kept so large that the size of the effective sample remains at the desired level after facing a normal loss i.e. nearly 30 percent. If we look at the figures relating to the voters' turnout in the preceding elections we find that the actual turnout in the elections was never higher than effective sample size of the present study. To put it differently, it would not be wrong to assume that the effective sample could be considered as an indicator of the prospective turnout. The highest turnout was observed in 1984, which was around 59 per cent for both the constituencies taken together. Therefore it would be safe to conclude that the effective sample of voters did represent the universe of actual voters.

Rural-Urban Distribution: The expansion of communication and means of transport in recent years has reduced the distance between rural and urban segments. The priorities of the voters differed in the form and content because of variations in socio-cultural and occupational environments, level of political awareness, nature of political affiliation, extent of electoral participation and responses towards electoral campaigns. Therefore it was treated as an important parameter in the present study.

Table 3.2
Rural-Urban Distribution of Voters

		Census ('000)	*Selected Sample*	*Effective Sample*	*Total Electors ('000)*	*Votes Pollled ('000)*
Rural	Male	2065 (78.3)	1060 (77.1)	898 (83.8)	—	—
	Female	1834 (79.6)	940 (83.5)	526 (81.3)	—	—
	Total	3899 (79.2)	2000 (80.0)	1424 (82.9)	1940 (75.7)	880 (81.6)
Urban	Male	570 (21.7)	274 (22.9)	173 (16.2)	—	—
	Female	452 (20.4)	185 (16.4)	121 (18.7)	—	—
	Total	1022 (20.7)	500 (20.0)	294 (17.1)	490 (24.3)	190 (18.4)
Total	Male	2635 (53.5)	1375 (55.0)	1071 (62.3)	—	—
	Female	2286 (46.5)	1125 (45.0)	647 (37.7)	—	—
	Total	4921 (100.0)	2500 (100.0)	1718 (100.0)	2430 (100.0)	1070 (100.0)

Figures in parenthesis represent column-wise percentages.

The Allahabad City North and the Allahabad City South assembly segments could be treated as urban segments while the electorate of the remaining eight assembly segments represented the rural electorate.

With the above classification the urban voters constituted 24.3 percent of the total electorate in both the constituencies under study. In the initial selected sample for the present study the urban voters' share was about 20 percent. In the effective sample it remained only 17.1 percent. After the elections it was found that the share of urban voters in the total votes polled in both the parliamentary constituencies under study was 18.4 percent, which was not far off from the effective sample. Thus, the rural-urban distribution of the effective sample was close to the actual voters' participation.

Gender Distribution of Voters: The male-female ratio in the total electorate was 55:45. In our initial selected sample this proportion was the same. But in the effective sample it was 62:38. Thus, it may be termed as a male biased sample. However, in earlier studies conducted during the two Lok Sabha elections of 1977 and 1980 in the metropolis like Bombay, the percentage share of women participation in elections was 40 and 39 percent respectively, which was closer to the share in our effective sample. Moreover, as noted earlier, if the effective sample was an indicator of the prospective turnout then there should be no hesitation in inferring that in the actual polling the male-female ratio might have been the same as observed in the effective sample.

Caste-wise Distribution of Voters: On the basis of caste, the Scheduled Castes respondents constituted 21.6 percent of the effective sample whereas in the population of the Allahabad district they constituted 21.4 percent. Respondents belonging to the OBCs constituted 41.8 percent while the Muslims 10.1 percent and other minorities mainly Sikhs and Christians 0.3 and the Upper Caste Hindus 25.8 percent. Nearly 0.7 percent of the voters refused to identify themselves in terms of caste. Some of them showing irritation said that casteism had ruined the country. They vehemently protested against the publication of caste figures in the newspapers. Some of them questioned the source of the caste-wise figures appearing in the newspapers and demanded that the election commission should ban such publications because such figures vitiated the social atmosphere, caused ill-will among different sections of the society and affected the impartiality of the elections.

It was found that there was sufficient difference between the rural and urban constituencies regarding the distribution of castes, although there was hardly any significant difference relating to scheduled castes and the Muslims. The picture however got reversed for the backward and the upper caste voters. The OBCs constituted 41.8 percent in the rural areas while in urban areas their proportion was only 10.9 percent. Contrary to this, the proportion of the upper castes in the urban areas was as high as 46.3 percent whereas in rural areas they constituted about 25 percent. That was why the political parties set up backward caste candidates in the rural area, and the upper caste candidates in the urban. Of the two Lok Sabha constituencies under study all the

Table 3.3
Caste-wise Distribution of Voters

	Distribution in Sample			*Distribution in Census (in lacs)*		
	Rural	*Urban*	*Total*	*Rural*	*Urban*	*Total*
Not Reported	2 (0.1)	10 (3.4)	12 (0.7)			
SC	303 (21.3)	68 (23.1)	371 (21.6)	6.83 (24.3)	1.17 (12.5)	8.01 (21.4)
OBC	682 (47.9)	32 (10.9)	714 (41.6)			
Muslims	129 (9.1)	44 (15.0)	173 (10.1)	3.89 (13.9)	2.47 (26.3)	6.36 (17.0)
UCH	307 (21.6)	136 (46.3)	443 (25.8)			
Others	1 (0.1)	4 (1.4)	5 (0.3)			
Total	1424 (100.0)	294 (100.0)	1718 (100.0)	28.09	9.41	37.50

Figures in parenthesis represent column-wise percentages.

assembly segments in the Phulpur Lok Sabha constituency were rural and the Congress, the BJP and the Samajwadi Party had set up backward caste candidates, while the BSP had fielded its National President Kanshi Ram. On the other hand, the Allahabad Lok Sabha constituency had two urban assembly segments out of five assembly segments and accordingly the Congress, the BJP and the Janata Dal had fielded the upper caste candidates while the BSP had a backward caste candidate (in the seat sharing arrangements the SP had got the Phulpur constituency while the JD the Allahabad constituency).

Occupational Structure of Voters: In the effective sample nearly one-third were found engaged in agriculture and allied activities, 23.5 percent, mainly women, were engaged in housekeeping, 15.0 percent were manual workers including agricultural labourers while 12.0 percent were in business and trade related activities. 5.0 percent were salaried persons, 2.0 percent were in professions like medicine, law, teaching etc. 3.1 percent were in the category of pensioners and others, 2.3 percent were unemployed and 3.6 percent were students (Table 3.4).

Table 3.4
Occupational Distribution of Voters

	Distribution in Sample		
	Rural	*Urban*	*Total*
Not Reported	2 (0.1)	1 (0.3)	3 (0.2)
Agriculture	579 (40.7)	1 (0.3)	580 (33.8)
Labour	246 (17.3)	7 (2.4)	253 (14.7)
Service	46 (3.2)	40 (13.6)	86 (5.0)
Trade	137 (9.6)	63 (21.4)	200 (11.6)
Student	32 (2.2)	31 (10.5)	63 (3.7)
Housewife	314 (22.1)	90 (30.6)	404 (23.5)
Unemployment	30 (2.1)	9 (3.1)	39 (2.3)
Professionals	19 (1.3)	17 (5.8)	36 (2.1)
Others	19 (1.3)	35 (11.9)	54 (3.1)
Total	1024 (100.0)	294 (100.0)	1718 (100.0)

Figures in parenthesis represent column-wise percentages.

Classification by Educational Level: In the effective sample 46.2 percent of voters were found illiterate. More than 90 percent illiterate voters were found in the rural areas. About 7.7 percent of the voters could read and write without having any schooling. Nearly 14 percent had passed the primary school level and the same proportion had cleared the high school examination. The proportion of the voters who possessed the educational status of levels higher than the high school was nearly 17 percent.

Table 3.5
Classification of Voters by Educational Levels

	Distribution in Sample			*Distribution in 1991 Census for the age 20+ (in '000)*		
	Rural	*Urban*	*Total*	*Rural*	*Urban*	*Total*
Not Reported	1 (0.1)	1 (0.3)	2 (0.1)	—	—	—
Illiterate	730 (51.3)	64 (21.8)	794 (46.2)	—	—	1541 (61.9)
Literate	123 (8.6)	10 (3.4)	133 (7.7)	—	—	171 (6.9)
Primary	214 (15.0)	37 (12.6)	251 (14.6)	—	—	165 (6.7)
High School	198 (13.9)	49 (16.7)	247 (14.4)	—	—	454 (18.3)
Above High School	157 (11.1)	133 (45.2)	291 (17.0)	—	—	158 (6.4)
Total	1424 (100.0)	294 (100.0)	1718 (100.0)	—	—	2490 (100.0)

Figures in parenthesis represent column-wise percentages.

Age-wise Distribution of Voters: For the age-wise distribution of the sample the respondents were divided into four categories—*(i)* 18-21 years; *(ii)* 22 -35 years; *(iii)* 36-60 years; and *(iv)* As above 60 years as shown in Table 3.6.

Table 3.6
Age-wise Distribution of Voters

	Distribution in Sample			*Distribution in Census*		
	Rural	*Urban*	*Total*	*Rural*	*Urban*	*Total*
18 - 21	207 (14.5)	34 (11.6)	241 (14.0)	246 (12.0)	82 (13.8)	338 (12.8)
22 - 35	544 (38.2)	112 (38.1)	656 (38.2)	725 (35.5)	207 (34.8)	932 (35.4)
36 - 60	575 (40.4)	119 (40.5)	694 (40.4)	790 (38.7)	234 (39.3)	1024 (38.9)
Above 60	98 (6.9)	29 (9.9)	127 (7.4)	279 (13.7)	724 (12.1)	351 (13.3)
Total	1424 (100.0)	294 (100.0)	1718 (100.0)	2040 (100.0)	595 (100.0)	2635 (100.0)

Figures in parenthesis represent column-wise percentages.

The age-wise distribution of the effective sample compared favourably with the distribution pattern in the census for U.P. as a whole. Although the age of the voters was recorded in the electoral list but for the purposes of this survey the age as reported by the respondents themselves was taken into consideration because it was considered more reliable.

III
Achievement Status of Voters

It has always been a challenging task for social scientists to isolate the factors affecting the voters' participation or their behaviour during an election. Such factors could be classified into two categories —ascribed and acquired. By combining these two factors various indices of the status of voters were developed. In studies pertaining to American voters the variables like, source of income, occupation, type of residence and educational level had been included to develop such type of composite index. Under the influence of such studies, in India also attempts had been made to develop Socio-economic Status (SES) index for voters in various election studies. However, in India, due to non-availability of reliable data on the source of income and the type of residence, it was preferred not to include them while preparing SES indices.

Keeping in view the social stratification in Indian society, in most of the cases caste had been taken as an indicator of social status and combining it with the educational and occupational standards the composite index for voters was constructed which had been termed as the socio-economic status index. In recent years, however, different patterns of mobility at different levels among all castes was visualised. Consequently it would not be justifiable now to accord weightage to different castes in terms of their traditional social hierarchy. This could be noticed as a common phenomenon, particularly in the cities. The individuals belonging to a caste generally considered to be low in social hierarchy could be seen on high government official positions and were part and parcel of the social elite participating in intellectual and other respectable pursuits. Also, individuals coming out from these castes had made a mark in politics and established their identity at national as well as local levels. It would not be appropriate, therefore, to take the caste in a generalised form as a determinant of one's social status in the society. Secondly, it was generally maintained that the political parties had, of late, acquired the identity of a caste or a group of castes. Even if it was true, the validity of the claim ought to be examined scientifically. If the caste were included as a variable in order to construct a composite index for voters, it would be difficult to isolate the impact of different castes on the electoral and political processes. Thirdly, in each caste there were different strata and as such their priorities and inclinations were not homogeneous. Although, they might appear as a homogeneous social group at times when there was political polarisation, the divergence prevalent among them should not be overlooked. Lastly, the voters belonging to Muslims, Christian, Sikhs and other religious minorities, as well as, the tribal groups did not have caste differentiation like Hindus and to take caste as a social variable for index construction for the voters belonging to these groups would make it unreal and subjective.

Having excluded the caste, there was no clear variable to indicate the socio-economic status of the voters. Therefore, in the present study, instead of Socio-Economic Status (SES) an Achievement Status Index (ASI) was constructed. In this index only two variables—occupation and education were taken into consideration. This Achievement Status Index was different from the SES index simply in the sense that caste was not included in it. This Achievement Status Index (ASI) reflected the achieved status of the respondents. Thus, with the help of this index it would be possible to isolate the stratification within the castes. The ASI could also be treated as a proxy indicator of one's economic achievements. The occupational hierarchy indicated the occupational mobility. At the same time the educational standards achieved by the respondents were also reflective of their economic prosperity. Thus the composite index (ASI) developed with the help of these two variables would to a large extent reflect the economic standards of the respondents. Here a question obviously arose as to why income of a household or of an individual which alone was sufficient for measuring economic prosperity could not be treated as an independent variable instead of using any proxy indicator in order to measure the economic achievement. Ordinarily it might appear to be true but there were numerous hindrances in assessing the income of the respondent voter or of his family. It had been found that the factors like unwillingness or inability to asses the income on monthly or yearly basis, tendency to report the level of income on the lower side, unstable forms of earnings, income being a joint family earnings, income generating through barter etc. made the collection of data regarding income of voters quite difficult and that too in the single visit survey method. Another reason for not collecting this information was that many of the respondents would feel offended at such queries as a result of which the investigators might face the risk of inability in eliciting the answers of the other queries also. Similarly, queries with regard to the size of land holdings were also beset with difficulties and hence were not included as an item for background information.

Occupation Scores: The relative hierarchy of occupations was determined by three variables — *(a)* the level of interaction with other voters, *(b)* exposure to propaganda and *(c)* entrepreneurial and leadership skills. Although no data was collected with regard to the variables stated above, the occupations had been ranked on the basis of observational data collected in course of field survey. Admittedly, such classification might be termed arbitrary. However, for the purposes of the study it had proved to be relevant.

In the light of what was stated above the occupations were ranked in a descending order. The agricultural and construction labourers were ranked lowest along with voters of other low level occupations and without any occupation. Since housewives possessed managerial skills while managing their domestic work independently they were assigned a higher rank. The peasants who managed their farm work were also placed in the same category because they also managed their farm on their own. But persons employed as class III or class IV employee in offices, institutions, establishment etc. were given higher weight than housewives and peasants because of their greater exposure to the election propaganda. In our sample there were sizeable number of students also because of the lowering of voting age recently. They were also placed in the same category along with the employees because of their exposure to election propaganda and interaction with more people of different walks of life. The traders however, were ranked higher than the employees in services and the students due to their greater interaction with the diverse sections of people. They also possessed entrepreneurial qualities of superior level. The Professionals, Government officials (class I and class II) and the big businessmen were accorded the top rank because they possessed all the qualities of other groups along with higher horizons of knowledge. Their leadership qualities were of the highest standard. On the basis of these observations were occupations were assigned weights and arranged in a descending order as shown in the Table 3.7.

Table 3.7
Weights to Various Occupations

Weights	*Occupations reported by respondent voters*
5	Professionals, Govt. Officials (class I and class II or equivalent) and Big Businessmen
4	Traders
3	Employees (class III and class IV or equivalent) and Students
2	Peasants and Housewives
1	Agricultural and Non-agricultural labourers, other low level occupations and without any occupation

Educational Standard Scores: Similarly, educational achievements were also ranked in terms of educational level attained by the respondent voters. The hierarchy and weights for educational levels have been given in the Table 3.8.

Table 3.8
Weights to Different Educational Standards

Weights	*Educational Standards*
5	Above high school
4	Up to high school
3	Up to Primary level
2	Literate without schooling
1	Illiterate

Achievement Scores: By adding the occupational and educational weights a composite score had been developed and termed as the Achievement Score of a voter. The range of achievement score, thus, would vary between 2 and 10. On the basis of the achievement score the achievement status index could be developed which would determine the achieved status of the voter. The status of voters thus worked out had been classified into three categories—*(i)* low achievement status with achievement scores ranging between

2 and 4; *(ii)* medium achievement status with achievement scores ranging from 5 to 7; and *(iii)* high achievement status having the achievement scores ranging between 8 and 10. With the help of this Achievement Status Index the prevailing pattern of stratification within the caste groups could be illustrated, as shown in the Table 3.9.

Table 3.9
Distribution of Voters in Different Caste Groups by Achievement Status Index

Community	*Achievement Status*			*Total*
	Low	*Medium*	*High*	
Upper Castes	105 (23.8) (12.1)	256 (53.4) (36.5)	101 (22.9) (50.2)	442 (100.0) (25.8)
Other Backward castes	405 (56.8) (46.8)	264 (37.0) (40.9)	44 (6.2) (21.9)	713 (100.0) (41.6)
Scheduled castes	278 (75.) (31.9)	74 (20.1) 11.5)	18 (4.9) (9.0)	368 (100.0) (21.4)
Muslims	78 (45.1) (9.0)	66 (38.2) (10.2)	29 (16.8) (14.4)	173 (100.0) (10.1)
Other Minorities	— (0.0) (0.0)	1 (25.0) (0.2)	3 (75.0) (1.5)	4 (100.0) (0.2)
Total	865 (50.5) (100.0)	646 (37.7) (100.0)	201 (11.7) (100.0)	1712 (100.0) (100.0)

The Table 3.9 shows that in the effective sample nearly 50 percent respondents were in the low, about 38 percent in the medium and approximately 12 percent in the high achievement status categories.

The caste-wise stratification on the basis of the achievement status index brought out some interesting facts. The high achievement status voters constituted 11.7 percent of the total effective sample and among them nearly 50 percent belonged to the upper caste, 22 per cent to the other backward castes, 14 percent to the Muslims and 9.9 percent to the SCs.

With regard to the medium status category the OBCs had 40 percent, upper castes 36.7, Muslims 10.2 and SCs 11.5. Thus in this category the proportion of OBCs was higher than the upper castes. The proportion of SCs was slightly higher than the Muslims but both of them were lagging far behind the OBCs and UCH. In the lower achievement status category which formed nearly half of the total sample the other backward castes constituted the largest share (46.8 percent) followed by SCs (31.9 percent). Surprisingly, the proportion of upper caste in the lower status category was higher (12.1 percent) than that of Muslims (9.0 percent).

If we look at the distribution of voters according to the achievement status categories within the caste groups we find that barring the upper caste groups in all the caste groups there was an inverse relationship between the achievement category and the size of voters. This shows that the proportion of voters got shrunk as one moved upward in terms of achievement status. It presents a pyramid shape distribution among scheduled castes, backward castes and Muslims. However, among upper castes the proportion of medium strata was largest while for the higher and lower categories it was found to be nearly equal. Thus, the distribution in this group acquired a diamond shape.

Although the distribution of voters among SCs, OBCs and Muslims have been pyramidical in shape but the difference in terms of concentration at the base should not be overlooked. This concentration was highest among scheduled castes with nearly three fourth of them (75.0 percent) lying in the low achievement status in the society. Among the OBCs also it was as high as 56.8 percent while this size reduced among Muslims to about 45 percent. In the case of medium achievement status it was found that the size was approximately similar among OBCs (37.0 percent) and Muslims (38.2 percent) while it was as small as 20.1 percent among in case of scheduled castes. However, in the top bracket of the pyramid the proportion of voters was largest among the Muslim population (16.8 percent) followed by backward castes (6.2 percent) and was smallest among scheduled castes (4.9 percent). Thus it can be said that among scheduled castes every 20th voter belonged to the high achievement status, among backwards it was every 16th and in case of Muslims every 6th and among upper castes it was every 4th voter. Thus Muslims appeared to be quite close to the upper castes in terms of proportion of the high achievement strata within the community.

IV
Concluding Remarks

The endeavour in the survey was to ensure objectivity of data. The sample was drawn from the updated voters' list. The investigators were intensively trained for the job. As a result the sample was close to the universe in respect of rural-urban differentiation, caste, gender and age-wise distribution and the classification by educational levels. Therefore the Achievement Status Index devised on the basis of this sample could not be faulted on the grounds of arbitrariness. The analyses of electorates' behaviour in successive election studies presented in the following chapters were based on the findings arrived at in this chapter. The Achievement Status Index and the stratification found thereby has helped to raise an edifice of the electoral behaviour in the state.

4

Electorate's Attitude Towards Electoral Processes

The present chapter is based on the findings of study conducted during the UP State Assembly elections of 1996. It has been divided in three sections. The first section deals with the design of the study while the analyses and results are presented in the second section. The implications in terms of attitude and behaviour have been spelt out in the concluding section.

Soon after the Lok Sabha elections held in April 1996 the electorate in Uttar Pradesh were called upon to elect the State Assembly in the month of October 1996. It was a mid-term election as the outgoing assembly was dissolved in about three years period[1]. This election was held under the President's rule and it was significant in view of the number of measures taken by the Election Commission to make electoral process as free and fair as possible. The Commission had imposed several restrictions to check various malpractices such as impersonation, booth capturing, expenditure in excess of the prescribed limit[2], use of violence and force etc. Due to strict monitoring of election processes by the observers of the Election Commission[3] the candidates were no longer in a position to provide free transportation and other incentives to the voters. In such a situation the behaviour of the voters was largely influenced by the motivational factors. Therefore this study was specifically focussed on identifying various determinants of voters' attitude towards political parties, their leaders and the electoral processes. The present chapter is based on the findings of the study.

I
Design of the Study

The Sample

The study was based on pre-election survey conducted during the week immediately before the polling date, similar as in the case of earlier study of Parliament elections discussed in the previous chapter. A three stage stratified sampling method was adopted to select the sample. In the first stage two assembly segments, one each from the two Parliament constituencies in the district of Allahabad,[4] were selected. These assembly segments were Allahabad City North (275) and Jhusi (270). In the second stage three polling booths were selected on random basis from each selected assembly segment. Then in the third stage updated voters lists of selected booths were used to randomly select 10 percent sample through systematic sampling method. A total of 208 voters from City North and 218 from Jhusi were selected. However, during the survey the investigators were able to contact and interview only 109 voters (male 66 and female 43) in City North and 120 voters (male 85 and female 35) in Jhusi. Thus, with a sample loss of about 30 percent the effective size of sample was 229 for the study. Table 4.1 presents distribution of the sample.

The Questionnaire

A structured questionnaire was developed to interview the sampled voters. After going through a pilot survey it was improved and standardized. The questionnaire was prepared in the Hindi language, which is the mother tongue of the people of the region. This gave additional advantage as most of the respondents themselves or their family members were able to go through the questionnaire, if they so desired. This was helpful in providing a foundation for confidence building between the investigator and the respondent.

Table 4.1
Sample Size and its Classification by Coverage

Assembly Segment	*Code No. of Sample Poling Booths*	*Localities Covered*	*Sample Size*	*Details of Covered Sample*					*No. of Selected respondents Not Available at the time of Survey*
				With Schedule Convassed	*Migrated*	*Found Dead*	*Untra-ceable*	*Total Covered Sample*	
City North 275	75	A Beli Road	90	32	06	—	06	44	46
	76	B Beli Road	60	44	04	—	04	52	08
	77	C Beli Road	58	33	12	01	11	57	01
Sub Total			208	109	22	01	21	153	55
Jhusi 270	237	Sudhnipur Kalan	96	45	04	—	01	50	46
	238	Sudhnipur Kalan	78	48	09	—	02	59	19
	240	Sudhnipur Kalan	44	27	—	—	01	28	16
Sub-Total			218	120	13	—	04	137	81
Grand Total			426	229	35	01	25	290	136

The questionnaire for this study was different from the previous study (Appendix 2). In the previous questionnaire (Appendix 1) the respondents were asked to express their opinions in terms of binary options i.e. in agreement or disagreement with a given statement. Besides, there were some projective questions also with a view to enable the respondents to express their view freely on certain aspects of political processes. In this study projective questions were not included in the questionnaire. Also, instead of binary options, scales were introduced to make the responses quantifiable. There was another reason for doing so. Often, the respondents preferred to situate themselves somewhere between the two extreme positions. Therefore recording the responses on scales was found a better method.

The questionnaire was divided into three parts. The first part was devoted to creating confidence in the respondent by the investigator. The second part consisted of items on opinions and attitudes of respondents on various issues of electoral processes while the third part was related with the background information of the respondents. The detailed description of the questionnaire is given in the following paragraphs.

Part - I

Confidence Building: In this part the respondents were specifically informed about the objectives of the survey and were taken into confidence that their responses would be kept confidential and utilized only for research purposes, so that the responses could be collected freely and unhesitatingly. There was no major item in this part so far as the data collection was concerned. There was a single question, "would you offer your cooperation in this study?" The respondents had freedom to respond according to their choice. If the response was positive then only the remaining two parts were to be canvassed. In case the respondent desired not to be interviewed, the remaining two parts obviously could not be pursued. Even so, the negative responses did throw light about the attitudes and behavior of non-participating electors.

Part - II

Opinion-Attitude Scale: The second part included thirteen items on opinion-attitude scales. The following issues were examined with the help of questions and statements included in this part of the questionnaire:

1. Awareness: To measure awareness regarding forthcoming election process, two items (nos. 1& 2) were included:

(i) Are you aware that the state assembly elections are to be held after some days?
The respondents' reply was recorded as "yes" or "no".

(ii) When would the voting take place in your area?
The respondents were asked to reply in terms of day/date/don't know.

2. Voting Right: The exercise of voting right was considered as a critical factor in understanding the voting behaviour. To measure it, the questionnaire included three items:

(i) Will you cast your vote?
A five-point response scale was used ranging from "will not go at all" (1) to "will definitely go to vote" (5)

(ii) The reason for whatever response to the previous question was also sought in the survey. For this purpose a separate question was included in the questionnaire asking the respondent, "Will you state the reason for doing so?" It was the only open ended question in the questionnaire so that the respondent could frankly come out in justification of his opinion.

(iii) How many times you have cast your vote in the preceding elections?
The response was recorded on a three point scale ranging from never (1) / sometimes (2) / always (3).

3. Participation in the Political Process: To measure voters' participation in the political activities like public meetings, rallies/demonstrations, party meetings, electioneering, donations and monetary contributions or simply identification with a political party, the questionnaire included separate five point scale for each activity (item-5).

4. Accessibility to Information: Accessibility to information has been classified into two categories, one related to the information about the forthcoming elections and the other regarding the ideas and programmes of various political parties and candidates. Accordingly two separate items (nos. 7 to 9) were included in the questionnaire.

(i) "How much information about the election you have received from the various sources of information?" The sources were classified into seven categories namely; family members/friends; local leaders; newspapers; radio/TV; market gossips; public meetings and any other. For each source four point response scale was used ranging from nothing-1 to very much-4.

(ii) "How did you get to know about the ideas and programmes of the candidates and the parties?" Responses in terms of 'yes' or 'no' were recorded for eight sources including: *(i)* election manifestoes; *(ii)* excerpts of manifestoes appearing in newspapers; *(iii)* public speeches; *(iv)* family members and friends; *(v)* posters; *(vi)* slogan shouting; *(vii)* propaganda on loudspeakers, and *(viii)* broadcasts on radio/TV. In addition to the above sources option of "not aware at all" was also included.

(iii) A specific item (no. 8) was also included in the questionnaire to assess the reach of party manifestoes. Respondents were asked "How many election manifestoes of different political parties you are aware of?" A four-point scale was used to measure the response ranging from none-1 to three or more-4.

5. Factors Influencing the Choice of the Voter: In order to examine the weight of certain factors influencing the voters' choice a three point response scale was introduced. The question put was "There are several grounds upon which the votes are cast. How do you view the following in this respect?" Seven factors were identified for investigations, namely, *(i)* local problem; *(ii)* ideology of the party; *(iii)* image of the candidate; *(iv)* proximity with the candidate; *(v)* caste or religion; *(vi)* monetary or any other direct gains, and *(vii)* other issue, if any. Responses were recorded for each factor separately.

6. Impact of Campaigning: A three-point response scale was included in the questionnaire to evaluate the impact of different methods employed by the political parties and the candidates to influence the voters. The question asked was, "To what extent the parties or candidates are employing the following to woo the voters?" The responses were recorded separately for seven such measures namely — *(i)* use of money; *(ii)* use of caste/religion; *(iii)* use of muscle power; *(iv)* use of posters/banners/ loudspeakers; *(v)* public meetings; *(vi)* mass contact, and *(vii)* other means.

7. Prevailing Political Environment: A set of fourteen statements was placed before the respondents. These statements were related to the political parties and leaders; poll arrangements; relevance of polls, and women reservation. Among these some were in the positive direction while some in the negative. The responses to these were recorded on a five point response scale (absolutely wrong-1 to absolutely correct-5).

8. Political Efficacy: A separate item was included in the questionnaire to assess the voters' opinion about their political efficacy in the present political system. Towards the end, the question asked was "How much faith do you have in the elections?" Responses were recorded on a five-point response scale (absolutely not-1, very high-5).

Part - III

Background Data: In this part of the questionnaire the data relating to the age, sex, educational level, marital status, caste, religion and occupation of the respondents were collected.

Data Collection and Analysis

Experienced field investigators were employed to collect the data. Respondents were contacted individually and the investigators filled up the questionnaires after putting the question in proper context.

The respondents were classified into rural and urban segments. These were further divided into male and female categories. The data were analysed on the basis of mean scores obtained from the responses ranging on three to five point scales. In case of combining the responses of two or more statements the direction of opinions was taken into consideration carefully. In such cases values were assigned in descending order for the responses of statements with negative orientation whereas ascending values were given to the responses of positive statements.

II
The Results

Attitude Towards Voting Right

It was a subject of concern that the people were losing trust in the elections. In order to gauge the opinion of the electorate in this regard two statements were placed before the respondents. First, "a single vote of yours hardly matters" and second, "every single vote is invaluable". The first statement was negative whereas the second was positive. If the responses to the first and second statements are allotted scores in the ascending and descending order respectively, as per the methodology stated earlier, the sum of the two will indicate the importance attached by the voters to their voting right. The mean value of these combined scores has been shown in the Table 4.2

Table 4.2
Mean Values of Voters' Attitude Towards Electoral Processes

Particulars	*Scale Range*	*Rural*			*Urban*			*Combined*
		Male N=85	*Female N=35*	*Total N=120*	*Male N=66*	*Female N=43*	*Total N=229*	*Total N=229*
Assigning Importance to voting right	2.10	8.44	7.29	8.10	7.83	7.53	7.72	7.82
Reporting inconveniences and hassles in voting	2.10	4.12	5.06	4.39	4.47	4.47	4.47	4.43
Extent of faith in elections process	3.15	10.22	8.00	9.58	10.00	9.67	9.87	9.72
Agreement on rise in electoral violence	2.10	7.26	6.26	6.97	7.83	8.12	7.95	7.43
Attitude towards political parties	2.10	4.22	5.23	4.52	4.21	4.72	4.41	4.47
Attitude toward political leaders	2.10	8.51	7.31	8.16	8.52	8.14	8.37	8.26

The mean values in this regard show that both rural and urban voters regard their right to vote highly. Even the rural women voters consider this right equally important. The enthusiasm for voting right was highest among male electorate in the rural areas. Hence the conclusion that the importance of the right to franchise is losing attraction could not be drawn by the fact that the voting percentage is lower. The problem lies elsewhere.

Attitude Towards Poll Arrangements

An attempt was made to examine whether there were any such defects, shortcomings or hassles in the existing arrangements for polling. The opinion was sought on two statements like: *(i)* "To wait in the queue for a long time at the polling station is painful" and *(ii)* "To cover the distance to reach the polling station is inconvenient". Both the statements were in the same direction on a five-point scale. Taking the opinion expressed in ascending order on both the statements, it was found that the mean value (4.43) regarding the inconveniences and hassles at polling stations is substantially low as shown in the above table. It shows that the arrangements in this respect were not discouraging the electorates from going for polls. This conclusion was valid for all sections of voters except for rural women voters in whose case the mean value was a little higher (5.06).

So we find that the electorate was neither indifferent towards his voting right nor was discouraged by the inconveniences and hassles caused by the polling arrangements.

Attitude Towards Electoral Processes

A very significant fact that came to light was that although the electorates reposed their faith in election they were not satisfied by the way in which our electoral system had evolved. In the questionnaire three statements in item number twelve were put before them—*(i)* "Elections are the means for the formation of a democratic government", *(ii)* "The decline in political culture can be checked only through elections" and *(iii)* "Trust in elections is on decline". The first two statements indicate a sense of satisfaction in the existing electoral system while the third, as against the two, is pessimistic in nature. By combining the scores of the above three statements, range being 3 to 15, we get the overall picture of electorates' opinion towards the prevailing electoral system. The mean value of the combined score for the electorate as a whole was found at the level of 9.72 which shows that they do not hold any extreme opinion in favour of or against the prevailing electoral system. If we look at it section wise, we find that both rural and urban male voters were marginally optimistic with a mean value (10.22 and 10.00 respectively) while the rural women voters were substantially pessimistic (mean value; 8.00) whereas urban women were closer to male voters (mean value; 9.67). Taking all these facts into consideration it appears that although the voters were not inclined to reject it, at the same time they were also not entirely happy with the nature and processes in the existing electoral system. This may be one of the reasons for fall of the voters' turnout.

Attitude Towards Political Parties and Leaders

The views and attitudes about the political parties and their leaders also determine the behaviour of the electorates. To evaluate the opinion of the electorate about the political parties two statements were put before them—*(i)* the political parties function in service of people and *(ii)* the political parties have come to be identified with the castes. The two statements are juxtaposed. After arranging the scores of responses in the ascending and descending order respectively (range 2 to 10), it was found that the voters as a whole hold a negatively inclined opinion about the political parties (mean value; 4.47). If we take different sections of the electorate independently the situation remained the same as shown in the above table. The rural and urban voters alike hold the political parties as irresponsible and unaccountable towards the society (mean value; 4.52 and 4.41 respectively). This trend was less prominent among the female voters The anger born out of this attitude was more explicit among male voters. However, the extent of adverse opinion against the political parties was at the similar level between the urban as well as rural male voters (mean value; 4.22 and 4.21 respectively).

In order to assess the opinion towards the leaders of the political parties two statements were put before the respondents—*(i)* the leaders have become selfish/ greedy and *(ii)* the political leaders are no more accountable to the society. Both these statements were negatively placed. By combining the scores with regard to the two (range 2-10), we find that there was a state of strong disillusionment among the electorates towards the leaders (mean value; 8.26). During the interview they used very strong words against them. This view prevailed with similar intensity among the rural male (mean value; 8.51), urban male (mean value; 8.52), and urban female (mean value; 8.14). However, among the rural women the intensity was slightly lower, the mean value being 7.14.

The state of disillusionment regarding the political parties had been validated in another way also in our survey data. It is a well-known practice that in a democratic system the political parties organise any number of programmes before and during the elections in order to muster mass support. Thus, the level of participation of electorates in such programmes can be treated as an objective indicator for assessing the electorates' inclination towards the political parties. In the present study the participation of electorates has been measured in respect of five forms of political participation i.e. participation in *(i)* public meetings, *(ii)* rallies/demonstrations, *(iii)* party meetings, *(iv)* electioneering and *(v)* donations. It was assumed that the participation in which maximum time and energy is consumed was an expression of greater participative activity of the electorate. From this point of view the level of participation a campaign worker during electioneering was considered as the most intensive participation whereas participation in a public meetings expressed the lowest level of participation. The participation in all these activities was measured separately on a five-point scale (range 1-5). The mean values of these scores have been shown in the Table 4.3. It was found that the participation in all these activities by the electorates was of minimal nature. In no case the mean value was higher than 1.56. Significantly, there was complete absence of participation among rural women in all the programmes organised by the political parties except in the form of attending public meetings that too at a very insignificant level (mean value; 1.03). In the urban areas, however, females were found participating at par with their male counterparts and surprisingly in some cases, for example, in making donations and also in electioneering the level of participation was higher than in all the other sections (mean values; 1.44 and 1.56 respectively). The table further shows that the mean values for participation in public meetings and rallies/ demonstrations were highest among rural male electorates (mean value; 1.78 and 1.27 respectively) while the urban male electorates dominated the party meetings (mean value; 1.36). In all the above cases the mean values for all the programmes were at a very low level which can not be considered as an active participation in programmes organised by the political parties. The insignificant level of such participation by all sections of electorates validates the conclusion that the voters nurse the feeling of indifference towards all the political parties.

Table 4.3
Means (Scale Range 1-5) of Items Related to Voters' Political Affiliation and Identity

	Rural			*Urban*			*Combined*
	Male N=85	*Female* N=35	*Total* N=120	*Male* N=66	*Female* N=43	*Total* N=229	*Total* N=229
Faith in elections	3.73	3.40	3.63	3.71	3.95	3.81	3.72
Commitment for voting	4.56	3.97	4.39	4.53	4.53	4.53	4.46
Participation in Public meetings	1.78	1.03	1.56	1.71	1.33	1.56	1.56
Participation in rally/ demonstrations	1.27	1.00	1.19	1.20	1.21	1.20	1.20
Participation in Party Meetings	1.28	1.00	1.20	1.36	1.35	1.36	1.28
Participation as campaign worker	1.49	1.00	1.35	1.45	1.56	1.50	1.42
Donations to Political Parties	1.13	1.00	1.09	1.27	1.44	1.34	1.21
Affinity with any political party	3.26	1.83	2.84	2.88	2.77	2.83	2.84

Inspite of all these it can not be concluded that the voters did not identify themselves with any political party. When asked "do you find yourself closer to any political party?" the responses on a five- point scale (range 1-5) did not confirm a state of rejection (mean value; 2.84). This situation was similar in rural as well as urban areas. The mean value shows that although they did identify themselves with some party, the level of attachment was neither high nor low. The level of attachment in rural areas was higher among men (mean value; 3.26) but very low among women (mean value; 1.83). In urban areas the level of identification with any political party was nearly at the same level between male and female electorates (mean values; 2.88 and 2.77 respectively). The above analysis validates the conclusion that there was indifference towards the political parties. Inspite of such indifference, however, in the present electoral system the electorates had no choice but to choose one party or the other as their preference.

Determinants of Voters' Choice

In the light of the analysis of electorate's attitude towards voting right, poll arrangements, electoral processes and political parties and leaders the question arises that if the political parties and their leaders were unable to attract the voters, what were the factors responsible for motivating the voters to vote? Why the commitment to vote at the elections was so intense? It requires an in-depth analysis. An effort in this direction was made in the study. It was found that in most cases the electorates avoided to state explicitly the factors that influenced their decision to vote. But when the same question was put before them in a general form they did not hesitate to open out. Keeping this behavioural pattern in view, the opinions of electorate were collected on some identified factors that were likely to influence the preferences of electorates in general in the forthcoming elections. These factors included—local issues, ideology of parties, image of candidates, personal loyalty to the candidate, inclination towards the caste/religion, pecuniary or other gains or any other factor. The responses to all these were collected separately on a three point scale (range 1-3). The mean values of responses for different sections of the electorate regarding various factors have been shown in the Table 4.4. It is evident from the table that the tendency among the electorate to vote on the basis of solution of local problems and pecuniary or other personal gains appeared prominently with the highest mean value (2.13). Besides, the voters attached more importance to the image of a particular candidate (2.00) than the ideology of his party (1.97). Caste and religious affinities and personal loyalties with the candidate were on the lower side of mean value (1.61 and 1.59 respectively). The trend was similar in all the different sections of the society, whether at rural-urban or male-female levels.

From the above table, some significant trends can be discerned. When the voters decided their choice in terms of local issues and personal gains it was the expression of their local interest. They attached more importance to the environment in which they were

Table 4.4
Means (Scale Range 1-3) of Determinants of Voting Decisions

	Rural			*Urban*			*Combined*
	Male N=85	*Female N=35*	*Total N=120*	*Male N=66*	*Female N=43*	*Total N=229*	*Total N=229*
Local problem	2.14	1.83	2.05	2.12	2.35	2.21	2.13
Ideology of Political Party	2.06	1.29	1.83	2.14	2.12	2.13	1.97
Candidate's Image	2.01	1.60	1.89	2.26	1.93	2.13	2.00
Personal Loyalties with candidate	1.59	1.49	1.56	1.80	1.37	1.63	1.59
Caste/Religion Affinity	1.88	1.69	1.83	1.47	1.21	1.37	1.61
Monetary or Other benefits	2.14	1.83	2.05	2.12	2.35	2.21	2.13
Other Considerations	2.06	1.29	1.83	2.14	2.12	2.12	1.97

living than to the national or larger regional issues. This shows that the issues that were dominant in panchayat elections held in recent past had continued to dominate and affect the assembly elections too. In course of the survey it was found that among the voters the local issues comprised mainly the benefits accruing as a result of numerous welfare schemes in the rural areas like roads, electricity, hand pumps etc. These infrastructural benefits for their village or specifically even for the particular habitation of theirs emerged as a dominant motivating force for exercise of their voting right. In this sense the factor labeled as local issues was similar to that of the personal interest or gains. That is why the mean values for both the factors, local issues and personal gains, have been similar. As regards the image of the candidate, it was found that the voters preferred a candidate who had promoted or could promote their personal gains. Thus, the image of the candidate was closely linked with his capacity to promote the personal gains of the electorates. Therefore the factors like the local issues and the image of the candidate converge on the point of personal gains. Factors like personal loyalties to a particular candidate emerge due to the prospect of likely benefits to accrue if the candidate got successful. Religious and caste affinities played a helpful role in this regard. It was because of this tendency the candidates with a criminal past got elected. The voters were not so much bothered about the character of the candidate. Instead they placed their personal gains in the centre and if a candidate with a corrupt and criminal past had served or was likely to serve in promoting their personal interest then he was their choice. In such circumstances a candidate with a tainted past could also be a winner at the polls. This trend makes ideology of a party, its views on national and international issues and its policies on socio-economic transformation as irrelevant.

III
Concluding Remarks

Our analysis has shown that in the present phase the prospect of direct and indirect personal gains is the key factor for deciding their vote by the vast majority of the electorate. In this endeavour the proximity with the candidate plays a significant role. The electorate feel that as against other candidates the caste candidate may be easily approachable for obtaining such gains. This factor motivates them to participate in elections enthusiastically against all odds. The electorates have an attitude of indifference, even contempt, towards the political parties, their leaders and the candidates in the fray in general. Yet, the prospect of obtaining personal gains through a candidate is a compulsive factor for them to join and participate vigorously in the elections under the banner of one party or the other. Although the participation level in the activities for political mobilisation before and during the elections is low, the percentage of vote casts is not so. This is very much in agreement with our earlier observation that the electorate in the present phase is possessed with indifference and contempt towards the political parties and candidates. It is the prospect of direct or indirect personal gains that drives them to go to polls. This behavioural pattern has found validity among rural and urban as well as male and female voters alike with some variations in case of rural women.

NOTES

1. The general elections for the last UP Assembly were held in November, 1993 in which the Samajwadi Party and the Bahujan Samaj Party had an electoral allaince. This allaince secured majority in the House and formed the government under the leadership of Mulayam Singh Yadav. If that government would have completed its full term the elections for next UP Assembly were to be held in November 1998.

2. **Account of election expenses and maximum thereof.**—Every candidate at an election shall, either by himself or by his election agent, keep a separate and correct account of all expenditure in connection with the election incurred or authorised by him or by his election agent between [2][the date on which he has been nominated] and the date of declaration of the result thereof, both dates inclusive.

   [2][Explanation 1.—Notwithstanding any judgment, order or decision of any court to the contrary, any expenditure incurred or authorised in connection with the election of a candidate by a political party or by any other association or body of persons or by any individual (other than the candidate or his election agent) shall not be deemed to be, and shall not ever be deemed to have been, expenditure in connection with the election incurred or authorised by the candidate or by his election agent for the purposes of this sub-section:

   Provided that nothing contained in this Explanation shall affect—

   (a) any judgment, order or decision of the Supreme Court whereby the election of a candidate to the House of the People or to the Legislative Assembly of a State has been declared void or set aside before the commencement of the Representation of the People (Amendment) Ordinance, 1974 (Ord. 13 of 1974);

   (b) any judgment, order or decision of a High Court whereby the election of any such candidate has been declared void or set aside before the commencement of the said Ordinance if no appeal has been preferred to the Supreme Court against such judgment, order or decision of the High Court before such commencement and the period of limitation for filing such appeal has expired before such commencement.

   [2][* * *]

   [2][Explanation 3.—For the removal of doubt, it is hereby declared that any expenditure incurred in respect of any arrangements made, facilities provided or any other act or thing done by any person in the service of the Government and belonging to any of the classes mentioned in clause (7) of Section 123 in the discharge or purported discharge of his official duty as mentioned in the proviso to that clause shall not be deemed to be expenditure in connection with the election incurred or authorised by a candidate or by his election agent for the purposes of this sub-section.]

   (2) The account shall contain such particulars, as may be prescribed.

   The total of the said expenditure shall not exceed such amount as may be prescribed. **(Section 77 of the Representation of the People Act, 1951).**

3. The Election Commission may nominate an Observer who shall be an Officer of Government to watch the conduct of election or elections in a constituency or a group of constituencies and to perform such other functions as may be entrusted to him by the Election Commission.

   The Observer, thus, nominated shall have the power to direct the Returning Officer for the constituency or for any of the constituencies for which he has been nominated, to stop the counting of votes at any time before the declaration of the result or not to declare the result if in the opinion of the Observer booth capturing has taken place at a large number of polling stations or at places fixed for the poll or counting of votes are unlawfully taken out of custody of the custody of the Returning Officer or are accidentally or intentionally destroyed or lost or are damaged or tampered with to such an extent that the result of the poll at that polling station or place cannot be ascertained. **(Section 20B (1) & (2) of the Representation of the People Act enforced w.e.f. 1.8.1996).**

4. The district of Allahabad has two Parliament Constituencies namely— Allahabad and Phulpur. Both the constituencies include five assembly segments each as shown in the Table 2.24.

5

Experimenting with Caste Re-Configurations

The present chapter is based on the findings of the election study conducted during the parliamentary election of 1998. It has been divided into four sections. In the opening section the important socio-political events that occurred during the period between the last election (1996) and the election under study have been discussed, the design of the study and the characteristics of the sample respondents have been explained in the second, the analyses of the data in the third while the emerging trends have been outlined in the last section.

The eleventh Lok Sabha could not survive even for two years and the people of India were forced to use their right to vote nearly three years ahead of the usual schedule[1]. This exercise cost the nation about Rs. 800 crores. In any case, it provided an opportunity to the social scientists to re-test the finding of their earlier surveys. Before proceeding to state and explain the design, findings and implication of the study it would be appropriate to narrate critically the important political occurrences that affected voters' behaviour in the election under study.

I
The Background

Hung Assembly in Uttar Pradesh: In the assembly elections, held in September 1996, no party was able to obtain majority. In the 425-member assembly the BJP was the single largest party with 170 members followed by the SP with 110 and the BSP with 67 members. The Congress party had a tally of 33 members only. The election results were almost a carbon copy of the 1993 assembly election results[2].

The three main contenders for power—the BJP, the SP and the BSP — were not in a position to forge a coalition among them to form a government. The state guesthouse incident of June 2,1995 in Lucknow had created an unbridgeable wedge between the BSP and the SP[3]. At the same time the BJP and the BSP also could not support each other. The Mayawati government of 1995, formed with the support of the BJP from outside, had vehemently attacked the BJP, unmindful of its support to her government. As a result the BJP withdrew its support which led to the fall of the government and imposition of the President rule. The hurt feelings were fresh enough not to permit any political arrangement between the two at that time.

Continuation of the President Rule: In such circumstances, the President rule was re-imposed for another six months after the elections. The assembly was kept in suspended animation and the Governor issued appeals repeatedly to the political parties to improvise a majority to form the government. In some quarters this was seen as a device to continue the President rule in the State. The Governor's insistence on demonstrating majority support to his satisfaction vis-a-vis the insistence of political parties on inviting them to form the government first and proving the majority on the floor of the assembly later had created a stalemate. The continued unwillingness to invite any party to form a government was seen as a device on the part of the Governor not to forego the power being enjoyed by him in the prevailing political uncertainty. It was also alleged that during the entire period of President rule it was the virtual rule of Mulayam Singh Yadav, the then defence minister in the Union Government, and that the Governor was acting as the proxy of the latter. Mulayam Singh Yadav and the United Front government at Delhi were happy with the continuing situation, as in their opinion they were successful in keeping the BJP out of power in the largest populous state of the country.

BSP-BJP Coalition: Towards the end of the President rule the national leadership of the BJP and the BSP devised a formula to form a coalition government in the State, which was formalised on March 14, 1997. Under this arrangement both the parties were to run the coalition for six months each. The BSP was to take the first term followed by the BJP. Both the parties were to have equal strength in the ministry. After a year the working of coalition was to be reviewed and, if found satisfactory, a decision could be taken for its continuation.

Thus, Mayawati was sworn in as the Chief Minister of UP on March 21, 1997, ending the ten-month long President rule in the state. The alliance as some opined, was opportunistic and likely to be short lived. Others thought, it was a reflection of improved relations at ground level between the upper castes and the Scheduled Castes, and if successful, in the long run it might give birth to a new coalition between two hitherto projected antagonistic social forces. It was particularly noteworthy in the sense that the BSP had projected, all along its rise and growth as a political movement and party, the upper castes as such, irrespective of the long standing socio-economic and even cultural stratification existing among them, as inimical and objects of hatred. The party was intolerant of what it called manuvad and coined slogans like "Tilak, Taraju our Talwar, Inko Juta Maro Char' and 'Brahman, Thakur, Bania Chor, Baki Sab DS-4' etc. This alliance seemed as if the politics of hatred between the upper castes and the Scheduled Castes was approaching to its end. The success achieved by this alliance in Farrukhabad Assembly by-election further endorsed the above phenomenon.

The Competitive Mobilization: Soon this optimism was belied. The undercurrents of mutually suspicious coalition partners remained and as soon as opportunities presented themselves fissures developed. The agreement on six months term in itself gave the impression of temporariness of the alliance. The provision of review of the alliance after a year further strengthened the temporary status of the coalition. All the political players felt that another election was round the corner. So a competition for expanding the existing popular support and breaking new grounds in that direction had started. The BJP, with the upper castes as its main support base, was around to further extend its ground among the OBCs and the SCs.

The BSP, on the other hand, was encroaching into the upper castes[4] and the OBCs, particularly among the Most Backwards and the Muslims[5], while consolidating its Scheduled Castes support base[6]. Likewise Mulayam Singh Yadav's effort was to keep the Yadavas intact, with as much support as possible among Muslims and extend the party's influence among non-Yadav backwards, the upper castes and the SCs. Thus, the political scenario was that of competing mobilization of support bases, in which the Mandir, Mandal and Manuvad receded in the background and new symbols were searched for.

Installation of Ambedkar Statues: In her previous term as the Chief Minister in 1995 Mayawati had got Ambedkar's statues installed and had noticed its utility as instrument of mobilisation of SC votes. Knowing that her term as Chief Minister would last for six months only she launched an un-ending extensive drive for the installation of Ambedkar's statues throughout the state. It was a well planned mobilisation strategy of Mayawati for consolidation of SC votes The administration in each district was to be responsible for providing government land and all sorts of necessary requirements including funds for the purpose. The statues were to be installed at prominent places like road crossings, public parks, educational institutions, kasbas and even villages. Indeed it had become a state sponsored Ambedkar's statue installation campaign.

At many places along with the installation of Ambedkar's statue, the adjacent public land was allotted to Ambedkar parks, Ambedkar libraries, Ambedkar research institutes etc. Funds for these purposes also were made available by the government. At the top of this agenda were the ambitious projects like the Ambedkar Park and the completion of the Parivartan Chowk at Lucknow. The charge of the Ambedkar Park was given to the Lucknow Development Authority. To begin with, it was a project of Rs. 15 crores. Later on it was raised to Rs. 25 crores, then to Rs. 45 crores, Rs. 85 crores and ultimately to Rs. 125 crores. The land allotted for the park was 28 acres in area. Rules and regulations relating to the development of parks were not observed. The CAG recorded objections against the reckless spending in this regard and an inquiry was instituted. Charges of corruption were made against the Lucknow Development Authority, Urban Development and Public Works departments. The media kept these issues relentlessly in the public eye.

Mayawati and the BSP might or might not have gained, apart from consolidation of SC votes, in extending their mass appeal among the other poor but the reaction of this drive on others, particularly on the SP, was prompt and emphatic. Mulayam Singh Yadav termed the whole drive as a type of land grabbing. He also said in no uncertain terms that if and when he returned to power he would get these statues replaced by that of Ram Manohar Lohia, who was one of the founders of the Socialist Party in India. The drive had also acted as a provocation in non-SC circles, so as to pull down the Ambedkar statues at some places. Ambedkar statue was blackened at Nana Saheb Park in Kanpur on August 5, 1997. In retaliation, the statues of Mahatma Gandhi, Indira Gandhi and Subhash Chandra Bose were pulled down and broken by Ambedkar supporters at Kanpur on August 7, 1997. The incident formed the subject matter of emotionally surcharged and heated debates in the Vidhan Sabha of UP after which the house agreed not to insult the personages of national leaders.

Initially the BJP was in a fix. The urban development minister and the PWD Minister in Mayawati government belonged to the BJP. These two ministers blessed the Ambedkar Park and Parivartan Chowk projects. Additionally, the BJP had Scheduled Castes MLAs in sizeable number and the party, being a partner in the coalition, did not want to accuse the Scheduled Castes Chief Minister of partisanship. However, finding that the SP was taking advantage by exploiting the resentment in non-SC section of population, Kalyan Singh of BJP, the Chief Minister in waiting, at last spoke out almost in similar way on this issue and he too was seen as opponent of the drive.

Creation of New Districts and Other Administrative Units: Mayawati's term of heading the coalition government with BJP saw another drive to extend her influence among some backward castes and for further consolidation of her position among the SCs. Like Ambedkar's statues new symbols in form of changing the nomenclature of some existing districts served the same purpose. The name of Bhadohi district was changed to Sant Ravidas Nagar. A new district in Faizabad was carved out with the name of Ambedkar Nagar. During this phase, she also created 3 divisions, 12 districts, 29 sub-divisions and a large number of development blocks, unmindful of the precarious condition of the state's exchequer. The criteria laid down for creations of new districts were not followed[7]. There was no administrative urgency at that time for the creation of such administrative units. However, these steps were helping in appeasing certain non-Yadav backward castes. Gautam Budh Nagar and Mahamaya Nagar, apparently symbolizing recognition of the Buddhist past, and Jyoti Ba Phule Nagar, recognizing the great nineteenth century social reformer of Maharashtra, brought in fact Mayawati closer to *Shakya-Saini-Kushwaha-Maurya-Mali* caste combination because this combination considered these great personalities as belonging to their own castes. Shahuji Maharaj Nagar, named after Chatrapati Shivaji's father, was created to appease the *Kurmi caste* in the state. Sant Kabir Nagar, the district named after Sant Kabir, was to please *Ansaris*, in common rural parlance known as *julahas*, the community which is most numerous among the Muslims in the state. The name Udham Singh Nagar was given to placate the Sikhs in the tarai region of the state. In this way Mayawati was trying to consolidate and expand her support base among non-dalit backward castes and minorities also.

Suddenly the Chandra Skekhar Azad Agriculture University, Kanpur, got a new nomenclature as Shahuji Maharaj University and Ruhelkhand University as Jyoti ba Phule University. Having done this much, as if to treat the coalition partners, she named the Gorakhpur University after the BJP leader Deen Dayal Upadhyaya.

The creation of new districts and other administrative units was done in spite of severe opposition. Mayawati was however, by taking these steps, was giving signal that she was to be seen as a strong dalit woman Chief Minister in the grade of Kalyan Singh and Mulayam Singh.

Ambedkar Gram Vikas Yojana: The Ambedkar Gram Vikas Yojana, a programme for providing basic infrastructural facilities to those villages where Scheduled Castes/Scheduled Tribes constituted majority of the population (50 percent or more), was launched in 1990-91 by the Mulayam Singh Yadav government. When Mayawati assumed power the limit was reduced from 50 to 30 percent. In this way the number of villages and the SC/ST population covered increased manifold. The programme included components like rural electrification, link roads, village streets and drains, primary schools etc. A separate department was created to monitor the implementation of the programme. In order to provide funds for the extended reach of the programme, the funds earmarked for Poorvanchal and Bundelkhand Vikas Nidhi were diverted. Frequent review meetings were held, mostly in the presence of the Chief Minister, and the bureaucracy was kept on his toes. This drive served the same purpose as did the Ambedkar statue installation i.e.

consolidation of the Scheduled Castes base. The programme as envisaged by Mayawati was meant to develop a feeling of empowerment among the Scheduled Castes in the remotest village of the state, which ultimately strengthened her power base and influence among them. In a way she was proving the basic point of the BSP ideology that state power would bring socio-economic gains, not vice-versa. The SCs living in such villages were enthused to find the top bracket of bureaucracy running to and fro to oversee the implementation of the programme at their doorstep all because their bahanji was the Chief Minister. It was certainly a change of direction of the state affairs.

The non-SC population in these villages was initially indifferent towards the programme. Later on, it was rationalized that the infrastructure created in the village under the Ambedkar village development programme would be more beneficial to them than to the SC households because they owned most of the resources. By and by a situation developed in which the non-SC vested interest in the rural areas began to mount pressure at the block and district level for the inclusion of their villages in the list of Ambedkar Gram Vikas Yojana. As no one in these villages was opposed to the programme so it did not encounter any opposition by the non-BSP parties also. But the villages not included in the list were feeling that their development was neglected. Not surprisingly, Kalyan Singh declared that when he would assume the power in the state he would take care of the development of the entire state (Dainik Jagran, August 8, 1997).

Politics of Harijan Act: As the BSP was consolidating its support base in the name of Ambedkar, the main opposition party in the state, the Samajwadi Party, raised the issue of repression of non-dalits under the provisions of the Harijan Act. The alleged ruthless implementation of the Harijan Act by the State machinery had angered sections of the upper castes and the backwards. By raising the banner of opposition in this regard the SP opened avenues for entry in the upper castes, particularly the Thakurs. Amar Singh, a spokesman of the party made specific allegation that by abusing the provisions of this Act a particular caste among SCs (the hint was on *chamars*) in league with the administration was falsely implicating the upper caste particularly the Thakurs (Lucknow, September 7, 1997). At a press conference (Dainik Jagran, September 7, 1997) Mulayam Singh drew similarity between the terror of *nasbandi* drive during Emergency Days and the one prevailing with the excesses of the Harijan Act at that time. The SP also launched *jail bharo andolan* between August 13 and September 10, 1997 in which the excesses committed under the Harijan Act were a major issue. At its public meetings the SP speakers highlighted this issue in their speeches. The opportunities offered, thus, for the SP to intrude into the upper caste support base bothered the BJP and other parties depending on non-dalit support base. The Samajwadi Janta Party and the Bhartiya Kisan Kamgar Party also launched statewide agitation on this issue. The BJP, through Kalyan Singh, took the stand that the party was indeed the well wisher of the dalits, however, the excesses under the Harijan Act would not be tolerated. On another occasion Kalyan Singh said that in rural areas the terror created by the Harijan Act was greater than that of dacioty (Dainik Jagran, September 6, 1997). As soon as Kalyan Singh came to power a government order was issued to all the district officials to prevent the misuse of the Harijan Act. In this way the BJP tried to assuage the hurt feelings of the upper caste with regard to excesses under Harijan Act by a government in which the BJP itself was a partner.

Thus, the competing parties carried on the mobilization politics along caste lines for or against the implementation of the Harijan Act during Mayawati's regime.

BJP in Power: The six month Mayawati's term as the Chief Minister, under the coalition arrangement with the BJP, was to expire on September 21,1997 and the BJP was to take over for the next six months. But as the date of handing over the Chief Minister's office drew closer, Mayawati started raising new conditions. She put forth a rider that with the change in the Chief Ministership a BSP member should replace the then Speaker of the Vidhan Sabha who belonged to the BJP. The BJP was not willing to accede to this demand. The Speaker Kesari Nath Tripathi himself declared emphatically that the speaker's office had a constitutional status and since he had been elected unopposed he was under no obligation to resign in any circumstances. Besides, a section of the BJP MLAs had threatened to resign from the assembly if the Speaker was forced to step down. In another move in the BJP the dissolution of the assembly itself was raised. The issue became so intricate that the break-up of the alliance loomed large as a possibility. In the end the BSP handed over the Chief Ministership to Kalyan Singh with the assurance from the BJP that no defection would be engineered in the BSP.

The whole game of Mayawati in the demand of change in Speaker appeared to be motivated by the desire to *(i)* prevent the defection in her party, particularly by the MLAs belonging to the upper castes and the OBCs who were formally elected on the BSP ticket but were suspected to be willing to cross over to the BJP at an opportune moment; *(ii)* pressurise the BJP government not to change the policies and programmes formulated by her in order to consolidate the support base of the BSP among the Scheduled Castes; and *(iii)* ensure not to upset the bureaucratic set up by fresh transfers and postings which she had formed as a dalit-oriented administration in the state. The intention behind placing these riders by Mayawati was to attack and harass Kalyan Singh, the Chief Minister in waiting, who had been critical towards her government throughout her Chief Ministership.

***Withdrawal of the BSP Support to Kalyan Singh Government*:** Within two days of assuming power the Kalyan Singh government issued an order to district officials to prevent the misuse of the Harijan act. A large number of top ranking administrative officers were transferred. The newly created districts by Mayawati were put under reconsideration. In another incident in the village Rohana of Muzaffarnagar district the police fired upon the dalits agitating against the alleged rape and murder of a dalit woman. All these steps and incidents together provided enough material for the BSP to conclude that the BJP was breaking the understanding arrived at the time of handing over of the Chief Ministership that it would not upset the policies framed by the Mayawati government. The BSP leader Kanshi Ram declared to launch an agitation against anti-dalit mentality of the Kalyan Singh government. Ultimately the support by the BSP to the Kalyan Singh government was withdrawn on October 19,1997.

Trust Vote, Defections and Violence in the Assembly: It was suspected that the then Governor of Uttar Pradesh, Romesh Bhandari, was in league with the United Front government at the Centre, particularly with the then defence minister and SP leader Mulayam Singh Yadav. With the withdrawal of the support by the BSP, the Kalyan Singh government was reduced to a minority. With Kalyan Singh still claiming majority, the Governor asked him to prove his majority on the floor of the house within 48 hours. Kalyan Singh accepted the challenge and by engineering defections in a number of parties proved the majority 222 to zero marred by violence during the proceedings in the house on October 21,1997.

The United Front government at the Centre in this situation concluded that the state should be put under the President rule once again on the ground *(a)* the defections were not constitutionally valid; *(b)* the proceedings of the Assembly were conducted in the state of confusion and violence; and *(c)* the house was devoid of entire opposition. In view of all these, the Union Cabinet recommended imposition of President rule under Article 356 of the Constitution. The President, however, returned the recommendations to the cabinet that the government in the State enjoyed the support of the majority in the House consisting of the elected representatives.

It was true that the Kalyan Singh government had tactically achieved the majority. The BSP, the Congress and the Janata Dal suffered defections. Some independents also supported the confidence motion. In order to stabilize the government, Kalyan Singh was left with no options but to appoint all the defectors as ministers due to which the size of the ministry was enlarged to 93. The ministry was later derisively designated as a 'jumbo ministry'.

Elections to the Legislative Council: On January 11,1998 the elections to the UP Legislative Council from local bodies were held in which the BJP won 25 seats, the SP 11, the Congress (I) one and independent one (I). The BSP failed to win any seat (Frontline, February 6, 1998). Kalyan Singh gained most from these polls. These elections were important in the sense that they indicated the social and caste equations emerging in the state.

The circumstances in which these elections were held gave birth to several controversies. More than a million members of local bodies were involved. The three major contenders the BJP, the SP and the BSP were to test which way the wind was blowing for the ensuing parliament elections. The BJP was not sure of the success. The Kalyan Singh government announced grants amounting to Rs. 250 crores to the local bodies of the state in order to fulfill its 'constitutional responsibility' just five days before the elections, scheduled at that time for December 29,1997. Kalyan Singh's gamble in this affair was, if the prospect of grants to the local bodies brought more votes to it, well and good. If Election Commission intervened, the elections would be shifted, probably after the Lok Sabha elections, avoiding the prospects of Lok Sabha polls with defeat in these elections (Frontline January 23,1998) The Election Commission, however, intervened and advanced the date of polling to January 11,1998. In the end the BJP won and faced the Lok Sabha elections with success in these elections.

Exploring Newer Caste Combinations: The 1996 Parliament and State Assembly elections in Uttar Pradesh had demonstrated that the politics of Ram Mandir and Hindutva of the BJP, the OBCs and Muslims combine of the SP under the umbrella of Mandal and the attack on the Manuvad and 85:15 slogan of the BSP had reached the plateau. It was best substantiated in the state assembly elections held in September 1996, a few months after the Lok Sabha elections. All the major parties, the BJP, the SP, the BSP, the Congress and the Janata Dal, won more or less the same number of seats in the assembly as in 1993 assembly elections (see endnote 2). Therefore, a change in strategy to increase the popular support base was necessitated by all. This gave birth to a new alignment of caste equations. Henceforth, it was not going to be upper caste alone for the BJP, OBCs and Muslims for the SP and SCs for the BSP (The Congress and UF were nearly wiped out). So a scramble for BJP to expand in OBCs and SCs, for the SP among upper castes and for the BSP among upper caste, OBCs and Muslims began. The events and incidents narrated above have to be understood in this context.

In this direction rallies and demonstrations of different castes were organised and patronised by the different political parties, the significance of which could be realised in the background of the events narrated. It has to be noted that these rallies and demonstrations openly exhibited the combination of such castes, which were previously inimical to each other.

In his campaign against the misuse of Harijan Act during Mayawati's regime, Mulayam Singh Yadav had projected *Thakurs* also among the victims. He was glorified as the friend and promoter of the *Thakurs* and addressed a number of *Kshatriya Sammelans*. in the state, cutting into the upper caste base of the BJP. Similarly the sections among trading community through meetings and conferences eulogized Mulayam Singh Yadav as their benefactor, again pushing into the BJP support base.

Mayawati launched rallies and conferences among MBCs and Muslims to strengthen and expand her base. She made sure that tickets were given to Muslims in sufficient numbers to make inroads into SPs support base. The BSP tickets were allotted to the upper caste candidates also. To make this point loud and emphatic the BSP launched a significant *Bhaichara rally* just before the Lok Sabha elections.

The BJP's primary worry was the likelihood rupture in its upper caste fort, most significantly among the thakurs. So Rajnath Singh, a thakur by caste, had to be installed as state president of the BJP. The number of *Thakurs* in the Kalyan Singh government also became considerable. At the same time Kalyan Singh, himself belonging to a backward caste—Lodh, along with other backward ministers, through the coalition partners, consolidated and extended the BJP support among the backwards. It already had a substantial base among the SCs.

II
Design of the Study

Sample Selection: As compared to the 1996 Parliament election study the size of sample in the present study was about one-third. This reduction occurred owning to two reasons. *(i)* In the 1996 parliamentary elections the sample was drawn from all the ten assembly segments of Allahabad and Phulpur parliament constituencies, whereas, in the present study, instead of all the segments, only six were selected (three in each parliament constituency); *(ii)* in 1996 five booths were selected from each assembly segment while in the present study only two booths each from the six assembly segments were selected. The number of assembly segments and the booths covered under the present study was reduced because the elections were to be held after only twenty two months of the 1996 parliament elections and only fourteen months after the state assembly elections. In view of the short intervals between the elections, It was felt that a reduced size of the sample would serve the purpose of the study. Thus, the total number of the selected booths was reduced from 50 to 12. However, the method of selection of the sample respondents from each selected booth was kept unchanged. With the help of updated voters' list a total of 600 samples (50 each from every sampled booth) was drawn through systematic sampling method.

Sample Loss: About 30 percent of the sample were lost and only 425 respondents constituted the effective sample (Table 5.1). The proportion of the sample loss was similar to that of the 1996 Parliament and State Assembly elections. Migration of households both among urban as well as rural areas was the major cause for such losses. Unavailability of voters continued to be a significant factor for sample losses This phenomenon was mainly the feature of urban areas. On the other hand, the continuance of names in the

Table 5.1
Factors Responsible for Sample Loss

Parliament Constituencies and Assembly Segments	*Size of Selected Sample*	*Size of Effective Sample*	*Reasons for Sample Loss* Migrated	Found Dead	Untraceable	Duplication	Not Available	Unwilling for interview	*Total Sample Loss* Number	%
1. Allahabad	**300**	**214**	**22**	**01**	**29**	**14**	**18**	**02**	**86**	**28.6**
City North	100	69	11	00	12	00	07	01	31	31.0
City South	100	65	09	00	15	01	09	01	35	35.0
Meja	100	80	02	01	02	13	02	00	20	20.0
2. Phulpur	**300**	**211**	**32**	**10**	**09**	**00**	**37**	**01**	**89**	**29.6**
Jhusi	100	72	07	09	03	00	09	00	28	34.0
Handia	100	75	11	00	03	00	11	00	25	26.0
Nawabganj	100	64	14	01	03	00	17	01	36	37.0
Total	**600**	**425**	**54**	**11**	**38**	**14**	**55**	**03**	**175**	**29.2**
(% dist'tion)	**(100.0)**	**(70.8)**	**(9.0)**	**(1.8)**	**(6.3)**	**(2.3)**	**(9.1)**	**(0.5)**	**29.2**	

electoral rolls even after the death of the elector was a feature in rural segments. The problem of duplication of names was not as serious as in the earlier survey of 1996 assembly elections. A substantial number of voters were not available at the time of survey being mostly away in search of employment and as per norms of the study[8] the substitution was also not available in the family. There were about 0.5 percent voters who refused to be interviewed.

Data Collection and Analysis

In this study the method applied for data collection was the same as in the 1996 Assembly elections. Experienced field investigators were employed to collect the data. Respondents were contacted individually and the investigators filled up questionnaires after putting the question in proper context.

For the purpose of analysis the respondents were classified into rural and urban segments, which were further divided into male and female categories. The data were analyzed on the basis of mean scores obtained from the responses on the scales of three or five points. In case of combining the responses of two or more statements the direction of opinions was taken into consideration carefully. In such cases values were assigned in descending order for the responses of statements with negative orientation whereas ascending values were given to the responses of positive statements.

Characteristics of Sample Respondents

There were 68.5 percent (291) rural and 31.5 percent (134) urban respondents in the effective sample (425). As compared to the sample for 1996 Parliament Election Study the urban bias was higher in the present sample. It must to be noted that the that in the previous survey the sample was drawn from the two urban and eight rural assembly segments while in the present study the sample was drawn from two urban but only four rural assembly segments. So it was obvious that there would be relatively higher urban bias in the sample. Another imbalance in the sample was in terms of gender distribution, which had reflected as the male bias. As compared to the 1996 parliament survey the female proportion in the present sample had increased to a large extent (30 percent), still it was lower than the proportion in the total electors in the district (45 percent).

The reason for this imbalance could be explained with the help of Table 5.2 in which it is evident that there was a sample loss of about 40 percent in case of female voters. As in the case of other surveys the female respondents, particularly in rural areas, continued to remain shy in responding to the questionnaire.

The caste-wise distribution of the sample had also changed. The proportion of Scheduled Castes had more or less remained the same (22.6 percent) which was a little less than their proportion in the population of Allahabad (24.6 percent). The proportion of the OBCs in the present sample got reduced to about 35 percent from 41.6 percent in the first survey. The percentage share of Muslims also went down from 10 percent in the previous survey to 6.4 percent in the present survey. The reduction in the proportion of the OBCs and the Muslims resulted in the increase in proportion of the upper castes from 25.6 percent to 34.4 percent. So the present sample had a prominent bias in the case of the upper castes.

In the earlier survey the respondents were classified in terms of the three caste groups (SC, OBC and Upper Castes) and the Muslims. It should be noted that each caste group consisted of a number of castes. In each caste group there had been internal conflicts and conciliation between the castes forming the group for power sharing. The dissatisfied section of a caste within a group did not hesitate to join hands with the other caste groups to gain a better share in power. This was a new factor in the emerging mobilization politics and therefore it became necessary to separate each caste from the other within each group. So the information about the caste of the respondents was obtained which was confined to four major caste groups in the earlier survey. The sample, thus, represented four castes among the upper caste group, twelve castes among the OBCs and five castes among the Scheduled Castes. A number of scholars have established that the Muslim community is as diversified caste-wise as the Hindu (Bhatty 1996; 244). However, the typical political situation prevailing in the state as a result of the domlition of the Babri Masjid and the perception that the BJP was a Hindu party aspiring to establish a Hindu rule has compelled them to take the stand that whichever party was in a position to defeat the BJP deserved their support. Therefore, irrespective of the division prevailing among them in terms of religious sects and social stratification, their electoral behaviour has been uniform i.e. to prevent the BJP from obtaining state power. Hence the Muslims were

Table 5.2
Distribution of Sample Respondents by Caste, Domicile and Gender

Castes	*Male*			*Female*			*Total*		
	Urban	*Rural*	*Total*	*Urban*	*Rural*	*Total*	*Urban*	*Rural*	*Total*
Upper Caste Hindus	**33 (41.8)**	**76 (34.5)**	**109 (36.5)**	**22 (40.0)**	**15 (21.1)**	**37 (29.4)**	**55 (41.0)**	**91 (31.3)**	**146 (34.4)**
Brahmin	21 (26.6)	58 (26.4)	79 (26.4)	10 (18.2)	6 (8.5)	16 (12.7)	31 (23.1)	64 (21.9)	95 (22.4)
Kshatriya	3 (3.8)	2 (0.9)	5 (1.7)	8 (14.5)	1 (1.4)	9 (7.1)	11 (8.2)	3 (1.0)	14 (3.3)
Vaishyas	4 (5.1)	10 (4.5)	14 (4.7)	3 (5.5)	3 (4.2)	6 (4.8)	7 (5.2)	13 (4.5)	20 (4.7)
Kayasthas	5 (6.3)	6 (2.7)	11 (3.7)	1 (1.8)	5 (7.0)	6 (4.8)	6 (4.5)	11 (3.8)	17 (4.0)
Dominant Backward Castes	**18 (22.8)**	**58 (26.4)**	**76 (25.4)**	**7 (12.7)**	**11 (15.4)**	**18 (14.3)**	**25 (18.7)**	**69 (23.7)**	**94 (22.1)**
Kurmi	9 (11.4)	11 (5.0)	20 (6.7)	1 (1.8)	4 (5.6)	5 (4.0)	10 (7.5)	15 (5.2)	25 (5.9)
Yadav	8 (10.1)	41 (18.6)	49 (16.4)	5 (9.1)	4 (5.6)	9 (7.1)	13 (9.7)	45 (15.5)	58 (13.6)
Kushwaha	1 (1.3)	6 (2.7)	7 (2.3)	1 (1.8)	3 (4.2)	4 (3.2)	2 (1.5)	9 (3.1)	11 (2.6)
Most Backward Castes*	**6 (7.6)**	**33 (15.0)**	**39 (13.0)**	**2 (3.6)**	**13 (18.3)**	**15 (11.9)**	**9 (6.0)**	**46 (15.8)**	**54 (12.7)**
Vishwakarma	3 (3.8)	9 (4.1)	12 (4.0)	—	2 (2.8)	2 (1.6)	3 (2.2)	11 (3.8)	14 (3.3)
Bind	1 (1.3)	10 (4.5)	11 (3.7)	—	4 (5.6)	4 (3.2)	1 (0.7)	14 (4.8)	15 (3.5)
Scheduled Castes**	**19 (24.1)**	**39 (17.7)**	**58 (19.4)**	**18 (32.7)**	**20 (28.2)**	**38 (30.2)**	**37 (27.6)**	**59 (20.3)**	**96 (22.6)**
Chamar	11 (13.9)	15 (6.8)	26 (8.7)	8 (14.5)	11 (15.5)	19 (15.1)	19 (14.2)	26 (8.9)	45 (10.6)
Pasi	7 (8.9)	13 (5.9)	20 (6.7)	9 (16.4)	5 (7.0)	14 (11.1)	16 (11.9)	18 (6.2)	34 (8.0)
Kol	—	11 (5.0)	11 (3.7)	—	4 (5.6)	4 (3.2)	—	15 (5.2)	15 (3.5)
Muslims	—	**13 (5.9)**	**13 (4.3)**	**3 (5.5)**	**11 (15.5)**	**14 (11.1)**	**3 (2.2)**	**24 (8.2)**	**27 (6.4)**
Others	**3 (3.8)**	**1 (0.4)**	**4 (1.3)**	**3 (5.5)**	**1 (1.4)**	**4 (3.2)**	**6 (4.5)**	**2 (0.6)**	**8 (1.9)**
All Castes Combined	**79 (18.6)**	**220 (51.8)**	**299 (70.4)**	**55 (12.9)**	**71 (16.7)**	**126 (29.6)**	**134 (31.5)**	**291 (68.5)**	**425 (100.0)**

* Some other Most Backward Castes, which were numerically very small in the sample, were also included like Gaderia, Nai, Kumbhar, Sonar, Bhujwa and Kahar.

** Some other Scheduled Castes, which were numerically very small in the sample, were also included like Dhobi and Khatik.

not classified in terms of their respective castes in the present study. There were some castes, which according to their size, had very few respondents in the sample, and it was not advisable to mention them separately. It has been assumed that detailed classification by major castes would be helpful in understanding the dynamics of electoral behaviour at grassroots level. Secondly, in this survey OBCs have further been divided into two groups—dominant backward castes and most backward castes. This classification was based on the findings of several other studies covering the same region (Sriniwas, Frankel, Jain)[9]. The detailed distribution of the sampled respondents by different castes has been shown in the Table 5.2.

III
The Results

The results of the survey have been analysed in two ways. As in the case of earlier survey, various aspects, such as political participation, affinity with the parties, determinants of voting decision and electoral environment, have been analysed in terms of mean values. In addition, the caste solidarity and party preferences have been explained on the basis of percentage distribution.

Political Participation: The mean values derived from the participation scores have been shown in the Table 5.3. It is evident from the table that the mean value for the monetary contributions to political parties was the lowest (1.00). It proves that the voters in general did not contribute funds to political parties. It also means that the political parties did not collect funds from the common electorate, the implication being that the political parties were funded by big business houses and the top rank leadership at district level belonged to the economically strong sections able to mobilize resources which might include unaccounted money.

The mean value for participation of the electorate in the electioneering as a campaign worker was marginally higher (1.14) than the monetary donations. In this case gender differentiation was clearly visible. Participation of women electorates in electioneering was negligible, which means electioneering was still a male dominated activity. There was no significant difference at rural and urban levels in this respect. The mean value of 1.14 denotes that the size of the section involved in the electioneering is very small. Had the mean value been 1.00 it would have meant that no one from the electorates participated in the electioneering. Had it been 5.00, it would have meant that the entire electorate participated in the electioneering. So the mean value of 1.14 means that the participation score for electioneering is effectively only 0.14 which implies that a very tiny minority was participating in the electioneering.

The overall mean values for activities like participation in the rallies and demonstration and the party meetings were equal (1.21). It appears that the same size of people and perhaps the same set of people were participating in various campaigns and mobilizations. There was however a difference at the urban and rural levels. It was found that the participation in the party meetings was greater than in the demonstrations and rallies in the urban areas. In the rural areas the picture was reversed. The implication is that the urban people take greater interest in the party meetings where policy decisions were taken than in the demonstrations and rallies where the decisions were propagated, whereas, in rural areas people were more interested in information regarding the decisions announced at the demonstrations and rallies. As regards the gender-wise preferences it was found that among the male electorates the mean value for participation in demonstrations had been higher, although marginally, than the participation in party meetings. Among the female electorates the value was higher in case of party meetings. The thirty-three percent reservation of seats for women in the panchayat elections[10] and progressively increasing participation of women in panchayat meetings at different levels might have inspired them to participate more and more in the party meetings. However, this did not mean that the participation level of women electorate was in any way higher than that of men. It was lower in both the cases as shown in the Table 5.3.

The mean value for participation in public meetings (1.48) was relatively higher than the other forms of participation. This form of participation attracted larger electorate in rural areas than in urban. In this case also the gender bias was evident. It was 1.60 for male electorates whereas it was only 1.18 in case of females. Among women it was higher in the urban areas while for men it was higher in the rural.

In the first survey, while constructing the political participation index in order to assess the intensity level of political participation of the voters, scores were assigned to various forms of political participation (Table 3.11). At that time those scores might have appeared to be arbitrary but the mean values of scores of different forms of participation presented in Table 5.3 confirm those observations.

Table 5.3
Mean Value of Various Forms of Political Participation

Range 1-5

Forms of	*Urban*			*Rural*			*Total*		
Participation	*Male*	*Female*	*Total*	*Male*	*Female*	*Total*	*Male*	*Female*	*Total*
Public Meetings	1.54	1.27	1.43	1.62	1.11	1.50	1.60	1.18	1.48
Demonstration/ Rallies	1.23	1.14	1.19	1.30	1.00	1.22	1.28	1.05	1.21
Party Meeting	1.35	1.13	1.26	1.21	1.11	1.19	1.25	1.12	1.21
Electioneering	1.22	1.05	1.16	1.19	1.00	1.13	1.20	1.00	1.14
Monetary Contribution	1.00	1.00	1.00	1.00	1.00	1.00	1.00	1.00	1.00
Affinity with Party	1.83	1.44	1.67	1.67	1.41	1.61	1.71	1.42	1.63

Affinity with the Parties: An endeavor was made to gauge the intensity level of the electorate regarding the affinity with a political party, irrespective of the fact whether on the part of the electorate there was participation of any kind in the activities of that party or not. The responses to the question relating to the subject were taken on a five-point scale, the mean value for which worked out to 1.63 as shown in the Table 5.3. It is only slightly higher than the level of participation or mobilization activities. The level of affinity with any political party was higher in urban than in rural areas. In case of male electorate it was higher in urban segments while for female it was nearly the same in both the areas.

Determinants of Voting Decision: Although the mean value of participation in the activities and the affiliation with a political party were found to be at a very low level, their participation level in voting was high. This was a perplexing phenomenon. The electorate was not participating in activities, was not mobilizing, did not posses high level of proximity with any political party, yet the participation in voting was high. The implication was that there were some factors other than those mentioned in the above paragraph which worked as the determinants of the vote. In other words, the participation of the electorate can not be understood or explained in terms of hitherto accepted norms and forms of the working of the party system. This phenomenon existed at the time of the last assembly elections also. Therefore as at that time a question as to how they viewed the factors like local issues, party ideology, personal loyalty to a candidate, caste and religious affinity, monetary gains and personal or community benefits as determinants of vote in general was put in the present questionnaire also. In the response on the both the occasions the local issues were accorded the top mean value. It will be appropriate here to explain the prevalent perception of the electorate regarding the term local issues. The policy makers would treat a road construction, brick laying, sinking a tube well or a handpump, construction of a dispensary or a school as welfare measures. The policy makers would think that by providing these infrastructural facilities the community would be benefited. But the voters' perception was different. They manipulated to get these public facilities constructed and installed in such a way that they could convert or use them like their personal assets Therefore all these facilities should not only be in their village but if possible right at their doorstep. If these installations were at a distance from their place of residence they got dissatisfied. It would not be out of place to mention that the behaviour of most of the village pradhans of appropriating the assets created for the welfare of the community reflects the same attitude. So, in the perception of the electorate the local them have got personalized. Thus, there was a vast difference between the perception of policy makers and the voters regarding the infrastructural facilities in a locality.

The policies of the parties have been viewed by the electorate as an important determinant of their vote. Its mean value was 2.10. The policies formulated by the parties attract attention of the electorate because the parties are caste based. At present, the socio- economic realities are in such a state wherein the interest of one section is in conflict with the interest of the other section and the parties create their support base amidst this conflict. They rationalize that unless the party captures the state power the interest of the section, which they are representing, would not be promoted and protected. For example, if the support base of a political party was among the Scheduled Castes, it would promise continuation of the reservation for them in the legislature, local bodies, government services, educational institutions, promulgation of reservation in private sectors, free electricity supply, link roads and schools in the *Harijan bastis*. At the time of elections this party would talk only of these issues. The Scheduled Castes electorate would smoothly identify such a party as their own and such policies as the determinants of their vote. Such a party would rarely talk about what measures it would take about the Non Scheduled Castes electorates. Similarly, a party enjoying an OBC support base would demand perpetuation of the Backward Caste Reservation and its further expansion. It would promise struggle against oppression in the name of enforcement of the provisions of Harijan Act. Such party would demand more and more remunerative prices for farm products, lowering the prices of fertilizers, pesticides and other agricultural inputs. Some parties, eyeing on the Muslim votes, would insist upon recognition of the Urdu language, appointment of Urdu teachers in schools and Urdu translators in the government offices, separate reservation for Muslims, scholarships for Muslim students etc. The parties likely to gain support from the upper castes insist upon recognition of merit, economic basis of reservation and in private they would denounce al kinds of reservations. All these issues cater to the imagination of different sections of electorate. It is to these policies which the electorates indicated as an important determinant to their vote.

In the respondents' opinion caste and religious affinity was a negligible determinant in the elector's vote. Its mean value was 1.10 on the scale of 1-3 as shown in the Table 5.4. It is difficult to comprehend this trend. In election after election it was found that the Muslim voters had opted en bloc to defeat a particular party perceived by them as their main enemy. Likewise, the caste groups had also voted almost en block. Numerous surveys would testify to this fact. Yet in the responses by the electors the caste was found an insignificant determinant in vote. It appears voters were hesitant in accepting the fact of caste based voting. They seemed to be conscious of the fact that to vote along caste lines was a bad electoral behaviour and it had to be kept hidden. They also seemed to be aware that it might harm the prospects of the candidate supported by them, for allied castes might feel hurt. Therefore in formal interviews the voters hid the fact that the voting was caste based, it might just be a tactics. However in private conversation voters did state that they would vote for a particular candidate because he happened to be their casteman or he was supported by their *biradari*.

Table 5.4
Mean Value of the Determinants of Vote

	Total			*Urban*			*Rural*		
	Male	*Female*	*Total*	*Male*	*Female*	*Total*	*Male*	*Female*	*Total*
Local Issues	2.47	1.90	2.24	2.35	1.71	2.09	2.51	2.04	2.30
Policy of Party	2.39	1.60	2.10	2.07	1.57	1.79	2.51	1.79	2.24
Proximity with the candidate	1.15	1.00	1.06	1.04	1.00	1.00	1.19	1.13	1.13
Caste/religious affinity	1.14	1.10	1.10	1.19	1.00	1.04	1.13	1.30	1.12
Monetary considerations	1.00	1.00	1.00	1.00	1.00	1.00	1.00	1.00	1.00
Personal or Community Gains	1.00	1.00	1.00	1.00	1.00	1.00	1.00	1.00	1.00
Any Other	1.00	1.00	1.00	1.00	1.00	1.00	1.00	1.00	1.00

In response to the above question the mean values for proximity with the candidate, monetary considerations and personal and community gains were 1.06, 1.00 and 1.00 respectively. The mean value for the proximity with the candidate was low for it might have had been covered under the item of caste and religious affinity. The response to monetary consideration fell in low mean value category because direct monetary gains were not in vogue then. These gains were in the shape of getting bank loans and other benefits through the government schemes and winning some contract in public works in case the candidate supported got successful at the polls. Even if direct monetary gains were offered this could not be disclosed in the first instance and secondly such transactions took place just before the elections and by that time the survey work was over. The mean value for the personal or community gains was found low as it was also covered by the local issues.

***Electoral Environment*.** By election environment is meant here all sorts of activities, fair or unfair, organized and run by the political parties and the candidates to woo the voters. On the basis of the observations made in the previous election studies six major factors were identified which determine the nature of election campaign. These factors were use of money, use of caste and religious sentiments, use of muscle power, use of posters/banners and loudspeakers, organizing public meetings and door-to-door campaigning. The opinions of the respondents regarding each factor were sought and recorded separately on a three-point scale. The mean value of each factor was worked out and on that basis the role of each factor was assessed.

In the opinion of the electorate, caste and religion constituted the most important determinant of the campaign (mean value; 1.98). Next important factors of almost equal mean value were door-to-door campaign, public meetings and use of posters and banners with mean values of 1.76, 1.75 and 1.71 respectively. The use of money as a factor of election campaign was found to be at a very low level (mean value; 1.20) while the use of muscle power was of no consequence (mean value; 1.00).

Table 5.5
Mean Value of the Perception about the Campaign Strategies for Wooing the Voters

Range 1-3

Forms of	Total			Urban			Rural		
Participation	Male	Female	Total	Male	Female	Total	Male	Female	Total
Use of Money	1.26	1.12	1.18	1.30	1.00	1.15	1.24	1.27	1.20
Use of Caste/ religion	2.02	1.60	1.84	1.79	1.18	1.54	2.10	1.94	1.98
Use of muscle	1.04	1.00	1.00	1.11	1.00	1.00	1.01	1.00	1.00
Use of Posters/ banners	1.78	1.52	1.66	1.71	1.30	1.54	1.81	1.70	1.71
Organising Public Meeting	1.86	1.47	1.69	1.86	1.16	1.57	1.85	1.71	1.75
Door-to-Door Campaign	1.84	1.59	1.72	1.81	1.34	1.62	1.85	1.79	1.76

It is to be noted here that while answering the questions seeking their own opinion with regard to the role of caste and religion the voters were circumspect and hesitant. But when the same subject was raised in terms of election environment in which their opinions were sought about what others were doing the answers were straight and frank. The caste and religion which were earlier denied, as a determinant of voting had in this section the most important factor used by the political parties and the candidates for their campaign.

Party Preferences and Caste Solidarities

In the analysis of the 1996 Parliament and State Assembly elections the caste as such was not taken into consideration. At that time three caste groups, the upper castes, the OBCs, the Scheduled Castes among the Hindus and the Muslims as a separate group as followers of a religion occupied the prime considerations. When the State assembly elections of 1996 produced the results which were a carbon copy of the 1993 State assembly elections, this fact instilled the realization that the mobilization for electoral purposes along these groups had reached a plateau. In order to move forward therefore and to avoid the prospect of a hung assembly in future it was necessary to make inroads into the dissatisfied elements in the groups other than their own. A scramble therefore began to penetrate in one another's citadels, for example the BSP campaigned for support in the more backward OBCs, the BJP extended its presence among the OBCs and the SCs. Efforts were made by the BJP to attract Muslims also. The Samajwdi party, which suffered in its lower caste support bases, tried to make up this loss by making inroads among the non-Brahmin upper castes. In such a situation all the parties lost some of their support to other parties and gained some support by snatching support from other parties. These were the new developments which necessitated the analysis of electoral behaviour on the basis of caste.

A specific question was put this time to the respondents, "which is the party of your choice at present". It was certain that the response of the respondents would be frank and straight this time because of the prevailing environment. The responses to this question have been analysed in three parts. In the first part, the responses of the over-all sample have been delineated in terms the party preferences. This part has been termed as the sample norm. In second part responses have been categorized in terms of the caste groups. In the third part the electorates' attitudes have been analysed in detail on the basis of caste-wise preferences.

Sample Norm

In the total sample 36.9 percent favoured the BJP, 22.4 percent Samajwadi Party, 12.9 percent BSP and only 2.5 percent Congress. As shown in the Table 5.6, about one-fourth (26.4 percent) of the respondents were not willing to indicate there preferences. During our survey, just a week before the polling day, they were found undecided. This indecisiveness might have been due to a number of reasons like: genuine indecisive state of mind, distrust in the interviewer and the apprehension of the harmful consequences in future. There were instances of remarks like "I will vote for anybody whom you would like to" (*Jhisko Aap Kahenge hum usi ko vote de denge*). Media took such remarks as an expression of indifference towards parties and as disillusionment with the system. In a study of 1967 elections D.L Sheth categorized voters, choices in elections as strong partisanship, weak partisanship and non-partisanship. 30 percent of the respondents were found non-partisans. He maintained that the emergence of a new political party mobilizes politically dormant group in society and cuts only marginally into the established support bases of the existing parties (Sheth 1975; 112). In three decades that have followed this election study, the Congress party underwent several vertical splits, a number of non-Congress parties merged into one to form the Janata party, to break up again in the shape of the BJP, the Janata Dal, the Samajwadi party, and the formation of a new Scheduled Castes based party, the Bahujan Samaj Party. Despite these developments the proportion of 'non-partisan voter' in the present study of 1998 elections remained close to the proportion found in 1967 which had surfaced owing to the emergence of numerous regional parties in the state. Not that all of them did not participate in the elections. Towards the end of the elections they would go along with the group to which they belonged. In the mean time they would keep the campaigners in suspense. This behaviour on their part was wrongly interpreted of their indifference.

Caste Group-wise Preferences

Scheduled Castes: Among the Scheduled Castes the undecided electorate constituted 27.4 percent, which was fairly close to the over-all average (26.4 percent). The BSP was the preference of 34.7 percent, the BJP 27.4 percent, SP 10.5 percent and the Congress merely 1.1 percent.

OBCs: The proportion of undecided electorate among OBCs was approximately the same as in the case of overall average (26.4 percent), whereas, nearly 33 percent preferred the Samajwadi Party and about 30 percent the BJP and 8 percent the BSP. Therefore there was no polarisation among the OBCs by and large.

Muslims: It will be seen that with only 11.1 percent undecided electorate, lowest in comparison with other three groups, 81.4 percent were in favour of the SP and 7.4 percent were favouring the BJP. It was clear that Muslim voters were most determined, clear headed and committed for the Samajwadi Party. Here was the only case of polarisation.

Upper Caste: Among the upper caste electorate the percentage of non-responding electorates was 24.7, quite close to the over all average (26.4 percent). Nearly 58 percent unhesitatingly revealed their preference in favour of BJP and about 10 percent for SP, about 7 percent for BSP and merely 1.4 percent favoured the Congress. Thus, there has been a tendency of polarisation in favour of the BJP among the upper castes as a group.

Caste-wise Preferences

Chamars: The most numerous among the Scheduled Castes in the region under study were Chamars. In our sample also they constituted 10.6 percant which was about half of the Scheduled Castes respondents. The proportion of undecided voters among them was 33.3 percent. As regards partisanship 35.6 percent preferred the BSP, 22.2 percent the BJP and only 8.9 percent the SP. This caste used to be a strong support base for the Congress. In this survey the Congress drew blank.

The large proportion of undecided electorate among Chamars has several explanations. The higher incidence of indecisiveness among Chamars could not be explained in terms applicable in the case of castes among the OBCs or the upper castes. The Chamars are mostly landless or tiny landholders of low quality. They are at the bottom in terms of social hierarchy. They are the victims in majority of the cases of atrocities committed against Scheduled Castes in rural areas. They constitute the largest proportion of agricultural labourers in rural areas and construction workers in the urban areas. High level of out-migration is prevalent among young male members of their households. With the above social profile the Chamars are the most vulnerable and socially insecure electorate. They considered the interviewers as outsiders and did not trust them. Hence to this specific question they preferred to be evasive to avoid the possible wrath of the other sections for having spoken out their preferences. Instead, they offered to vote for any one whom the interviewer would suggest. They regretted that it was presumed that they were the BSP's vote banks and that their stated stand to the contrary would not be trusted by non-SCs. Their indecisiveness should be understood in this light also. This caste has been identified as the backbone of the BSP in UP. They feel proud to identify themselves with Mayawati. Among those who stated their preferences, 35.6 percent favoured the BSP and 22.2 percent the BJP. These two facts would surprise anyone conversant with the ground realities. The BSP enjoys commanding position in this caste and the BJP is supposed to be the most abhorrent party among them. It can be explained in this way—it could really be presumed that the bulk of the non-committed percentage would go to the BSP and the party would certainly enjoy more than 50 percent support from them. The BJPs significant presence could be due to the support to Mayawati during the guesthouse incident in 1995 and unconditional support to the government that she formed. The BSP had also entered into an arrangement to form a coalition government with the BJP for six months term in 1997. So the aversion towards BJP had lessened. The dominant section of the BJP was giving signals of sympathetic attitude towards the Scheduled Castes and they appeared keen on power sharing and electoral adjustments with it. Moreover, the upwardly mobile sections from among them, mainly due to job reservations, were aware of the assessment that the BSP was not likely to capture power on its own, either at the centre or the state. So they were soft towards the BJP foreseeing some kind of understanding.

An incident needs mention here. In a village 'Dauna' falling in the Bara assembly segment of the Allahabad Parliamentary constituency a middle aged Chamar woman was paraded naked by the landowners belonging to an OBC Kurmi caste, the caste to which the local BSP MLA belonged. It was an intolerable, humiliating, inhuman behaviour on the part of the persons concerned. The local MLA did not come out in support of the woman, fearing the loss of the Kurmi support. The local BJP workers led by a Brahmin leader initiated the protest and they launched the campaign against the incident, which attracted wide publicity and attention of the Government. For a long time the local BJP functionaries enjoyed the confidence of the Chamars whereas the Kurmis remained formally with the BSP. It did not create a base for the BJP among the Chamars in general but it was a situational alignment temporarily. It had made impact in the 1996 elections and still continued during the present survey also.

Nearly 9 percent support to the SP is insignificant. It will be seen from the table that among all the castes every party is able to extract nearly this size of support, the implication being, the party functionaries are able to mobilise this much of support through their social personal contacts. The hostility of the Chamars towards SP, the symbol of which was Mulayam Singh Yadav, was the product mainly of not very cordial relations between the two parties in the coalition government, which was installed in 1993, and when Mayawati withdrew the support, the government had fallen in 1995. She was mandadled by SP workers and her life was allegedly in danger. This incident had attracted condemnation from public in general and non-SP formation in particular. Such incidents are not forgotten easily and stay long in public memory. If the Chamars did not forget and forgive Mulayam Singh Yadav it was understandable.

Pasi: The Pasis are the next largest group after the Chamars among the Scheduled Castes. In our sample they constituted 8.6 percent which was   percent among the total Scheduled Castes respondents.

The proportion of undecided voters among them was 22.3 percent. The party wise preferences for the BSP, the BJP and the SP were 38.2, 32.6 and 8.9 respectively. This caste also used to be a traditional Congress vote bank but in this survey no respondent preferred its as his party.

Like Chamars, the Pasis are also at the bottom of the social hierarchy and mostly landless too. However, the degree of their socialization with other castes was higher than the Chamars. Their participation in the Freedom Struggle was also greater. In the post-independence period they have provided leading personalities for the Congress party. They have displayed entrepreneurial acumen in the informal sector. From another angle the landed aristocracy has used them as musclemen. During the recent phase of the caste based competitive mobilization the trend to search and establish historical roots of the castes was encouraged. It has been stated that the pasis were a martial race and ruled different pockets of the country. It is being established recently that the region around Lucknow was such a pocket where one Raja Suhail Deo of Behraich ruled during the Muslim period. A fort located near Lucknow is said to have been constructed by a Pasi ruler named Maharaja Bijli Pasi. Virangna Uda Devi is said to have fought against the Britishers for freedom of the country during 1857 Struggle. The authors of the history of this caste have theorized that since the rulers of their caste fought against the foreign rulers but were subdued by them and also because the upper caste joined hands with the rulers of the day, this caste was forced into submission and suffered the humiliation of living under the status of the untouchables.

The majority support for the BSP was understable because the BSP took the lead in the Scheduled Castes, consolidation as a political force and the Pasis found respectability in that setup. But since the Pasis had closer links with the Congress and a share in power also in the past, it was easy for them, when the Congress declined to shift to the BJP. Like Congress BJP also had some penetration among the Pasis, therefore it was not surprising that when the Congress support had evaporated among the SC the BJP filled in that vacuum which is been reflected as 23.2 percent support for it in our sample.

Kol: The Kols constitute the largest group among the Scheduled Castes in the district. In our sample also their proportion was 3.5 percent which was around 15 percent of the total Scheduled Castes respondents. During the survey 13.6 percent among them were found in the category of undecided voters. The largest proportion of support was in favour of the BJP (33.3 percent) while the BSP and SP received support in equal measure (26.7 percent).

Although the Kols are listed as the Scheduled Castes in the State and receive all the benefits which accrue to such castes but they assert themselves to be *adivasis* (the tribals). The neighbouring Bihar and Madhya Pradesh governments have recognised them as such. The Kols in the state are struggling to win that status.

Their leaders go into the past and claim that their forefathers had ruled over one sixth part of the country. The ramparts of the fort situated in the village Kharka falling under the jurisdiction of the police station of Khiri in the Allahabad Parliament constituency is claimed by them to have belonged to one of their kings in the distant past. They consider below their dignity to be bracketed with other Scheduled Castes. However, most of them are landless and illiterate. Their condition in general is not better than that of other Scheduled Castes. Their social accessibility in other castes is relatively easy and in some cases they can be seen as domestic workers. They are concentrated mostly along the southern borders of the district in the two assembly segments of Meja and Bara. A substantial number comes from the adjoining state of Madhya Pradesh as seasonal migrant labourers to work in the fields as well as open quarries of stone and silica sand. In terms of asset ownership they are worse off than the Chamars and the Pasis. Even now the majority among them lives in makeshift hutments without any doors. So far it has not been possible to absorb a section among them in the mainstream of the development.

Inspite of the above conditions the easy accessibility in and acceptability by other castes, the urge for identity as past rulers of the region as well as the feeling of aversion of being bracketed with the Chamars and Pasis inclined a substantial section among them to own the BJP as their party. For the same reason the SP was able to muster support in equal measure with the BSP, even though the Kols had fallen in the Scheduled Castes group. The sitting MLA of the Meja assembly segment hailed from this community and belonged to the Communist Party of India (Marxist). It can be safely concluded that the BSP did not command majority in this caste among the Scheduled Castes.

Yadavas: In Uttar Pradesh the backward castes comprise around 42 percent of the population with the Yadavas heading the list at nine percent (Hasan 1989; 154). The Yadavas are an important force everywhere in the state except in western UP and the hill districts. In the two Parliament constituencies in the district of Allahabad the proportion of the Yadavas in the total electorate was reported to be around 10.5 percent (Aggarwal & Chowdhry 1996; 233-236). In our sample the Yadavas constituted 13.6 percent of the total respondents. Among them only 8.6 percent were undecided as against the sample norm of 26.4 percent. More than half (53.5 percent) were in favour of the Samajwadi party but a sizeable proportion (37.9 percent) favoured the BJP also. There was, however, no support either for the Congress or the BSP among the Yadavas.

The Yadavas were the forerunners in organizing backward castes in this part of the country. The All-India Yadav Mahasabha was organised in 1923. It had many adherents among the Ahirs of north India. An Ahir conference was held in Lucknow, followed by an Ahir *mahotsav* in Allahabad in 1923, where a provincial *mahasabha* was inaugurated (Hasan 1996; 128). Sometime in the 1940s, the Yadavas had "subsumed their various sub-caste identities into a pan-Yadav identity .....which celebrated their 'glorious' links to Lord Krishna, primarily to equip them psychologically to overcome their lower status in the ritual caste order." (Ramaseshan 1994;...). Like the Jats in western UP, the Yadavas in other parts of the state did not consider themselves socially inferior to any other caste. They asserted their superior social status vis-à-vis Dalits. At the same time, they used their backwardness in relation to the upper castes in order to demand the benefits of reservation (Hasan 1998; 131). The Yadavas, alongwith the Kurmis, were not in an immediate sense, beneficiaries of the Green Revolution. In fact, it was happened only in the late seventies and early eighties, a good ten-odd years after the first fruits of the new agricultural strategy came to be tasted with great relish in the western parts of the state. For the first few decades after Independence, Jats were the undisputed leaders of the backward castes. The Yadavs were consistently out of the folds of the Congress (Lal 1998; 35). They were first attracted by the Praja Socialist Party, then to Sanyukt Socialist Party under the leadership of Dr. Ram Manohar Lohia, then to Bhartiya Kranti Dal of Charan Singh and after the formation of Lok Dal they joined it. But in the eighties they started challenging the Jat leadership. The split in the Lok Dal following the death of Chowdhary Charan Singh must be viewed essentially as Yadav revolt against Jat leadership (Jain 1996; 147). During the years of the Janata Party/Dal goverments in the Centre as well as the State, a large number of Yadav leaders emerged on the political scene which commanded considerable support among OBCs. After the split in the Janata Dal the Yadavs moved with the Samajwadi Party of Mulayam Singh Yadav. The period of eighties and early nineties could be seen as the phase of ascendcy of Yadav leadership in UP and Bihar. Mulayam Singh Yadav in UP and Laloo Yadav in Bihar became the undisputed symbols of OBC politics. With the rise of Mulayam Singh Yadav in state politics the Yadavas gained extraordinary strength in UP. Mulayam Singh Yadav maintained his caste identity and his caste fellows sustained him (Wright 1995; 19). Thus, Mulayam Singh Yadav, the Yadava caste and the Samajwadi Party merged into one. Differently put, the Samajwadi party became the party of the Yadavas and Mulayam Singh Yadav emerged its undisputed leader/supremo.

The Yadavas have had a rather split personality in historical terms. Although primarily an agrarian caste, the process of their urbanization has apparently been more directly evident than in the case of the other intermediate castes (Lal 1998; 33). The reason was that apart from the agricultural occupation the Yadavas had side by side a subsidiary occupation of dairy farming. They not only supplied milk to the households within their village but also to the nearby markets and towns and to the families of the government officers and employees stationed there. Thus, they had greater exposure in the urban/semi-urban centres and easy accessibility to the government functionaries. This brought awareness among them with regard to the happenings at the political levels and opened opportunities for employment in the lower jobs. Among the backward castes they alone had cash in hand in their possession all the time. All these factors contributed in the emergence of an upward mobile section within the Yadavas.

The Yadavas have always been an enterprising caste. With the rise of Mulayam Singh Yadav as Chief Minister the upward mobile section among Yadavas got entrenched in other occupations and that too in a short period. The fact of the Yadavas being the ruling caste in the name of the Samajwadi party was fully exploited with the connivance of the bureaucracy in obtaining the lucrative contracts of public works, excise, mining and factory scraps; acquiring licenses for wholesale trade of drug and pharmaceuticals, soft drinks; fertilisers; automobiles and not to mention penetration in small scale retail businesses. The reference area does not lack from the "rags to the riches" story in the nineties itself. It is noteworthy that the neo-rich Yadavas of nineties were more subtle, more urbane and more aggressive than the neo-rich of the seventies and eighties mostly concentrated in the rural areas. The gains of earlier neo-rich Yadavas were mainly from new technology in agriculture, higher prices for farm produce, contracts in social forestry, rural road construction, canal and irrigation related works and maintenance of public buildings in rural areas. But the factors responsible for the emergence of neo-rich in the nineties were entirely different. The benefits accruing to them in economic fields were closely linked with the political connections at higher levels. This section of Yadavas could be seen as active players between politics, administration and business.

The fact that the BJP was able to secure 37 percent support among the Yadavas in the survey was unusual in the background of the fact that this caste was the mainstay of the Samajwadi party. It seems to have happened because the competition to get rich quick among the neo-rich Yadavas was very severe, so much so that whoever failed to take advantages from political connections through the Samajwadi party looked for alternatives. Since the BJP was in the leadership of the governments at the centre and the state, they took the easy route of leaning towards the BJP. This situation afforded the BJP with an opportunity to penetrate in the caste that was the hardcore of the OBCs, mobilization. It was possible that a fair share of our sample might have fallen in the area of influence of such Yadav electorates.

Kurmis: Along with the Yadavas the Kurmis are another dominant backward caste of the region. In Allahabad and around, they are considered to be the most prosperous cultivator caste. They constituted 4 percent of the electorate in Allahabad and 8 percent in the Phulpur parliament constituecy. By taking both the constituencies together it was found that Kurmis constituted nearly 5.8 percent of the total electorate in the district (Aggarwal & Chowdhry 1996; 233-236). In our sample the Kurmi respondents constituted a share of 5.9 percent. The proportion of undecided electorate (52.0 percent) was nearly double as compared to the sample norm. One-fifth among them (20.0 percent) revealed their preference in favour of the BSP and 12 percent each in favour of the SP and the BJP. A small section (4.0 percent) favoured the Apna Dal. The Congress had no support in this caste also.

It had been observed that in the polarized atmosphere of UP, the forces, which were still without a stable political party, were the 'Kurmis' and the 'Koeris'. They constituted "floating" vote banks—they form part of those dominant power groups with the backwards who fell out with the traditional representatives of the backwards in the post-Mandal phase without going over to the BJP or the BSP. All the three formations were trying their best to woo them. It was clear that these forces were likely to go with any party which appeared close to coming out of the current deadlock. They constituted in many ways that crucial 'third' element which might tilt the balance of social forces in the state (Misra Amresh).

As the Yadavas had challenged the Jat leadership in UP in 1980s, so the Kurmis staged a major protest against Yadavas in the nineties. They were feeling uncomfortable in the Samajwadi Party because of the predominance of the Yadavas. After being 'nudged out' of Mulayam Singh Yadav's Samajwadi Party, the Kurmis in Uttar Pradesh sought to have a tie-up with Kanshi Ram's Bahujan

Samaj Party. The Kurmis claimed that they provided the security to dalits to fearlessly exercise their franchise (Lal 1998; 5). Therefore a section among them was inclined towards the BSP and another in favour of the BJP. Yet another section was identifying itself with the Apna Dal led by Sone Lal Patel, a Kurmi by caste. In the Phulpur constituency the Samajwadi Party, the BSP and the Apna Dal fielded Kurmi candidates. Here a candidate of this caste on the BJP ticket represented one assembly segment (Soraon). In the Allahabad parliamentary constituency one assembly segment (Bara) was represented by a candidate of this caste on the BSP ticket consecutively for three terms. Thus, all the major parties, the BJP the SP and the BSP had bases among the Kurmi caste in this area. It is also to be noted that the Phulpur Parliamentary constituency was being represented by the Kurmi candidates for the last four elections in a row. The Kurmi's therefore considered Phulpur as their stronghold. This consideration was the most important determinant of their electoral behaviour. The large proportion of indecisive electorates among them was due to the fact that three candidates from among them were contesting in Phulpur and a decision had to be taken by the caste regarding the candidate to be supported. Towards the end the decision went in favour of the Samajwadi Party candidate, who was a Kurmi by caste, because there was a strong Muslim and Yadav support in his favour. As a result the other Kurmi candidates fared badly. In the end the caste leaders felt elated that this strong hold of theirs continued to be represented by one of their castemen no matter what his party was. The observation that the Kurmi caste constituted a floating vote-bank stood valid.

Kushwaha: Among the OBCs the Kushwahas as a caste were small in size. In our sample they constituted a share of 2.6 percent only. They included sub-castes like Kushwaha, Maurya, Kachi, Koeri and Mali. The proportion of undecided electorates among them was 36.4 percent which was 10 points higher than the sample norm As regards partisanship, the Samajwadi party was favoured by 36.4 percent and the BJP by 27.2 percent. The BSP and the Congress had no support among this caste.

The Kushwahas are also predominantly a cultivating caste. The majority among them owns smaller size of land-holdings. Although a few of them may be found with larger size land holdings. Generally they produce market-oriented cash crops like vegetables. They are known for their expertise in intensive agriculture. Their exposure to urban market is vast. Possibly for this reason they are ahead of other OBCs in education. They may be in government services but a large number among them find self-employment as registered medical practitioners, compounders, pathology assistants, and other independent service providers particularly in rural areas.

In recent years they have endeavored to organize different sub-castes and create state and national level platform to register their independent identity by organizing conferences and publishing journals to be able to enter into the competitive politics. Allahabad district has also witnessed such conferences in the recent past. For this purpose they have amalgamated five sub-castes, namely—Kushwaha, Maurya, Shakya, Saini and Mali. They trace their origin from the mythological figure Kusha, a son of Lord Rama. In mention is made about King Shursen of Mahabarata as their ancestor. Gautam Budha, Chandragupta Maurya and Samrat Ashoka are also listed in the lineage. Jyoti ba Phule, a social reformer of Maharashtra and Mali by caste is among the modern symbols.

As a caste they are religious, peace loving and most acceptable among other castes. Socially they feel closer to Kurmis. Like Kurmis they too are a part of the floating vote bank which is being reflected in the high proportion of undecided voters among them. The assembly segment of Nawabganj in Phulpur constituency is at present represented by a candidate of this caste. He had contested the election on the Congress ticket but later on, with the split in the Congress legislature party resulting in the formation of the Loktantrik Congress Party, he joined the latter and was appointed a minister of state in the BJP-led government in the State.

Vishwakarmas: As a caste, Vishwakarmas are rural artisans. Of late, their economic conditions have deteriorated. They are not able to withstand the onslaughts of mechanisation in their trade. Like other artisan castes in the countryside this artisan caste has also been reduced to the level of rural labourers. They are, however, at present a shade better than others in artisan castes in the sense there is still a market for their low skilled products in the rural areas. Recently they have made, like many other communities, an attempt to establish their social identity by posing Giani Jail Singh, the former President of India, as pride of their caste. They relate themselves with the mythological figure, Lord Vishwakarma. This caste can provide a good case to study the political behaviour of rural artisans categorised under the OBCs. Half of these electorates were reluctant to favour any party

Table 5.6
Caste-wise Distribution of Electorates by Party of their Choice

Castes and Caste Groups	*N*	*Undecided*	*% of respondents preferring the* BJP	SP	BSP	Congress	Others
Brahmin	95	21 (22.1)	65 (68.4)	6 (6.3)	2 (2.1)	1 (1.1)	—
Thakur	14	4 (28.6)	7 (50.0)	2 (14.3)	1 (7.1)	—	—
Vaishya	20	5 (25.0)	10 (50.0)	4 (20.0)	—	1 (5.0)	—
Kayastha	17	6 (35.3)	2 (11.8)	2 (11.8)	7 (41.2)	—	—
Upper Caste Hindus	**146**	**36** **(24.7)**	**84** **(57.5)**	**14** **(9.6)**	**10** **(6.8)**	**2** **(1.4)**	—
Kurmi	25	13 (52.0)	3 (12.0)	3 (12.0)	5 (20.0)	—	1 (4.0)
Yadav	58	5 (8.6)	22 (37.9)	31 (53.5)	—	—	—
Kushwaha	11	4 (36.4)	3 (27.2)	4 (36.4)	—	—	—
All Dominant OBCs	**94**	**22** **(23.4)**	**28** **(29.8)**	**37** **(39.4)**	**5** **(5.3)**		**1** **(1.1)**
Vishwakarma	14	7 (50.0)	1 (7.1)	—	4 (28.6)	2 (14.3)	—
Bind	15	2 (13.3)	6 (40.0)	7 (46.7)	—	—	—
Other MBC	25	8 (32.0)	9 (36.0)	5 (20.0)	3 (12.0)	—	—
All MBCs combined	**54**	**17** **(31.5)**	**16** **(29.6)**	**12** **(22.2)**	**7** **(13.0)**	**2** **(3.7)**	—
Chamar	45	15 (33.3)	10 (22.2)	4 (8.9)	16 (35.6)	—	—
Pasi	34	8 (23.5)	11 (32.4)	2 (5.9)	13 (38.2)	—	—
Kol	15	2 (13.3)	5 (33.3)	4 (26.7)	4 (26.7)	—	
All SCs combined	**96**	**26** **(27.4)**	**26** **(27.4)**	**10** **(10.5)**	**33** **(34.7)**	**1** **(1.1)**	—
Muslims	**27**	**3** **(11.1)**	**2** **(7.4)**	**22** **(81.4)**	—	—	—
Others	**8**	**7** **(87.5)**	**1** **(12.5)**	—	—	—	—
All Castes combined	**425**	**112** **(26.4)**	**157** **(36.9)**	**95** **(22.4)**	**55** **(12.9)**	**5** **(1.2)**	**1** **(0.2)**

at the time of our survey. Nearly 29 percent favoured the BSP, about 14 percent, the Congress and nealy 7 percent preferred the BJP. It is to be noted that the Vishwakarmas do not desire to associate themselves with the party of dominant castes among the OBCs, the Samajwadi Party. Even the BJP, the upper caste party, is not preferred much among this caste, while the Congress has been favoured by relatively larger section. Only BSP had penetration among them of some effective size. This caste had not made up its mind yet and they did not seem committed to any party. They were found willing to gain benefits from public policies and rural development programmes for self-employment ventures and in this endeavor they wished to get support from the leaders of all the political parties. The fact of 50.0 percent vote among them makes them a part of the floating vote bank.

Bind: Binds constituted 3.5 percent of our sample. Among them 13.3 percent were undecided, 46.7 percent favoured the Samajwadi party and 40.0 percent supported the BJP. The BSP and the Congress had no support among them.

Under the category of the Binds have been included the sub-castes Bind, Mallah, Nishad and Kewats. They trace their origins right from the days of Lord Rama, who was the guest of honour of the Nishad King Guha of Shringverpur situated at the banks of the river Ganga falling in the Phulpur parliamentary constituency.

Economically, it is a weak caste. Most of them posses a marginal size of land holdings. Generally they belong to poorer category of population, and are engaged in sharecropping. In this area, the carpet weaving on labour cost at household level is wide spread among this caste. They have been politically associated with and sympathetic towards the BSP since its inception. Beni Madhav Bind from amongst them had contested elections as an independent and the BSP candidate in Phulpur constituency in the past. In 1996 assembly elections he was a BSP candidate from Handia assembly segment under Phulpur Parliamentary constituency and polled impressively. In the present election (1998) he was fielded by the BJP from the Phulpur Parliamentary constituency. Another factor affecting the electorates' behaviour of this caste was the candidature of Phoolan Devi, 'the bandit queen' from the adjacent Parliament constituency of Bhadohi, which she had won in the 1996 elections as the Samajwadi Party candidate. She participated in electioneering in the constituencies under study also and made quite an impact. As a result of these two factors the BSP was totally out of picture among this caste in this election. Nearly 40 percent were favouring the BJP while 46.7 percent preferred the Samajwadi party.

Brahmins: According to the 1931 census, the Brahmins forming over 9 percent of the population in UP, represented 40 percent of the entire Brahmin population in India, making UP the area of maximum Brahmin concentration. In Allahabad parliamentary constituency the Brahamins constitute nearly 15 percent and in Phulpur around 11 percent. Taking together both the constituencies they comprise 13.2 percent of the total electorate. In our sample they constituted a share of 22.4 percent which is in excess of their actual proportion in the total electorate by around 9 points.

Among the Brahmins 22.1 percent of the respondents were undecided. This figure is below the sample norm (26.4 percent). Yet, in view of the fact that the Brahmins had been one of the leading sections in the game of power play and also politically most conscious, this figure is on the higher side. This could be partly explained in terms of the fact that no political party of significance had set up a Brahmin candidate in the Phulpur constituency and therefore, the affinity with the candidate among them was missing in this constituency. Also, the pollsters were forecasting a hung parliament as the outcome of the election. A section among Brahmins, therefore, was not willing to commit itself with any party so that it might not mar the prospects of promotion of their self-interest

As regards partisanship, 68.4 percent supported the BJP. It was a fairly high proportion of support in favour the BJP, but it was not high enough as was the general perception among people about the Brahmins, support. The high proportion (22.1 percent) of undecided respondents among them could also be a factor in lowering the proportion of the support to BJP among the Brahmin electorate. The fact that SP, the main rival and the BSP, enjoyed merely 6.3 and 2.1 percent support respectively establishes that by and large the Brahmin voters had owned the BJP as their party.

Thakurs: Among the upper castes numerically the Thakurs are next in rank to the Brahmins in UP. Known as Kshatriyas and Rajputs from the ages in the popular parlance, they are called Thakurs in this region. The share of this caste in the total population in the state has been estimated as 6.7 percent. In Allahabad parliament constituency they constitute nearly 5 percent and in the Phulpur constituency around 4 percent. Thus, taken together, the Thakurs constituted 4.5 percent of the electorate in Allahabad. In our sample they comprised 3.3 percent.

Among the Thakurs a high 28.6 percent were undecided, which was higher than the sample norm by 2 points. Half of them preferred the BJP and 14.3 and 7.1 percent favoured the SP and the BSP respectively. The Congress could not muster support among this caste. Considering the incessant political attack on them together with the Brahmins, from the OBCs and the lower castes, the support percentage to the BJP appeared to be on the lower side. During our survey it was found that the general perception among them was that the BJP was a party dominated by the Brahmins and they would have little place in this party. So they were looking out towards the SP and the BSP also. Naturally, the non-BJP parties were working overtime to bring them on their side and thus upset the upper caste apple cart of the BJP. There had been Thakur faces like Amar Singh in the SP to attract this caste towards the party. He organised numerous campaigns and conferences among them and picked up opinion makers in favour of the SP. The SP had set up some candidates in the State from amongst them to fetch the caste vote. The 14 percent support to the SP in this caste was the result of such efforts and a clear tendency of penetration by the SP among them was visible. It appeared during the survey that this caste was in the process of disenchantment with the BJP and in future by and by might break away from it but as yet it was not strong enough to cause substantial danger to the BJP. It is to be noted that no party had fielded a Thakur candidate in either of the two constituencies in Allahabad. Therefore the caste affinity factor was not present among them. Hence, in this environment, the proportion of about 28 percent electorate among this caste as undecided was not surprising.

Vaishyas: Among the Vaishyas the undecided percentage was 25.0 percent which was marginally below the sample norm. In the distribution of partywise preferences it was found that 50 percent were in favour of the BJP, 20 percent of SP and 5 percent of Congress. BSP was not favoured at all by this caste. Vaishyas are a trading community, concentrated in urban areas and 'kasbas' but spread sparsely in the villages also. The Vaishyas or 'banias' were traditionally the support base of erstwhile Bhartiya Jansangh, the predecessor of the Bhartiya Janata Party. In fact, during the days of the Bhartiya Jan Sangh, the party was dubbed as the party of 'banias' and the electoral successes of the party were confined to the urban areas only. In the wake of Mandal and Mandir movements during which the upper caste shifted their allegiance from the Congress to the BJP, the Vaishya community became one of the many support bases for the party. But when Mulayam Singh Yadav headed the state government for the second term he removed many causes of resentments which this trading community was facing. He abolished the octroi system, removed the inter-district barriers, suspended the section 3/7 of the Essential Commodities Act and withdrew the cases against the traders filed under this section. All these measures created a favourable atmosphere among the traders for the Samajwadi Party, which resulted in a support base for it among the Vaishyas.

The Vaishya community consists of several sub-castes like Agarwal, Kesarwani, Gupta, Jaiswal, Sahu, Gupta (teli) etc.The last three of them were included among the OBCs who enjoyed the reservation privileges as a result of the enforcement of Mandal Commission recommendation. Therefore, the Vaishyas have now two divisions—the upper caste Vaishyas and the backward caste Vaishyas. But, as traders, whenever the common interests and demands necessitate, they join hands, which happens quite often. Of late in, order to enhance their strength and political clout, attempts were made to bring the Sindhis, Punjabis and Khatris in their fold, particularly at the time of election. These are also predominantly the trading communities. Another factor helping the SP was the fact that the candidate in the Allahabad countituency was an upper caste Vaishya. He had the resources to mobilize this community in his favour. In the 1991 parliament elections he was the BJP candidate and had been defeated by a small margin by the Janata Dal Brahmin woman candidate. The Vaishya community suspected that the Brahmins belonging to the BJP did not support their own candidate; instead they supported the Janata Dal candidate for caste considerations. In another instance, the wife of the same Vaishya leader was fielded by the BJP as the candidate for the post of Mayor in Allahabad which she lost. In that case too the Vaishya community suspected that the BJP Brahmins supported the SP candidate, a Brahmin by caste, along the caste lines. So there was enough material for a section of the Vaishya community to suspect betrayal by the Brahmins of the BJP. Hence, the 20 percent support for the Samajwadi party emerged.

The fact, however, remains that the trend of polarisation in favour of the BJP still continues. Just before the elections and the present survey the three prominent leaders of the trading community, Ravi Bhushan Wadhavan, former Mayor of Allahabad; Sunil Seth Bagga, President, Allahabad Vyapar Mandal (both Samajwadi Party activists) and Satish Jaiswal, former two times MLC on Congress ticket, jointed the BJP. The BJP thus gained more than the loss caused by Shyama Charan Gupta's joining the Samajwadi Party.

Kayasthas: As in the case of Vaishyas, the candidate—caste factor played a decisive role in case of Kayasthas' electorate behaviour also. It was presumed on the past pattern of their electoral behaviour that they would stay with the BJP in the forthcoming elections. Nevertheless, the BSP, in view of a sizeable presence of the Kayastha voters in the assembly segments of Allahabad North and Allahabad South, fielded Dr. K. P. Srivastava, a Kayastha, as its candidate for the Allahabad parliamentary seat. The BSP hoped that its traditional Scheduled Castes votes joined by the Kayastha votes would raise the possibility of success in elections. Kayasthas are mainly city dwellers, well educated, employed in government jobs in large numbers, engaged in liberal professions and wield considerable influence at the places where they work. In all the trade unions of white-collar employees the Brahmins and the Kayasthas have been front runners for different offices for a long time in Allahabad. The community expected that the BJP would accord recognition to them in some elections—from the Mayor of Allahabad to the state Assembly. Having lost patience they obtained the BSP ticket for the Allahabad Parliamentary constituency. The candidate, Dr. K.P. Srivastava, who comes from a liberal profession was elected president of the Kayastha Pathshala Trust, a premier educational trust of long history and standing. He had been the member of the BJP for the past seven years. From BJP to BSP was a big shift of political positions. Therefore as the BSP candidate he could carry only 41.2 percent of the Kayastha electorate in his support. A substantial section of 35 percent among them remained undecided at the time of our survey. The BJP and the SP equally shared the support of another 24 percent. Nearly 40 percent openly favoured the BSP while the BJP and the SP were reduced to merely 12 percent each. The role of candidate—caste factor affecting the electorates' behaviour can not be better exemplified than this instance.

IV
Emerging Trends

It was found that the choice of electorate had mainly been confined to three political parties—the BJP, the SP and the BSP. The Congress and other regional parties were not able to attract any noticeable support. In terms of overall average the BJP was the most favoured party among the electorate (36.9 percent) followed by the SP (22.4 percent) and the BSP (12.9 percent) respectively. Usually a week before the polling one-fourth of the electorate remain undecided about the party they would vote for, which was reflected in our sample norm also.

The pattern of electorates' preference establishes that the unity among four major caste groups have broken down. New forms of caste alliances that were experimented during the 1996 parliament election were further strengthened. The strong polarisation among the upper caste Hindus in the name of Hindutva, the OBCs in favour of Mandal and the Scheduled Castes under the banner of the BSP have been diluted. But this dilution did not happen on economic basis. No class differentiation has taken place. Instead, the erstwhile caste federations have weakened and some castes, as an independent social group, preferred to move out from the federations and now join such federations which they were not known to join hands with. For example, Kayasthas with the SCs and the Binds with the upper castes. This could be seen as the process of reconfiguration of the castes and social groups.

A typical feature in the state was that in each caste federation there were at least two principal castes at par with each other in terms of numerical strength as well as social and economic influence, such as Brahmins—Thakurs (upper castes), Yadavas - Kurmis (OBCs) and Chamars—Pasis (SCs). These principal castes provided the main support base for the parties identified with them at the time of elections. In course of time, in each of these three federations one of the two principal castes almost monopolised the organisational power and office of the respective party, as a result of which the tendency to move away in the other caste emerged, leading to cracks in the caste federations e.g. the Kurmis moving away from the Samajwadi Party, the Thakurs from the BJP and the Pasis from the BSP. It is worth mentioning here that the two principal castes in each of the three federations easily aligned with and cultivated each other in day-to-day life. In controlling the levers of power, however, they were seen fiercely competitive and even antagonistic. This appeared to be a dichotomous relationship that in contention for the capture of power they united but when the enjoyment of benefits of power was monspolised by one of them the other moved away. This happened because during the last decade each one of the three caste-federations had been in power in the state at one point of time or the other. The United Front run government led by Mulayam Singh Yadav from 1989 to 1991, The BJP led by Kalyan Singh was in power from 1991 to 1992. Mulayam Singh Yadav again headed the government of the SP-BSP combine between 1993 and 1995 and then Mayawati led the BSP government with the support of the BJP from outside during 1995. In 1997, Mayawati again led the government of the BSP-BJP combine and lastly, Kalyan Singh of the BJP came to power for second term in 1997 with the support of splinters of the BSP, the Congress and the Janata Dal and some independents. Thus, the parties symbolising the three caste federations were in power twice with different allies at different times, shaking the castiest mould in the process. A common feature during the entire period was that the leader of the party in power invariably used the state power to consolidate his or her position in his or her own caste. More and more people of their caste could perch themselves visibly in positions of power at different levels and thus establish a hegemony of their caste in the party of the caste federation. Thus, other castes in the federation felt marginalised. Initially murmuring, then open protest followed by rallies against the government of their own became a general phenomenon in state politics. Depending upon the level of dissatisfaction all the three caste federations had their monolith image broken by such rallies, secret configurations and war of statements etc. During the Mulayam Singh Yadav government the Kurmis revolted against Yadavas by forming the Apna Dal under the leadership of Dr. Sone Lal Patel, shattering the image of OBC unity. Then, during the Mayawati government, the BSP became suspect in the eyes of some Scheduled Castes other than Chamars. Accusations regarding the domination of Chamars in the BSP gave rise to Pasi conferences and new symbols like Maharaja Bijli Pasi, Veerangana Uda Devi etc. came into prominence. Similarly, for the BJP, the general perception was that it had become a party dominated by the Brahmins, and as a result, during the period prior to election, a number of Kshatriya conferences were organised, led by non-BJP leaders in which Mulayaam Singh Yadav was extolled as their leader. The biggest revolt, however, was faced by the SP. In case of the BSP and the BJP only some section broke away and the bulk remained with the party of the respective federations. This situation of losing the support of a section in the caste federation was on the one hand weakening the federation while on the other hand there was enough space available to create a new support base in other caste federations by wooing the disgruntled elements. A new scene emerged on the political horizon—non-OBC leaders were projected on the SP platform, non-upper caste leaders were sought after and projected on the BJP platform and the 'manuvadi' faces were found among the BSP candidates' list. The new trend was emerging. The outsiders came with their caste support to join the alien caste federation expecting that the two joining together would gain electoral success. To some extent it worked on the local level. But on the higher level it resulted in the formation of something like a syndicate of caste leaders from different caste federations in different parties.

NOTES

1. Elections for the last parliament were held in April 1996.If it would have completed its full term the next election should have been held in April 2001.
2. Comparative Picture of U.P. Assembly in 1993 vis-a-vis 1996

Party	*Seats*	
	1993	*1996*
BJP	176	174
Samata	—	25
SP	109	110
BSP	67	67
Congress	28	33
JD/LKD	24	31
CPI/CPM	5	5
Independents		

3. In June 1995 in the state guest house at Lucknow the BSP leader Ms. Mayawati was assaulted by the supporters of the then Chief Minister Mulayam Singh Yadav for withdrawing the support from the government.
4. In Allahabad laying down the foundation stone of the community hall of Kayastha Patshala Trust Mayawati as chef minister announced Rs. 1 million grant for the construction of hall. She appreciated the contribution of Kayestha community on educational, social and political walks of life. She assured to hold a kaystha conference in Lucknow and to consider the proposal for declaring Chitragupta Jayanti and Bhaiya Dooj as a public holiday (August 22, 1997).

5. The state minister for minorities welfare and wart, Buriyad Husain Ansari that 1996-97 the state has allocated a fund of Rs. 144380 million for disbursing scholarship to about 35 lakh minority students. This amount was nearly droplet than the previous year's allocation. (DJ, August 19, 1997).
6. The state minister for minorities welfare and wart, Buriyad Husain Ansari that 1996-97 the state has allocated a fund of Rs. 144380 million for disbursing scholarship to about 35 lakh minority students. This amount was nearly droplet than the previous year's allocation. (DJ, August 19, 1997).
7. In 1992 the state government had laid down six criteria for creating on new district i.e., *(i)* Population—15 lakh, *(ii)* Area—500 sq.kms. *(iii)* Tehsil—3 *(iv)* Block—10 *(v)* Police station—12 and *(vi)* Number of Lekhpals—300.
8. It had been observed that in a single visit survey it was not possible to interview every selected voter primarily due to his non-availability at the time of the visit of the investigator. In such cases it was decided that if a selected voter was not available at the time of the visit of the interviewer another member be interviewed in his or her place. The interviewers were directed to take care that in such cases a male voter was substituted by a male and a female by a female voter. Another conditions for the substitution was that the substituted interviewee must have been included in the voter list. It was assumed that the substituted voter being a member of the same family was not likely to display any adverse or different trend for the purpose of the study.
9. Prof. M.N. Sriniwas has noted that among this group "there are at one extreme the dominant, landowning, peasnt castes which wield power and authority over local Vaishyas and Brahmins, whereas, at the other extreme are the poor, near-Untouchable groups living just above the pollution line (Sriniwas 1966; 10). Similarly Frankel has observed that in concrete terms it is possible to divide the Shudra category into two clearly identifiable sub-categories—what are called the Upper Shudras and the Lower Shudras. In the North India, the Upper Shudras comprise such economically powerful and politically aggressive groups as the Jats, Yadavs ,Kurmis and Koiris while the Lower Shudrass include the humble Hajjam, Kumbhar, Lohar,Teli, Tatwa, Dhanuk and Mallah.(Frankel 1989; 54). Meenakshi Jain has pointed out that the main beneficiaries of the land reforms were the erstwhile tenants among Jats, Yadavs, Kurmis, Koiris, that is, those belonging to the upper strata of the Shudra castes (Jain 1996; 138). Here the term Shudras have been used for the OBCs.
10. One-third of the seats for panchayat bodies at all levels has been reserved for women through the Panchayati Raj Adhiniyam U.P. (1994) in accordance with the 73rd Constitution Amendment Act, 1992.

6

Shift in Party Preferences

This chapter is based on the findings of the election study of the 1999 Lok Sabha elections. It is divided into four sections. The first section provides a brief description of the major events at national and state level that occurred during the period between the 1998 and the 1999 Lok Sabha elections and influenced the behaviour and preferences of the electorate. In the second section the design of the study and the characteristics of the sample respondents have been explained. The results of the analysis have been presented in the third section which includes political participation, determinants of voting, electoral environment, shift in party preferences and the losses and gains to parties, followed by a concluding section.

The tenth Lok Sabha elected in 1991 had enjoyed a full term of five years and the elections for the eleventh Lok Sabha were held in April 1996. But after only 20 months the mid-term polls for the twelfth Lok Sabha were held in February 1998 and this body also could not survive long and again the elections for the thirteenth Lok Sabha were necessitated after a gap of only 18 months in October,

1999. Thus, in a short span of about three years, people of India were forced to go to polls thrice to elect the members for the Lok Sabha, putting a heavy strain on the public exchequer and administrative machinery. Without going into the right or wrong of this situation, the present study was undertaken with the purpose to analyze whether the trends which had emerged during the last three years period i.e. between 1996 and 1998 were still valid or not.

I
The Background

A brief resume of important events in the intervening period would be necessary to serve as the background in which the activities relating to political mobilisation took place. In the following paragraphs we propose to take up some major events into account which influenced the electoral behaviour to a great extent. The narration of the events covered has been divided in two parts. In the first part the events having national importance have been described. In the second part the events relating to the state of Uttar Pradesh have been taken up and their likely consequences on the electoral behaviour have been analysed.

National Context

Hung Parliament and a Coalition Government: After the election for 12th Lok Sabha the country got a hung parliament again in which the BJP emerged as the largest single party. The BJP and its allies obtained 252 seats[1], which was twenty short of the minimum number (272) required for simple majority in the Lok Sabha. After strenuous efforts the BJP was able to manage the support of some more small parties and independents in its favour. The Telgu Desam Party was promised the post of the Speaker in the Lok Sabha and in return its members were to abstain at the time of the vote of confidence. With these permutations and combinations, A. B. Vajpayee was administered the oath of office as the Prime Minister on March 19, 1998. At the time he was enjoying the support of 276 MPs. The new combination was later converted into National Democratic Alliance (NDA) with a set of policies to be pursued. Thus, the country was given one more coalition government[2].

In the formation of the government all leading alliance partners were allotted ministership. However, the formation of this coalition government was at variance with the preceding ones in following respect—*(i)* the leadership of the coalition was with the largest party —the BJP, which was far bigger than the rest of the alliance partners; *(ii)* barring a few, there was some sort of pre-poll understanding between the coalition partners; *(iii)* the coalition was able to formulate a national agenda in which the BJP had given up the controversial issues like abrogation of article 370 in respect of Jammu and Kashmir, a common civil code and the construction of Ram Temple at Ayodhya; *(iv)* a co-ordination committee of the alliance was constituted with a non-BJP convenor (George Fernandes—the Samata Party leader) and *(v)* unlike the coalitions in the past this coalition was not dependent upon any outside support as was the case in the Chandrashekhar, Deve Gowda and Gujral governments.

In this coalition Jayalalita's AIADMK and its Tamilnadu allies had a strength of 27 MPs and enjoyed the status of the second largest group after the BJP. Prior to the formation of the government, Jayalalita, on the strength of her 27 MPs, indulged in hard bargaining. The alliance was subjected to her numerous tantrums. When the President demanded from Vajpayee the endorsement letters from the parties supporting the government she delayed this letter for 48 hours. In the end, after bargaining in respect of the ministerial berths of her choice, she offered 'unconditional support'. At one time, she would talk of outside support and on the other, the distribution of portfolios to her MPs. Her conduct throughout the government formation was such that observers got the impression that this government was not going to last long.

Jayalalita's Pressure-Politics: At the same time Jayalalita's tantrums created a situation that the parties of her own alliance refused to toe her line of unsettling the NDA government. With the efforts of the BJP and allies the wedge between Jayalalita and her Tamilnadu allies was deepened, so much so, that when Jayalalita threatened to withdraw the support to the Vajpayee government, the parties of Tamilnadu (MDMK, PMK and TRC) refused to do so. By the end of August 1998 she was reduced as the leader of only 18 MPs belonging to the AIADMK only. Even so this number was critical enough for the survival of the Vajpayee government. Knowing this she continued to bargain and on every following occasion she bargained on harder terms.

The government was upset with Jayalalita's behaviour. Vajpayee's prestige was declining day by day. Newer and newer problems were emerging, demanding immediate attention and solution. In the midst of these troubles the government was able to resolve the Cauvery water dispute between Tamilnadu, Karnataka, Andhra Pradesh and Kerala. Jayalalita opposed this award and pulled out her ministers from the government. The DMK, the rival party of the AIADMK, and a constituent of the erstwhile United Front, wasted no time in changing the side and extended its support to the beleaguered Vajpayee government. A split in the Janata Dal followed this move and one faction of it extended its support to the Vajpayee government and declared its intentions to join the coalition government. It took nearly ten months for the government to manage additional support to counter Jayalalita.

In the process of bargaining Jayalalita was pursuing her personal agenda dressed in the garb of political demands. She was facing several serious corruption charges and the DMK government had constituted special courts to bring expeditious end to these. Jayalalita pressed for the dismissal of the DMK government under article 356. The Vajpayee government refused to oblige. She made petitions in the High Court and failing there she pressed for replacement of the Chief Justice of Tamilnadu High Court. Here she succeeded. She was also successful in forcing the central government to go in appeal in the Supreme Court against the decision of the High Court. Besides, she demanded the transfer and posting of 25 bureaucrats of several departments investigating the charges levelled against her. When the government refused to oblige her on this issue she withdrew her party support to the government.

All this drama was widely publicised through the electronic and print media. The government was losing its credibility among the people. From the point of view of the public opinion, Jayalalita's pressure politics and more often the Central government's surrender before her was giving a message to the people that the charges of corruption on the political leaders do not affect them. The state power is used only to exonerate them, not to punish them.

Pokhran-II: Immediately after taking over, in the circumstances narrated above, on April 8, 1998 the Prime Minister ordered Chidabaram, the Chief of the Department of Atomic Energy (DAE) and APJ Abdul Kalam, the head of the Defence Research and Development Organisation (DRDO), to conduct the nuclear tests. On May 11, 1998 at 3.45 p.m. the simultaneous underground nuclear explosions were successfully conducted in the deserts of Pokhran in Rajasthan. Two days later, without bothering about the US sanctions, two additional tests were conducted. The official announcement said, "This completes the planned series of underground tests" (India Today, May 25, 1998, 22).

This operation, code-named *Shakti*, accorded India as the world's sixth nuclear weapon state. In an opinion poll conducted by ORG—MARG for India Today on May 13, 1998 in 12 major cities[3], about 87 percent of the respondents approved of the testing of the nuclear bombs, 86 percent supported the weaponisation of the bomb, 92 percent said that after the tests they felt more proud to be an Indian and 88 percent said that as a result of the test India would emerge stronger (India Today, May 25, 1998). The country was in a state of euphoria, from beginning to the end the confidentiality of the test was maintained, so much so, that the US satellites could not detect the preparation for and conduct of tests. This also created a tremendous sense of pride and trust in the government. The Prime Minister, in an interview to the India Today said, "no price is high enough when it comes to securing national interests" (India Today May 25, 1998). The demand of signing the CTBT under the pressure of western powers was rejected unless the total disarmament including the nuclear disarmament was programmed and accepted by all nuclear powers. It was pointed out that the security situation and needs must be taken into account while passing judgment on our nuclear testing. The Finance Minister declared that the nature of our economy was such that we could withstand the economic sanctions. The stand on all these issues created a sense of pride and strength in ordinary Indian. Thus, within a period of one month, a Prime Minister humbled by Jayalalita at the time of the formation of the government became an object of pride for the nation.

Onion Crisis and Assembly Elections in Four States: Another major event of the period was the 'Onion Crisis' and the defeat of the BJP in the Assembly elections in four states (Madhya Pradesh, Rajasthan, Delhi and Mizoram) in November 1998.

The onion is an important item of daily consumption in the Indian households. Normally it is available in plenty to reasonable prices. It is grown mainly in the states of Maharashtra, Orrisa, Uttar Pradesh, Karnataka and Gujrat[4]. In December 1997, onions were priced between Rs. 9 and 12 per kg. in retail market. In January 1998 the prices rose to Rs. 20-25 per kg. due to unseasonal rains affecting the production adversely. The then Gujral government was forced to impose a ban on the export of onion (January 12, 1998). The ban was repealed in early March by the same government but this time it was accompanied by heat wave affecting the crops[5]. By August 1998 the prices touched Rs. 26 per kg. There were unseasonal rains delaying the kharif crops. The government woke up to the crisis and imports were then planned as prices continued to shoot up. In October 1998 the prices crossed the level of Rs. 50 per kg. mark[6]. Anticipating the crisis in the Indian market the international prices also went up. At the time of Dewali festival the retail price of onions in Delhi touched Rs. 60 per kg. Side by side, the prices of other vegetables also rose as a substitution effect. All in all, the middle class consumer and the urban poor were severely hard hit. Their anger centred against the failure of the Union Government for failing to control the prices. The BJP got serious drubbing in Delhi, Rajasthan and Madhya Pradesh assembly elections and Congress secured clear majorities in all these states[7]. Thus, the 'onion crisis' and the defeat in assembly elections exposed the incompetence of the government in handling the situation and as a consequence faced a serious loss of credibility.

In certain sections the argument was advanced that the onion price rise was to the benefit of farmers, implication being that the government should not intervene. The counter argument was that the price rise was to the advantage of the traders with capacity to hoard, with marginal benefits to the retailers. A conspiracy theory was also advanced. In 1980, the onion prices had gone up to Rs. 5 per kg. under Charan's Singh care-taker government and Indira Gandhi had capitalsed on the issue and won the elections. In private, the Congress leaders were saying that the onion issue could have the same electoral effect. Some Congress leaders were propagating that the onion price hike was an outcome of the Pokhran blasts. The party's foreign affairs cell chairman Natwar Singh said that the government had hurled so many onions and potatoes to stem radioactivity in Pokharan that now people were suffering (India Today November 9, 1998 p. 22).

In an opinion poll conducted for India Today by ORG-MARG after the onion crisis, the respondents were of the opinion that Sonia Gandhi would make a better Prime Minister than Atal Behari Vajpayee. A year earlier it was the other way round. The results were not favourable to the government. The BJP and its allies were projected to obtain 135 seats against 252 in February 1998 while the Congress and allies 305 against 142, UF 52 against 112 and others

60 against 41. The vote percentage being 26, 45, 9 and 20 as against 36, 26, 25 and 13 respectively (India Today, December 28, 1998, 20-26). Had the elections taken place at that time the BJP-led government would have lost the elections.

Conversion Controversy: Conversion of the Hindu poor, particularly the tribals, was in vogue during the British rule and was considered by the freedom fighters as a tool in the hands of the British to perpetuate their rule in India. A large number of educational institutions, hospitals and orphanages in the service of the poor, the neglected and the deceased were organised and run by the Christian missionaries. In the post-independence period also such activities continued unabated, particularly in the states like Mizoram, Nagaland and Meghalaya, Kerala and in the tribal belt of the Chotanagpur plateau and Orissa through Madhya Pradesh, Maharashtra and Gujarat. One BJP Rajya Sabha MP, Dilip Singh Judeo alleged that nearly 4.5 lakh Hindus were being converted to Christianity each year. (India Today, January 25, 1999). Such allegations gave birth to agitation against the Christian Missionaries in different parts of the country. In fact, protests against conversions, sometimes loud and sometimes feeble, had always been there in a section of the Hindu population. However, during the period under consideration, the violent and criminal activities including murders, looting, rape of nuns, burning of mission homes increased, attracting the attention of the nation[8]. It certainly lowered the image of the country as a secular democracy throughout the world.

The arguments for and against flew in abundance. The opponents and critics of the activities of the Christian missionaries, mainly the Vishwa Hindu Parishad (VHP) and the Bajrang Dal said that *(a)* the Christian missionaries were taking advantage of the poor, innocent and illiterate tribals; *(b)* the conversions by them did not take place because of change of faith but due to pecuniary allurements; *(c)* such conversions were actually the conversion of nationality itself; *(d)* it was the point of larger conspiracy hatched by the Catholic Church, financed by them, and thus to cause subversion of the social balance in the country; *(e)* with the rise of Sonia Gandhi on the national scene politically the Christian missionaries had been emboldened to indulge in mass conversions.

On the other hand, the Christian missionaries, the liberals, and the leftists argued that *(a)* the charge of mass conversion was factually incorrect, as the Chistians as a whole were as tiny in number as nearly 1.0 percent in the total population. This was in fact a decline in population compared with the previous decades; *(b)* in principle conversions were not in vogue, the churches in India had evangelism as their objective which meant they were only propagating the gospel of Jesus leaving every body free to accept or reject; *(c)* the missionaries were only active in the service of the people who were in utter neglect and suffered poverty, illiteracy and disease *(d)* as secularists contended that instead of attacking the churches and the Christians the Hindu fundamentalists should go to the tribals, and work for them, fight hunger, poverty and decease there and keep them in Hindu folds; *(e)* the charge went on alleging that, all this noise of conversion was a handiwork of the BJP's front organisations to scare the Hindus of the dangers coming with the rise of the Congress under the leadership of Sonia Gandhi and to consolidate their caste Hindu support base as they had done at the time of the demolition of the Babri Masjid in 1992.

In the midst of this fierce debate and abhorrent criminal activities the Prime Minister Atal Behari Vajpayee suggested the need for a national debate on the issue of conversions. The opponents turned down the suggestion as uncalled for and demanded that what was needed was the prosecution of the guilty. Incidentally, while the debate was going on, mass re-conversions termed as *shuddikaran* did take place at some places in Gujarat and Madhya Pradesh. It also resulted assertion among Christians in the form of taking out processions, public meetings, and closure of all the Christian educational institutions, activating the minority commission and sending delegations to the Prime Minister and the Union Home Minister.

Fall of the Government: Sensing the vulnerability of the BJP-led coalition government, Jayalalita put forth new demands, such as, appointment of as many as 25 bureaucrats to the post of her choice. Throughout the year her kept increasing, some of them impossible, like removal of Ram Krishna Hegde from the ministry and shifting of George Fernandes form the Defence to less important ministry, even reinstatement of the sacked Naval Chief Vishnu Bhagwat, thus, tying to show that she was the most powerful person. Subramaniam Swamy was also active with his single point programme to pull down the BJP government. He persuaded Jayalalita and Sonia Gandhi to join a tea party organised by him in

New Delhi. To begin with, it served as the process of pulling down the Vajpayee government.

As it turned out, Jayalalita withdrew the support from the government, going with the opposition. The President asked Vajpayee to prove the majority support of the government. After the confidence debate, the government fell by one vote. The expectation was that Sonia Gandhi would be installed as the next Prime Minister and asked to prove her majority on the floor of the Lok Sabha. However, the president taking a different route, demanded from her the written endorsement of her likely supporting parties. That became difficult Tamil Manila Congress refused to support any government which included AIADMK; the Janata Dal said that it would not support a government that included Lalloo Prasad Yadav, the Samajwadi Party Chief Mulayam Singh Yadav said he would not support a government that included the Bahujan Samaj Party (BSP), the Revolutionary Socialist Party and the Forward Block said they would not support a Congress led government. In this situation, Sonia Gandhi could not produce the written support of 272 MPs as required to form the government. The President in this situation dissolved the house and ordered fresh polls with the Vajpayee government to function as care-taker government until the elections.

In this whole episode no party came out unscathed. The President's neutrality was also questioned. His demand that Vajpayee seek confidence vote was seen as partisan. The speaker Balyogi acted upon the advice of the ex-speaker P. A. Sangma in Girdhar Gomango's matter whether the latter had a right to vote in the house. Mayawati openly declaring in the house to remain neutral and at the time of actual voting ordering her MPs to vote against the motion and then claiming that she had taken the revenge on BJP. Sonia Gandhi claimed the support of 272 MPs but failed to produce the endorsement letters in support of this claim, and Mulayam Singh Yadav informing the President that his 20 MPs would not support a Congress government because they were never consulted nor asked.

Kargil War: Just before the general elections, the Indian army fought a successful war against the Pakistan-backed intruders on the Line-of-Control (LOC) in the Kargil-Drass sector of Kashmir. The war started as a proxy war in the last week of May 1999 and turned into a full-fledged war that stretched upto mid-July 1999. Ultimately India won the war by pushing back the intruders across the border. This war cost heavily on the Indian exchequer and the lives of a good number of military and para-military officers and personnel were sacrificed for the supreme cause of national security. The war created a euphoria and generated a strong feeling of nationhood throughout the country during the war period. However, the failure of military intelligence was also pointed out by some quarters.

After the war was over it was found in an opinion survey that 83 percent of the people were of the view that the government managed the war very well. As a result the BJP and its allies were in advantage in terms of the ensuing elections. The Congress on the other hand was attacking the government on the grounds of the failure and coordination of various intelligence agencies.

Uttar Pradesh Context

State's Financial Crisis: During this period the financial crisis erupted in an unprecedented way. At one stage the government was forced to defer the payment of salary for about two months to nearly half the state government employees numbering around 10 lakhs. The crisis continued to rise unabated. Although the state's revenue receipts rose by 44 percent over the past five years but on the other hand expenditure grew by more than double (89 percent). As a result, fiscal deficit increased from Rs. 3710.93 crore in 1992-93 to Rs. 11,023.98 crore in 1997-98. The state's external debt had almost doubled from Rs. 26, 920 crore in 1993-94 to Rs. 50,524 crore in 1997-98 (India Today, December 21, 1998, 40). In such a situation the people of the state were getting panic about the future, and the credibility of the state government was sliding down fast. At the same time the state as well as the central government was also getting desperate. Some strong measures were announced like closing down the loss-making public-sector units, curb in the allowances of ministers and bureaucrats, ban on leave encashment facility, decision to transfer the bonus and increased DA into the employees' provident fund[9] instead of cash payments. These measures were hitting hard the employees the of government sector, which was the largest organised sector in the state.

The measures taken by the then BJP Chief Minister Kalyan Singh were not supplemented by similar discipline among his ministerial colleagues. They insisted and even prevailed on the government to fill 70,000 vacancies of class III employees which would cost Rs. 4000 crore annually. Kalyan's 92 member jumbo ministry itself was causing burden of about Rs. 3 crore each annually. The expenditure on parks, stadiums and statues continued as in previous days[10]. Irrational spending of public funds on unwarranted populist measures did not stop.

The contradiction between the strong measures for financial discipline and the populism by the government aided by the extravagance of ministers and bureaucrats was making the state government unpopular. Kalyan Singh was repeatedly saying that his government had inherited debt ridden economy and empty coffers which had forced him to take strong measures but all these measures were termed as '*nautanki*' by the opposition.

Deterioration in Law and Order: The then Union Home Minister Indrajeet Gupta in 1997 had once commented that Uttar Pradesh was heading towards anarchy and chaos. The BJP was in the forefront in demanding the change of Governor Romesh Bhandari. Mayawati government was also not successful in improving the law and order situation in the state. When Kalyan Singh came to power he used the rhetoric that his top priority would be to provide bhaye mukta samaj (terror free society). During his first six months the situation did not improve. According to the police, between January and June 1999 there was an increase of 6.06 percent in murders, 10.79 percent in dacoties, 13.02 percent in lootings and as much as 38 percent in organized rioting, compared to the corresponding period the previous year (India Today, July 6, 1998, 44). Murders, kidnappings, extortion and lootings, that too in broad daylight, became common in the state, particularly in the capital city of Lucknow[11]. The business community, engineers and contractors and bureaucrats too were living under constant fear and terror. The credibility of the police and the administration was at a record low. The administration resorted to arming the traders and arms licenses were issued in large number[12]. Besides issuing the firearms the police imparted training to them. These innovative measures to control crime were initiated for the first time in the history of the state and probably of the country since independence[13]. The decision to arm the citizens was criticised as it would lead to anarchy and promote a different kind of gun culture in the state. But more importantly, the message percolating was that the law enforcement agencies had failed to control the crime and if trained police force was unable to check the mafia dons how the traders and citizens could succeed.

Kalyan Singh was desperate over the crime situation in the state and in a law and order review meeting in Lucknow on April 30, 1998 he announced "I want performance, results, I want to take a vote that you will create a dhamaka (impact) in the state. If noted criminals can be liquidated in encounters, do it. If you take the life of one person who had taken the lives of 10 others, then people will praise you. And I am here to protect you". This announcement was termed as the license to liquidate and armed with the chief minister's license to kill, the state police eliminated 200 'hardened criminals' in various encounters. The opposition parties on the other hand made hue and cry against these killings as 'fake encounters' and turned the issue into a political campaign, demanding the dismissal of Kalyan Singh's BJP government which they accused of targetting minorities in the fake encounters.

Kalyan Singh constituted a Special Task Force (STF) to curb terrorism in the state and launched operation 'Bazooka' to eliminate the dreaded mafia don Sri Prakash Shukla, which was completed by killing him in an encounter in Ghaziabad on September 22, 1998. But still a large number of mafia dons were operating freely in the state. The criminal-politician-bureaucrat nexus had come into its naked form in the state. Nearly two dozen MLAs who supported the Kalyan Singh government during trust vote were the history sheeters and among them ten were cabinet ministers (Indian Today, July 6, 1998, 44). Many Legislators were reported to be running mafia gangs and some ministers were believed to give shelter to the criminals in Lucknow (India Today, February 2, 1998, 48-49).

Dissidence against Kalayan Singh's Leadership: Between the 1998 and the 1999 Lok Sabha elections, the chief minister, Kalyan Singh, dominated the political scene single handedly. On some occasions his style of functioning and his individual personality helped in projecting him as a strong administrator and shrewd politician, which was gainful for the BJP. But at many times his autocratic and unaccommodating behaviour, ignoring the party organization and depending on personal loyalists, was the reason for embarrassing the party.

During this second term of Chief Ministership, Kalyan Singh accorded special importance to a lady corporator Kusum Rai, representing the Rajajipuram ward in the Lucknow Nagar Nigam. This 35 year old BJP leader developed intimate relationship with the chief minister and in no time she was able to wield so much clout that she started holding *'darbar'* at her residence. In official circles she was dubbed as 'Super Chief Minister' with a mini-secretariat functioning under her command. Kalyan Singh elevated her to the post of the Chairperson of State Social Welfare Board, which was equivalent to the office of the minister of state. Her husband was appointed officer on special duty in State Information Department. The lady became a reliable instrument for getting prize postings and transfers in nearly all the government departments. Besides, she unhesitatingly interfered in the functioning of administration and quite often she instructed officials to release the criminals under custody mostly in Lucknow and the districts of Eastern U.P. Kusum Rai, through these operations, managed to collect huge amount of assets. The Income tax Department issued a notice asking her to disclose the sources of her wealth allegedly amounting to Rs. 100 crore which included prime real estate acquired through benami transactions and a petrol pump in her native district Azamgarh in Eastern U.P. Kusum Rai had been a major cause of friction between Kalyan Singh and his opponents. Due to arrogance and in-accessibility the Chief Minister Kalyan Singh faced stiff opposition from the legislators of his own party. On March 31, 1998, after the resignation of a minister Devendra Singh Bholey, 19 MLAs and 3 MLCs of the BJP submitted a memorandum to central the leadership on April 5, 1998 for replacement of Kalyan Singh. The memorandum was supported by a signature campaign in favour of the cause. The central leadership gave no encouragement to the dissidents. Prime Minister Atal Behari Vajpayee ruled out any change in the state leadership in the near future. This gave Kalyan a new strength and instead of negotiating with the dissidents he nominated the controversial lady, Kusum Rai, as the chairperson of State Social Welfare Board. This action caused further heartburn among, dissatisfied BJP MLAs.

Again in the month of May 1998 the dissidents met the BJP President, Kushabhau Thakre, and submitted their resignation in protest against the continuation of Kalyan Singh. Following the mass resignations, the central leadership summoned Kalyan Singh and asked for cancelling many of his controversial appointments, including that of Kusum Rai, to give a patient hearing to the aggrieved MLAs, and resolve the infighting in consultation with Kalraj Misra and Lalji Tondon. The central leadership gave the impression that if he did not agree the party might go for a President's rule in the State. The dissidents on the other hand started claiming that they had the support of 60 MLAs, a third of the total BJP strength in the assembly and if the central leadership did not pay heed to their demands they might proceed for a split in the BJP.

Kalyan Singh did not appreciate the suggestions of the central leadership. Instead he condemned the entire dissidence as an upper-caste gang-up against him. Within the BJP backward leaders like Uma Bharati and Ganga Charan Rajput also stood with the Kalyan's classification. Kalyan was giving the message to party leadership that if they removed him backward castes would turn against the BJP. Several castes had also mounted a campaign in favour of Kalyan Singh. Posters in the form of open letters to the BJP leadership gave the warning that the backward castes were deserting the party. Sakshi Maharaj, a lodh by caste and a BJP MP openly started sharing the public meetings with the Samajwadi Party leader Mulayam Singh Yadav to forge a backward unity in the state against the upper caste dominated party of the BJP.

The forward—backward divide in the BJP was visible on the occasion of the 67th birthday of Kalyan Singh on January 5, 1999, which was being celebrated with great fanfare. Co-incidentally, the birthday of Murli Manohar Joshi, also fall on the same day. The dissidents chose to celebrate Joshi's birthday at a parallel function in Lucknow. It was the show of strength on both sides.

The Brahmin leaders were advocating that under Kalyan's leadership major support base of the BJP, the Brahmins, were frustrated and angry and were getting ready to desert the BJP. On the other hand, leaders like Sakshi Maharaj were thundering that the party would not be allowed to be run as a private limited company of the Brahmins.

All these developments created a forward-backward division within the party from national and state to the panchayat level in the state. The forward caste sympathisers of the BJP were thinking that they were being humiliated under Kalyan's leadership and at the same time backward support base of the party was viewing that a leader belonging to the backward caste was being humiliated by the forwards. The BJP was the loser at both ends.

The BSP's Worries: The party decided to stage a gherao at Raj Bhawan on May 21, 1998 against two main issues. First, the Kalyan Singh government had insulted the Dalits and their leader Baba Saheb Ambedkar by halting the work in progress in the construction of the 100 crore rupee Ambedkar Park. The party alleged that special attention was being paid to parks and statues in the name of Gandhi and Deen Dayal Upadhyay and development of the Lakshman Park. Secondly, after the issuance of the government order by the Kalyan Singh government that the injustices in the name of Harijan Act should be prevented, the incidents of atrocities against the Dalits had increased. The BJP government did not allow holding demonstration or gherao in the capital and arrested Mayawati and her party workers.

Mayawati was also seen worried when she said that the Governor of the state Suraj Bhan was using his position to make inroads into the BSP's vote bank while the Kalyan Singh government was 'pursuing anti-dalit politics'. Suraj Bhan was taking keen interest in the programmes for the Dalits and the minorities. He appointed an officer to monitor the filling up of reserved vacancies in government departments. He also directed the government to restore the reservation of 21 percent posts for Dalits in a police station, a scheme launched by BSP Chief Minister Mayawati and discontinued by Kalyan Singh a year ago (India Today, October 19, 1998, 36).

The Memorial of Kothari Brothers: The BJP was concerned about the consolidation of its Hindu vote that was attracted towards the party after the Ayodhya movement. In the memory of Kothari brothers described as 'Ayodhya Martyrs' by the BJP, a memorial in Lucknow was erected. On October 30, 1998, the Minister of Urban Development, Lal Ji Tondon, unveiled a towering black granite-and-marble memorial inside a round-about to glorify the 'martyrdom' of the Kothari brothers who had died in police firing during the kar seva in Ayodhya on October 30 and November 2, 1990. Brushing aside all criticism Tondon argued that unarmed people dying for their faith are martyrs (India Today, November 16, 1998, 42).

The state chief of Samajwadi Party, Ram Sharan Das, called the Ayodhya martyrs' memorial as a 'criminal act' of the BJP Government to glorify those whose actions led to communal violence and social disturbances. Das also declared that if his party returned to power in the state it would demolish all the symbols of communal hatred. Congress legislature party leader Promod Tewari decried the memorial as 'shameful' saying it was improper to build a monument in the honour of those killed while violating constitution and law.

Controversy Over Recitation of Vande Mataram and Saraswati Vandana: In November 1998 the Kalyan Singh Government decided to make the recitation of Vande Matram and

Saraswati Vandana compulsory in government-run primary schools and junior high schools. The decision was criticised by the Muslim clergies and intellectuals. They, along with the opposition parties, particularly the SP and the Left parties, alleged that this decision should be seen as part of a bigger design of the Central government to *Indianise* education in the country and the move was seen as an experiment to use Uttar Pradesh as a laboratory to create divisions on communal lines. On the other hand the state minister for Basic Education, Ravindra Shukla, emphasised that 'Vande Matram' was a patriotic song and therefore ulemas and clergies must realise that it was a part of our culture. As the controversy raged, the Prime Minister Atal Behari Vajpayee, during his Lucknow visit clarified that making the recitation compulsory was not necessary (India Today, December 1998, 34-35). However, the controversy paid dividends to the BJP in terms of consolidation of Hindu votes.

II
Design of the Study

Objectives

(*a*) Whether the caste reconfigurations devised by various political parties were still valid in the similar way;
(*b*) What were the features of gains and losses in the support base of different political parties;
(*c*) Whether the stalemate due to the triangular nature of contest between the BJP, the SP and the BSP still continued;
(*d*) Have frequent elections affected the form and the level of electoral participation of voters;
(*e*) Did any significant change take place in electioneering strategies of political parties and electoral environment resulting therefrom;
(*f*) Did the national and the state leadership of different political parties affect the voting behaviour at the grass root levels; and
(*g*) What could be the larger socio-economic and political implications of the patterns of voting behaviour.

Methodology

This study was basically a comparative analysis in relation to the 1998 study. So the sample of the previous survey (1998) was repeated with the similar method of substitution (details have been discussed in chapter V). Simultaneously, the questionnaire was also kept unchanged, only a few new questions or options were added which were considered to be necessary to remove the data gaps of the previous study. The duration of the survey was also the same. Incidentally, the team of investigators was also the same. Thus, it can be assumed that the data of 1998 and 1999 surveys were comparable to a large extent. By repeating the sample with the same team of investigators turned out to be an added advantage. The acquaintance between the two made the communication straight and the data collected became more realistic.

The Sample

In this repeated exercise, about 22 percent of the sample were lost due to various reasons as shown in the Table 6.1. Thus, a total of 331 respondents were interviewed during this survey instead of 425 in the previous survey.

Table 6.1
Factors Responsible for Sample Losses

Cibstutyebcues	*Effective Sample During*		*Sample Loss in 1999 (%)*	*Reason for Sample Loss during 1999 survey*				
	1998 Survey	*1999 Survey*		*Migrated*	*Found Dead*	*Untrace-able*	*Not Available*	*Total*
Allahabad	201	156	12.9	15	4	—	7	26
Phulpur	210	175	10.0	—	3	5	13	21
TOTAL	411	331	11.4	15	7	5	20	47

Characteristics of Sample

Rural-Urban Distribution: Among the effective sample of the 1999 survey 74.0 percent respondents were the residents of rural areas while 26.0 percent were found to be the urban dwellers as shown in the Table 6.2. This ratio was more close to the rural-urban ratio of Allahabad district (79:21). In the earlier survey during the 1998 the proportion of urban-based respondents was higher (31.5 percent).

Table 6.2

Caste-wise Distribution of Respondent by Domicile and Gender

Caste	*Rural*			*Urban*			*Total*		
Groups	*M*	*F*	*T*	*M*	*F*	*T*	*M*	*F*	*T*
SC	28	21	49 (20.0)	13	12	25 (29.1)	41	33	74 (22.4)
OBC	77	25	102 (41.6)	15	07	22 (25.6)	92	32	124 (37.5)
UCH	59	09	68 (27.8)	25	10	35 (40.7)	84	19	103 (31.1)
Muslims	15	10	25 (10.2)	00	01	01 (1.2)	15	11	26 (7.9)
Others	01	00	01 (0.4)	02	01	03 (3.5)	3	1	4 (1.2)
Total	180	65	245 (74.0)	55	31	86 (26.0)	235 (71.0)	96 (29.0)	331 (100.0)

Gender Distribution: The male-female ratio in the effective sample was found to be 71:29, which obviously shows the male bias of the sample. The gender distribution was nearly the same as it was in the earlier survey (70:30). The gender ratio in Allahabad was ......

Caste-wise Distribution: The sample represented 22.4 percent respondents belonging to the scheduled castes. In the previous survey also the proportion was nearly the same (22.6 percent). The representation of Muslims in the sample had increased a little, from 6.4 percent to 7.9 percent in this survey, bringing it more close to the ratio in the universe. The proportion of OBCs in the present sample was 37.5 percent while it was about 35 percent in the previous survey. The upper caste Hindu respondents had been reduced from 34.4 to 31.1 percent in the present survey. Thus, the caste composition of the sample in both the surveys was similar to a large extent as shown in the Table 6.3. At the same time, this caste composition was closer to the caste composition of Allahabad and Phulpur constituencies taken together.

Occupational Distribution of the Sample: As regards occupation, nearly one third were cultivators, about 20 percent were labourers, predominantly the rural labourers while, respondents employed in any kind of service or engaged in trading business constituted the proportion of about 10 percent each. Students were 4.2 percent while unemployed were 3.0 percent. Nearly two thirds of the women respondents reported themselves as housewives constituting about 20 percent of the effective sample.

Table 6.3
Occupation-wise Distribution of Respondents

	Rural			*Urban*			*Total*		
	M	*F*	*T*	*M*	*F*	*T*	*M*	*F*	*T*
Agriculture	88	06	94 (38.4)	05	00	05 (5.8)	93	06	99 (29.9)
Labour	34	15	49 (20.0)	08	04	12 (14.0)	42	19	61 (18.4)
Trade	22	01	23 (9.4)	10	00	10 (11.6)	32	01	33 (10.0)
Service	16	01	17 (6.9)	16	01	17 (19.8)	32	02	34 (10.3)
Professionals	02	01	03 (1.2)	01	00	01 (1.2)	03	01	04 (1.2)
Students	04	00	04 (1.6)	08	02	10 (11.6)	12	02	14 (4.2)
Unemployment	07	00	07 (2.9)	03	00	03 (3.5)	10	00	10 (3.0)
Housekeeping	03	41	44 (18.0)	00	22	22 (25.6)	03	63	66 (19.9)
Others	04	00	04 (1.6)	04	02	06 (7.0)	08	02	10 (3.0)
Total	180	65	245	55	31	86	235 (71.0)	96 (29.0)	331 (100.0)

III
The Results

The results of the survey have been analysed in two ways. As in the case of earlier survey, various aspects such as political participation, affinity with the parties, determinants of voting decision and electoral environment have been analysed in terms of mean values. In addition, the shift in party preferences and gains and losses to various parties have been analysed with the use of cross-tables.

Political Participation

The mean value of participation in all the activities improved marginally in1999. This improvement may have occurred because the electoral contest in 1999 was quadrangular whereas, in 1998, the Congress remained marginalised as in 1996 and the contest was limited to three parties only—the BJP, the SP and the BSP. The emergence of Congress had brought some more people, yet small in number, in the electoral contest. Also, from the very beginning the BJP-led government was under so much pressure by the threats of Jayalalita that its fall seemed imminent all the time. All the parties were foreseeing a possible mid-term poll due to which they kept going the mobilisation activities without any break. It might have led to improvement in the mean values for different forms of political participation.

The comparison of the mean values of different forms of political participation for 1998 and 1999 are shown in the Table 6.4. We find that in 1998 the participation in the form of attending public meetings had the highest mean value, followed by participation in rallies/demonstrations, attending party meetings and functioning as an election campaign worker. In 1999 the participation in rallies and demonstration replaced the participation in public meetings. The mean value of other forms of participation remained in the same order as in 1998. By observation one can see that of late the response to the public meetings addressed by the local district level leaders or even second rank leadership of the party was poor. But if a party announced that a leader of a national standing of the party would address the rally, the local leaders made all out efforts to ensure maximum participation from their areas to make the rally a success and to catch the eye of the top leadership. The importance of local leaders by such intensive activity becomes a parameter to assess their status in the region where they come from. It is a route to win the party tickets to contest elections at different levels. It is thus that the public meetings are losing relevance and rallies for the leaders have come to occupy the centre stage.

It would be relevant to point out here that the political participation index developed during the 1996 parliament study in order to assess the intensity level of political participation of the voters stood valid for 1999 also. At that time those scores might have appeared to be arbitrary but the mean values presented in Table 6.4 confirm those observations.

Table 6.4
Mean Values of Items of Political Participation and Party Affiliation in 1998 &1999

(Scale range 1-5)

Sl. No.	*Forms of Participation*	*Classification of Electorate*	*1998*	*1999*
1.	Participation in public meeting	Rural	1.42	1.86
		Urban	1.47	1.56
		Total	1.44	1.78
2.	Participation in rallies/ demonstration	Rural	1.16	2.04
		Urban	1.24	1.73
		Total	1.18	1.96
3.	Participation in party meetings	Rural	1.14	1.33
		Urban	1.26	1.24
		Total	1.18	1.30
4.	Participation in electioneering	Rural	1.08	1.33
		Urban	1.16	1.14
		Total	1.11	1.28
5.	Donation to political parties	Rural	1.00	1.24
		Urban	1.00	1.04
		Total	1.00	1.19
6.	Affinity with any party	Rural	1.53	1.24
		Urban	1.70	1.04
		Total	1.58	1.19

Affinity with the Parties

Interestingly, the mean value of the response to the affinity with any political party had declined as compared to 1998 survey as shown in the Table 6.4. At the same time the value was less than any form of participation in 1999 while it was higher than all the forms of participation in 1998. The decline in affinity reflects that the caste-candidate factor was becoming stronger which is evident in the Table 6.5 also. As we would see in the following section of this chapter that in the present phase the party affinity is at its lowest. In reality in order to fetch votes the caste of the candidate forms the core of the support. The votes thus secured would not automatically become the support of the party. If the candidate would change the party his caste electorate would also shift with him. They would become the flag bearers of the new party. It is no more an act of political immorality to quit one party and join another for the success in elections. Thus, not the party a candidate belongs to, but his caste to which he belongs, is crucial. So the decline in the mean value for the party affinity is obvious.

Together with the observation made above another critical factor has to be noted here. The caste has a social network, which becomes an important social resource for its members. Membership of a caste makes a person part of a person-based social network which controls insiders' information about economic opportunities, transmits skills and provides varied types of human and material support (Panini 1996; 39). Some members of the caste for various reasons get in the key positions of this network and the rest are on the periphery. In case the caste candidate gets into power those in key positions earn high rewards while others are benefited according to the roles they play. During the tenure in power the candidate as the representative of his caste, rewards the castemen while in the elections he makes promises. So not the policy of the party announced in the manifestoes but likely gains to accrue in the process of distribution of the favours through the state power is crucial to the voters' behaviour. This could also be a reason for the decline in the mean value for party affinity.

Determinants of Voting Decision

The consideration of local issues, which emerged with highest mean value in 1998, continued to be so in the 1999 survey also. At the same time the level of the mean value (2.88) had been very close to the maximum value of the range. This trend conveys a message that the problems at local level continued to be unattended and people were becoming desperate due to which the local problems became the issue of top priority even in the parliament elections. It would be appropriate to mention here, as observed in the study of the 1998 elections, the local issues were in reality perceived as indirect personal gains. It has been explained at length in the preceding chapter and needs no elaboration.

Next to the local issues the policy and programmes of the political party were placed as second important factor. The mean value in this case had also increased in 1999 as compared to 1998 from 2.10 to 2.78. In the earlier study it was pointed out that the parties had been successful in mobilizing their support base by projecting their programmes and policies, which they had implemented during their terms in the government. It can also be hypothesized that the competitive populism by different parties in the state had increased further. This issue has also been discussed in detail in the previous chapter The situation remained unchanged.

The issues like personal loyalties to the candidate, affinity with caste and religion, monetary considerations and personal as well family benefits continued to be accorded less values in determining the decision to vote as in the elections of 1998.

Table 6.5
Mean Values of Determinants of Voting Decisions in 1998 and 1999

(Scale range 1-3)

Sl. No.	*Determinants of voting*	*Classification of Electorate*	*1998*	*1999*
1.	Local Issues	Rural	2.30	2.90
		Urban	2.09	2.83
		Total	2.24	2.88
2.	Policy and programes of Political Party	Rural	2.24	2.82
		Urban	1.79	2.69
		Total	2.10	2.78
3.	Proximity with the Candidate	Rural	1.13	1.35
		Urban	1.00	1.13
		Total	1.06	1.29
4.	Caste/Religion Affinity	Rural	1.12	1.38
		Urban	1.04	1.15
		Total	1.10	1.32
5.	Monetary Benefits	Rural	1.00	1.23
		Urban	1.00	1.07
		Total	1.00	1.19
6.	Personal or Community Benefits	Rural	1.00	1.29
		Urban	1.00	1.02
		Total	1.00	1.24

Electoral Environment

As explained in the previous chapter the election environment was analysed on the basis of six major factors, which determine the nature of election campaign. These factors were-use of money, use of caste and religious sentiments, use of muscle power, use of posters/ banners and loudspeakers, organizing public meetings and door-to-door campaigning. The opinion of the respondents regarding each factor was sought and recorded separately on a three-point scale.

The mean values of each factor for 1998 and 1999 have been shown in the Table 6.6.

The use of caste and religion was accorded the highest value similar to the earlier survey. However, the value of the mean (2.38) increased substantially and approached closer to the maximum value of the range. This shows that caste institutions were increasingly used for wooing the voters during the 1999 elections. This observation may appear to be contradictory to the earlier observation that since newer caste configurations were under progress the bonds between voters and parties had loosened. But this was not true. In fact newer caste configurations in themselves became the strong basis for parties depending on caste institutions for their mobilization strategy as has been explained in detail in the following section of this chapter.

The increased emphasis on door-to-door campaign and public meetings might be the result of the contest turning to quadrangular from triangular. Another explanation could be that during the transitory phase of caste reconfiguration it required caste leaders to put in extra effort to maximize the reach among the fellow castemen and to convince them of the benefits accruing from and the chances of success of the new combination being pursued.

The increased value of mean for the perception about the use of posters/banners and the money in the electioneering was due to the increase in the expenditure limit for electioneering in parliament elections. Besides, it also indicates that the control of the Election Commission had also weakened and the parties had devised ways to convince election observers about their expenditure being under the prescribed limits.

Another important result was that the value of mean for the voters' perception about the use of muscle power had also increased a little. This small increase had larger implications regarding the transformation of political and socio-economic environment of the state, which has been discussed in the head of criminalisation in politics in the concluding chapter.

Shift in Party Preferences

It was evident in 1998 that the configurations around the Mandir-Masjid, Mandal and anti-Manuvad were not as effective for mobilization as earlier. A re-configuration was experimented at the time of 1998 elections. This process encouraged shifts in preferences

Table 6.6
Mean Values of the Perception about the Campaign Strategies of Different Parties for Wooing the Voters

(Scale range 1-3)

Sl. No.	*Campaign Strategies*	*Classification of Electorate*	*1998*	*1999*
1.	Use of Money	Rural	1.20	1.59
		Urban	1.15	1.60
		Total	1.18	1.59
2.	Use of Caste and Religion	Rural	1.98	2.38
		Urban	1.54	2.37
		Total	1.84	2.38
3.	Use of Muscle Power	Rural	1.00	1.19
		Urban	1.00	1.09
		Total	1.00	1.17
4.	Use of Poster/Banner/loudspeaker	Rural	1.71	1.86
		Urban	1.54	1.81
		Total	1.66	1.85
5.	Public Meetings	Rural	1.75	2.02
		Urban	1.57	2.06
		Total	1.69	2.03
6.	Door-to-Door Campaign	Rural	1.76	1.99
		Urban	1.62	2.09
		Total	1.72	2.01

of various degrees in some sections. The day-to-day mobilization strategies on the caste basis by the political parties further strengthened this trend. One of the main objectives of this study was to measure such shifts and its consequences on the political parties.

For this purpose the question that was asked for assessing the partisanship during 1998 survey "which party do you prefer in the present phase?" was retained in the 1999 survey also. Since the sample of 1998 was repeated during 1999 survey, the responses to this question could be compared to understand the shifts in the patterns of partisanship. Alongwith this repetition a new question was included in the questionnaire of 1999 survey "do you still have affinity with the party which you preferred during the last election?" The response to this new question would enable us to assess the proportion of shifters as well as the partisans with stable party preferences. By combining the responses of these two questions the trends in stable partisanship and the shifts in party preferences could be analysed. The responses to both the questions have been shown side by side in the Table 6.7. The responses have been presented in terms of caste and caste-groups in this table.

The table has two parts. Part A is related to the responses of the first question, which provides the information regarding the patterns of partisanship during 1998 and 1999 survey. Part B furnishes the data on the pattern of shifts in party preference in 1999 as compared to 1998.

In Part-A of the table the respondents have been classified into two categories. The first category represented those respondents who did not disclose their preference and preferred not to respond. They have been termed as 'undecided' and they represent the attitude of 'indecisiveness'. The second category stood for the respondents who unhesitatingly indicated their party preferences. They have been termed as 'partisan voters'. The party preferences have mainly been distributed between four parties namely—BJP, SP, BSP and Congress. All other preferences beyond these four parties have been classified into a common group of 'others'. One separate group has also been created for those respondents who categorically stated that they did not prefer any party in the present political system and they have been classified as 'none' in the table.

In Part B of the table the respondents have been classified into three categories in terms of their responses regarding the shift in party preferences. The first category represents those voters who did not shift from their earlier choice. They reflect the attitude of stable or committed partisanship. The second category represents such respondents who admitted that they were not satisfied with their earlier choice and decided to shift their allegiance in the forthcoming elections. These voters have been termed as the 'shifters'. The third category is constituted of those respondents who did not disclose their decision regarding the change in party preferences. They might represent the attitude of lack of political identification but, at the same time, they might be honest in their response that they were neither committed nor had they shifted. They might form the part of those respondents who have been classified as 'undecided' in Part A of the table. Such respondents have been termed as 'non-partisan' electorate.

The proportion of respondents in different categories for overall sample has been termed as the 'sample norm'. By combining the data of the two parts of the table and then comparing it with the sample norm we could get following five possible scenarios among different caste and caste-groups:

(i) The proportion of the 'committed' is above the sample norm which means the electorate in the group is overwhelmingly satisfied with its earlier party preference. This attitude must correspond with the data of Part A meaning thereby the pattern of partisanship between 1998 and 1999 should not vary substantially. If it is not so, it implies that shifting in the preference must have taken place between the dates of survey and polls in 1998 and those preferences are still continuing. This situation may reflect the trend of polarisation in the group for a particular party.

(ii) The second scenario could be that the proportion of the 'committed' in Part B is less than the sample norm and at the same time the proportion of the 'shifters' is higher than the sample norm. It means that substantial shifting in terms of party preference has taken place within the group, which should be reflected in terms of variations in the patterns of partisanship during both the surveys.

(iii) The third scenario could be that the proportion of the 'committed' and the 'shifters' in Part B, both are above the sample norm, which means the proportion of 'non-partisan' voters is less than the sample norm. In such cases the proportion of 'undecided' shown in the first category of Part A would reduce in 1999 as compared to 1998.

(iv) The fourth scenario could be that the proportion of the 'committed', the 'shifters' and the 'non-partisans' in Part B all the three is close to the sample norm. This implies that the party preferences have become somewhat stable and the indecisiveness among the electorate of that group presented in part A would decline.

(v) The fifth scenario could be that the proportion of the 'committed' is closer to the sample norm but the proportion of the 'shifters' is higher than the sample norm. Such a situation implies that there has been a major shift in the party preference and some new party has acquired prominence without changing the general pattern of party preference.

In the light of above explanations and with the help of Table 6.7 the phenomena of shifts in party preferences have been analyzed.

Table 6.7
Partisanship and Shift in Preferences by Castes and Caste-Groups during 1998 &1999

Caste and Caste Groups	Year of Survey	N	PART-A							PART-B		
			Undecided	% of respondents prefering						Committed	Shifters	Non-Partisan
				BJP	SP	BSP	Cong.	Others	None			
Brahmin	1998	95	21	65	6	2	1	—				
		(22.4)	(22.1)	(68.4)	(6.3)	(2.1)	(1.1)					
	1999	74	5	62	1	—	6	—	—	70	2	2
		(22.5)	(6.8)	(83.8)	(1.35)		(8.1)			(94.6)	(2.7	(2.7)
Thakur	1998	14	4	7	2	1	—	—				
		(3.3)	(28.6)	(50.0)	(14.3)	(7.1)						
	1999	5	1	2	2	—	—	—	—	5	—	—
		(1.5)	(20.0)	(40.0)	(40.0)					(100.0)		
Vaishya	1998	20	5	10	4	—	1	—				
		(4.7)	(25.0)	(50.0)	(20.0)		(5.0)					
	1999	21	4	13	3	—	1	—	—	17	3	1
		(6.4)	(19.0)	(61.9)	(14.3)		(4.8)			(80.9)	(14.3)	(4.8)
Kayastha	1998	17	6	2	2	7	—	—				
		(4.0)	(35.3)	(11.8)	(11.8)	(41.2)						
	1999	3	—	2	—	—	1	—	—	3	—	—
		(0.9)		(66.7)			(33.3)			(100.0)		
Upper Caste	1998	146	36	84	14	10	2	—				
Hindus		(34.4)	(24.7)	(57.5)	(9.6)	(6.8)	(1.4)					

	1999	103 (31.1)	10 (9.71)	79 (76.7)	6 (5.83)	—	8 (7.77)	—	—	95 (92.2)	5 (9.7)	3 (2.9)
Kurmi	1998	25 (5.9)	13 (52.0)	3 (12.0)	3 (12.0)	5 (20.0)	—	1 (4.0)				
	1999	24	—	2 (8.33)	6 (25.0)	—	3 (12.5)	13 (54.2)	—	21 (87.5)	2 (8.3)	1 (4.2)
Yadav	1998	58 (13.6)	5 (8.6)	22 (37.9)	31 (53.5)	—	—					
	1999	38	5 (13.2)	2 (5.26)	28 (73.7)	—	3 (7.89)	—	—	35 (92.1)	3 (7.9)	
Kushwaha	1998	11 (2.6)	4 (36.4)	3 (27.2)	4 (36.4)	—	—	—				
	1999	10	2 (20.0)	2 (20.0)	4 (40.0)	1 (10.0)	1 (10.0)	—	—	9 (90.0)	1 (10.0)	—
Dominant BC	1998	94 (22.1)	22 (23.4)	28 (29.8)	37 (39.4)	5 (5.3)		1 (1.1)				
	1999	72	7 (9.72)	6 (8.33)	38 (52.8)	1 (1.39)	7 (9.72)	13 (18.06)	—	65 (90.3)	6 (8.3)	1 (1.3)
Vishwakarma	1998	14 (3.3)	7 (50.0)	1 (7.1)	—	4 (28.6)	2 (14.3)	—				
	1999	11	3 (27.3)	7 (63.6)	1 (9.09)	—	—	—	9 (81.8)	2 (18.2)	—	

Table Continued....

Caste and Caste Groups	Year of Survey	N	PART-A							PART-B		
			Undecided	% of respondents prefering						Committed	Shifters	Non-Partisan
				BJP	SP	BSP	Cong.	Others	None			
Bind	1998	15	2	6	7	—	—	—				
		(3.5)	(13.3)	(40.0)	(46.7)							
	1999	12	3	8	1	—	—	—	—	12		
			(25.0)	(66.7)	(8.3)					(100.0)		
Other MBC	1998	25	8	9	5	3	—	—				
			(32.0)	(36.0)	(20.0)	(12.0)						
	1999	29	7	4	15	—	1	1	1	23	5	1
			(24.1)	(13.8)	(51.7)		(3.5)	(3.4)	(3.5)	(79.3)	(17.2)	(3.5)
Most Backward	1998	54	17	16	12	7	2	—				
Caste		(12.7)	(31.5)	(29.6)	(22.2)	(13.0)	(3.7)					
	1999	52	13	19	17	—	1	1	1	44	7	1
			(25.0)	(36.5)	(32.7)		(1.9)	(1.9)	(1.9)	(84.6)	(13.5)	(1.9)
Chamar	1998	45	15	10	4	16	—	—	—			
		(10.6)	(33.3)	(22.2)	(8.9)	(35.6)						
	1999	36	5	4	1	16	10	—	—	28	5	3
			(13.9)	(11.1)	(2.8)	(44.4)	(27.8)			(77.7)	(13.9)	(8.4)
Pasi	1998	34	8	11	2	13	—	—				
		(8.0)	(23.5)	(32.4)	(5.9)	(38.2)						
	1999	23	3	—	1	17	2	—	—	22	—	1

Kol	1998	15 (3.5)	2 (13.3)	5 (33.3)	4 (26.7)	4 (26.7)						
	1999	14	1 (7.14)	2 (14.3)	5 (35.7)	—	5 (35.7)	—	1 (7.1)	12 (85.7)	2 (14.3)	—
Other SC	1998											
	1999	1	—	—	—	—	—	1 (100.0)	—	1 (100.0)	—	—
Scheduled Castes	1998	96 (22.6)	26 (27.4)	26 (27.4)	10 (10.5)	33 (34.7)	1 (1.1)	—	1 (1.4)			
	1999	74	9 (12.2)	6 (8.11)	7 (9.5)	33 (44.6)	17 (23.0)	1 (1.4)	1 (1.4)	63 (85.1)	7 (9.5)	4 (5.4)
Muslims	1998	27 (6.4)	3 (11.1)	2 (7.4)	22 (81.4)	—	—	—				
	1999	26	2 (7.7)	—	20 (76.9)	—	2 (7.7)	—	2 (7.7)	23 (88.5)	2 (7.7)	1 (3.8)
Others	1998	8 (1.9)	7 (87.5)	1 (12.5)	—	—						
	1999	4	2 (50.0)	1 (25.0)	1 (25.0)	—	—	—	—	3 (75.0)	1 (25.0)	—
Total	1998	425 (100.0)	112 (26.4)	157 (36.9)	95 (22.4)	55 (12.9)	5 (1.2)	1 (0.2)				
	1999	331	43 (13.0)	111 (33.5)	89 (26.9)	34 (10.3)	35 (10.6)	15 (4.5)	4 (1.2)	293 (88.5)	28 (8.5)	10 (3.0)

Note : Figures in parentheses represent the percentage to the number of respondents of the concerned caste or caste group.

The analysis has been done at three levels—over-all, caste group-wise and caste-wise.

Over-all Shifts

As stated earlier the pattern of shifts and partisanship in over-all sample has been termed as the 'sample norm'. We find that at the over-all level 88.5 percent stated that they have not change did their party preference. Only 8.5 percent shifted from their earlier choice and the remaining 3.0 percent did not respond to the question.

The proportion of 'undecided' fell from 26.4 to 13.0 percent. The preference for the BJP declined from 36.9 to 33.5 percent and in case of the BSP, from 12.9 to 10.3 percent. The SP gained from 22.4 to 26.9 percent and the Congress from 1.2 to 10.6 percent. Among others the Apna Dal registered an increase from 0.2 to 4.5 percent. Significantly, 1.2 percent declared themselves as non-partisans, which means that they did not prefer any political party. On this basis following conclusions can be drawn:

(i) during the past year the and a half commitments for partisanship had considerably enhanced among the electorates;
(ii) the proportion of the 'shifters' was fairly low[14];
(iii) the proportion of the 'undecided' declined to about half;
(iv) the BJP and the BSP had suffered a loss in their support bases;
(v) the Conress, the Apna Dal and the SP had increased their support bases;
(vi) the most significant gain was in the case of the Congress whereas the gains by the Apna Dal were also noteworthy;
(vii) a small section among the electorates was found dissatisfied with the present party system ;

Caste Group-wise Shifts

Scheduled Castes: Among the scheduled castes the proportion of the undecided fell from 27.4 to 12.2 percent. This shows that the predilection for partisanship among this group was pronounced as compared to the earlier survey. The BJP had suffered a serious blow, its decline being as low as 8.11 percent from 27.4 percent. In case of the SP, the loss was marginal, from 10.5 to 9.5 percent. The BSP consolidated its support base among the SCs gaining from 34.7 to 44.6 percent. The 10 percent point increase in the support of the BSP could be explained on the basis of the enthusiasm and self-confidence generated among the Scheduled Castes as a result of the role of the BSP in pulling down the BJP led government at the Centre. There was a steep rise in the support from 1.1 to 23.0 percent in favour of the Congress among the SCs. It could also be mentioned here that the support for the Congrees was coming mainly from this section for the proportion of support among the SCs was more than the double of the sample norm (10.6).

The section among the SCs which remained unadjusted in the BSP dispensation and which was earlier supporting the BJP appeared to have shifted towards the Congress. The Congress was emerging as the alternative to the Vajpayee government at the Centre and therefore there was an expectation of likely gains to accrue if and when the Congress came in power.

Dominant OBCs: Among the dominant OBCs, the castes like Yadavas, Kurmis and Kushwahas are included. In this group about 90 percent electorates said that they had not shifted from the choices of preceding election in 1998. A section of about 8 percent among them had shifted their preferences while 1.4 percent did not disclose their preferences. Thus, the commitment for partisanship was higher than the sample norm (88.5 percent) which shows that in their opinion the chances of success of the party with which they identified themselves were greater. The same reason might have been the cause behind the rise in partisanship at these elections when compared with the earlier election. The proportion of undecided electorate had been reduced by nearly 14 percent points i.e. from 23.4 to 9.7 percent. As in the case of the SC group, the BJP lost its support heavily among this social group too (from 29.8 to 8.33 percent). The BSP also lost ground in this group by about 4 percent point (from 5.3 to 1.4 percent). Thus a total of 32 percent points (14 points from undecided to partisanship, 14 and 4 points as shift away from the BJP and BSP respectively) was shared by the Apna Dal (17 points), the SP (13.4 points) and the Congress (9.7 points). Like the BSP in the case of Scheduled Castes, the SP consolidated its position further in this group and the Apna Dal as a rather new entrant effected a very significant penetration. Again as in the case of the SC, group the Congress party which had been out of power for a decade appeared to have found a base for itself in this group which implied that the party appeared to be in the process of revival

Most Backward Castes: The castes included in this group in our sample were Vishwakarmas, Binds, Gaderia, Nai, Kumhar, Sonar, Bhujwa and Kahar. Nearly 85 percent electorates belonging to MBC group did not shift their preferences. But the shift in the preferences was highest in this group (13.5 percent). It was more than fifty percent of the sample norm (8.5 percent). This section among the MBCs had not been able to settle its opinion as to which party would provide maximum benefits to them. It might have been because of this fact that only about 25 percent decline was found in respect of undecided electorates whereas in case of sample norm it was 50 percent. Therefore the feature of indecisiveness continued to prevail among this group. The proportion of undecided among this group declined from 31.5 to 25.0 percent, which means a section of 6.5 percent moved from undecided category to the partisanship. Among the MBCs, the SP gained the most i.e from 22.2 to 32.7 percent, followed by the BJP, which increased its support base from 29.6 to 36.5 percent. The BSP lost its entire support of 13.0 percent and the loss for the Congress was of 1.8 percent points, from 3.7 to 1.9 percent. Thus a total of 21.3 percent points (6.5 from undecided to decided, 13.0 and 1.8 as the shifts away from the BSP and Congress respectively) was shared by the SP (10.5 percent points) and the BJP (6.9 percent points). It seems that in future the size of the section of the undecided might get reduced as their preferences are getting reduced to either the SP or the BJP.

Upper Caste Hindus: The Upper caste group included the Brahmins, Thakurs, Vaishyas and Kayasthas. The shift in the party preferences had been very low among this group, 4.9 percent. It was lowest among all the groups. Obviously, the proportion of committed partisan electorate was highest in this group (92.2 percent) which was about 4 percent point higher than the sample norm. Here also 2.9 percent electorates did not disclose their preferences. The proportion of undecided declined sharply from 24.7 to 9.7 percent. Thus the size of partisan electorate among this group increased by 15 percent points. The losers in terms of support base were the SP and the BSP, the loss being 3.8 and 6.8 respectively. The BSP lost its entire support. The BJP and the Congress were the gainers. The BJP increased its support from 57.5 to 76.7 percent whereas the Congress gained from merely 1.4 to 7.8 percent. Just as the BSP consolidated its support base among the Scheduled Castes and the SP among the dominant OBCs, the BJP extended its base among the upper castes. The SP support declined and the Congress became the second largest party among the upper castes dislodging the SP from that position.

Muslims: The shift of preferences among the Muslims was 7.7 percent, which was less than the sample norm (8.5 percent). The commitment for partisanship in the group was at par with the sample norm (88.5percent) which means the proportion of those unwilling to disclose their preferences was higher (3.8 percent) than the sample norm (3.0 percent). The proportion of the undecided declined from 11.1 to 7.7 percent. The BJP lost its entire support base of 7.4 percent. The SP also lost its support base by about 5 percent points i.e. from 81.4 to 76.9 percent. The Congress gained from nil to 7.7 percent. The BSP continued to draw a blank. Half of the 15.3 percent points (3.4 from undecided to decided and 7.4 and 4.5 shifting away from the BJP and the SP respectively) were gained by the Congress. The remaining half stated that they were not with any party. This attitude on their part was not an expression of non-partisanship or political indecisiveness. Any available party did not represent their partisanship, according to them. It was an attitude of protest.

The size of shift among the Muslims was equal to the overall average but the message it contained was significant. Muslims had the perception that if Mulayam Singh Yadav would have supported the Congress at the Centre the Congress would have been able to replace the BJP. Hence Mulayam Singh Yadav was pointed as a villain who was responsible for non-BJP government not being formed at the centre. Secondly, they were arguing that since SP the was a regional party it could not form a government on it s own at the centre while the Congress was contesting on all India level and under the leadership of Sonia Gandhi, it could defeat the BJP at the centre. Thirdly, Salman Khursheed, being the state president of the Congress, was also attracting Muslims in favour of the Congress. All these factors were a motivating force for a shift in Muslim choice, particularly in favour of the Congress. The Congress candidate, Rita Bahuguna Joshi, in Allahabad was also one important factor for the Muslims' moving in her favour whose family had strong political support base among Muslims. But in the other constituency. Phulpur, the Muslims did not prefer the Congress. They remained with the SP and that was the main reason of low proportion of shift among them in the overall sample. It was a tactical move by the Muslims to defeat the BJP in which they succeeded. So, in the same district, the behavioural pattern of the same community differed which has been dealt in detail in the later section.

Caste-wise Preferences: The preceding analyses of the shift in party preferences on the basis of caste groups do not enable us to get a clear picture of the ground realities as regards the shifting in the party preferences among different castes independently. The pattern of shifting in different castes belonging to the same caste group was markedly different as evident in the Table 6.6. So to get a more realistic picture the analysis of caste-wise shift in party preferences was necessary. In the Table 6.7, the voters' preferences for parties among different castes provide sufficient explanation to the phenomena of significant shifting from the previous choice.

The parties in the contest in some cases changed the candidates in the election under study. It affected the candidate- caste factor of the electorates' preference. Therefore, the changes in the candidature of different parties had also to be discussed before the discussion of electoral behaviour along caste lines.

The BJP retained its candidates in both the constituencies Professor Murli Manohar Joshi, a Brahmin (upper caste) from Allahabad and Beni Madhav Bind belonging to Most Backward Caste from Phulpur. The SP changed its candidate in both the constituencies. In Allahabad Reoti Raman Singh, a Bhumihar (upper caste) was fielded replacing Shyama Charan Gupta, a Vaishya (upper caste). In Phulpur, although the candidate was replaced by Dharamraj Patel in place of Jung Bahadur Patel, but the caste of the candidate did not change. The BSP changed both the candidates. In Allahabad there was a change from K.P. Srivastava, a Kayastha (Upper Caste) to Ram Dulare Patel, belonging to dominant backward caste, a Kurmi and in Phulpur from Ram Pujan Patel a Kurmi to Tulsi Ram, a Yadav (dominant backward caste). In this election the Congress emerged as a viable alternative to the BJP at national level. The party had fielded a strong candidate from Allahabad. Rita Bahuguna Joshi the daughter of late H.N. Bahuguna and the then mayor of the Allahabad and Brahmin by caste replacing Dal Bahadur Singh, a Thakur (upper caste). In Phulpur, the Congress contested the election with Ram Pujan Patel, a Kurmi, instead of J. N. Mishra, a Brahmin. The Apna Dal did not change its candidate from Phulpur, Dr. Sone Lal Patel, the national president of the party.

Chamars: The shift in party preferences among the Chamars was 13.8 percent, which was over 60 percent higher than the sample norm. At the same time the indecisiveness among them had decreased, as a result the proportion of partisanship increased. The BJP had suffered a major setback in this caste, its half of the support base had eroded and reduced to 11.1 from 22.2 percent. The situation of the SP was no better in the earlier election also, but howsoever small a support base was there that too reduced sharply and it came down from 8.9 to a mere 2.8 percent. This caste had been the major support base of the BSP. In the present election it increased the support for the party from 35.6 to 44.4 percent. The most significant, however, was an impressive gain by the Congress. The Congress did not have any support among the Chamars during the previous survey whereas this time it gained nearly 30 percent in its favour.

The sharp shift in partisanship among the Chamars was the result of a number of developments. The BSP gained because Mayawati emerged as a bold and decisive leader in pulling down the Vajpayee government. But the Congress gained more mainly because of certain local factors. First, at the local level the candidates fielded by the BSP belonged to the castes which had been antagonistic in their social behaviour towards the Chamars. The BSP leaders had repeatedly been reminding their followers about the misdeeds of Mulayam Singh Yadav and his *goondas* during the guest house incident in 1995. Similarly, the role of Jang Bahadur Patel and other Patel leaders of the district, while defecting from the party in favour of Mulayam Singh Yadav, was also considered as an act of betrayal to the party. The prominence given to these incidents by the BSP leaders during mobilisation campaigns created a typical mind set of the Chamar community against the Yadavas in general and the Kurmis in particular in Allahabad. So the candidates of the BSP in both the constituencies were one major factor responsible for detraction of a section of the Chamar voters from the BSP. Secondly, the Congress was emerging as a viable alternative at the national level and its leader Sonia Gandhi was raising hopes for a change which might have appealed to some voters among the Chamars, particularly to those who had been the support base of the Congress during the pre-BSP days. The Congress was also cultivating those earlier links. Thirdly, the Congress candidate from Allahabad, Rita Bahuguna Joshi, belonged to the Bahuguna family, which had personal friends among the community leaders in all parts of the district. Since she was seen as a prospective winner, those links were motivated to campaign in favour of the Congress. Apart from

Table 6.8
Party Candidates and their Caste in Allahabad and Phulpur Parliament Constituencies

Political Parties	*1998 elections*		*1999 elections*	
	Candidates	*Caste*	*Candidates*	*Caste*
		ALLAHABAD		
Bhartiya Janata Party	Dr. Murli Manohar Joshi	Brahmin (upper caste)	Dr. Murli Manohar Joshi	Brahmin (upper caste)
Samajwadi Party	Shyama Charan Gupta	Vaishya (upper caste)	Reoti Raman Singh	Bhumihar (upper caste)
Bahujan Samaj Party	Dr. K.P. Srivastava	Kayastha (upper caste)	Ram Dular Patel	Kurmi (dominant OBC)
Congress	Dal bahadur Singh	Thakur (upper caste)	Dr. Rita Bahuguna Joshi	Brahmin (upper caste)
		PHULPUR		
Bhartiya Janata Party	Beni Madhav Bind	Bind (Most Backward Caste)	Beni Madhav Bind	Bind (Most Backward Caste)
Samajwadi Party	Jung Bahadur Patel	Kurmi (dominant OBC)	Dharma Raj Patel	Kurmi (dominant OBC)
Bahujan Samaj Party	Ram Pujan Patel	Kurmi (dominant OBC)	Tulsi Ram Yadav	Yadav (dominant OBC)
Congress	J. N. Misra	Brahmin (upper caste)	Ram Pujan Patel	Kurmi (dominant OBC)
Apna Dal	Dr. Sone Lal Patel	Kurmi (dominant OBC)	Dr. Sone Lal Patel	Kurmi (dominant OBC)

these explanations, it had also been noticed that at the national level the Congress was able to penetrate swiftly among the Chamar Community.

Pasi: Among the Pasis there was no shift in party preferences. The indecisiveness among them had also been reduced sharply from 23.5 to 13.0 percent. The BJP drew a blank in 1999 survey whereas in the previous survey the party was preferred by about one third of them. The SP had a very small support in this caste in the earlier survey. However, the party was able to retain its small support base with a marginal loss. The Pasi caste had polarized in favour of the BSP this time, raising the support from 38.2 to 73.9 percent. It was a significant gain for the BSP. The Congress, which had no support in the earlier survey became the choice of about 8.70 percent of this caste the present survey.

The data shown in the table with respect to 1998 survey was collected a week before the polling. In that survey the electorate of this caste had indicated 32 percent preference for the BJP. In the present survey the BJP had no support at all. At the same time the electorate had stated that they did not change their party preferences of 1998 elections. If what had been stated was true, the 32 percent which preferred the BJP in 1998, in the period of one week i.e. between the survey and the actual polling, they had shifted from the BJP to the BSP in 1998 itself.

Kol: There was a noticeable shift in the party preferences among the Kols. As a result the commitment for partisanship was less than the sample norm. However, the indecisiveness among them had declined by about a half (from 13.3 to 7.1 percent). During the previous survey nearly one-third of the Kols had favoured the BJP while now the proportion was reduced to less than 15 percent. But the more significant loss of support was in the case of the BSP, which was completely wiped out in the 1999 survey The Congress was the real gainer, which had no support in 1998 survey. It gained the support of more than one-third of the Kols during this survey. The SP was also able to improve its support base among the Kols from 26.7 to 35.7 per cent.

Yadavas: A large proportion the among Yadavas stated that they had not changed their preferences during the two points of our survey, the percentage (92.1 percent) being higher than the sample norm. But at the same time a sizeable proportion of 7.9 percent, quite close to the sample norm, had shifted from their earlier choice.

Significantly, there was no respondent in this caste who was unwilling to disclose his or her party preferences, which shows the attitude of boldness in expressing his choices. The proportion of the undecided had increased in this caste. Possibly, the candidate-caste factor was responsible for the increase in proportion of indecisiveness. The BSP had set up Tulsiram Yadav as its candidate and Dharmaraj Patel was contesting on behalf of the Samajwadi Party. The nature of the contest might have caused indecisiveness with regard to whether to vote for the casteman or the party of the caste. Although the BSP candidate was not able to win the preferences for the party at the time of the survey, he was however able to create indecisiveness among a section of the Yadavas. The share of the support for BJP had reduced from 37.9 to a mere 5.3 percent whereas the SP had increased it from 53.5 to 73.7 percent. The Congress managed to draw a noteworthy support of 7.9 percent, whereas earlier there was no support for it.

The decline in the support base of the BJP represents the higher level of shift, which is in contrast with the higher level of commitedness. It appears that during the survey in 1998 the Yadavas, who were in favour of the BJP, might have shifted in favour the SP at the time of polling which was held a week after the survey. The higher proportion of the non-shifting among the Yadavas in 1999 could be explained with this last moment shift in choices in1998. A similar shift had taken place at the last moment in case of the Pasis also as stated earlier.

Kurmi: Among the Kurmis 87.5 percent stated that they had not shifted their party preference. This proportion was close to the sample norm. A significant feature with regard to the party preference in this caste was the total absence of indecisiveness. In 1998 survey the proportion of undecided was 52 percent which was completely absent during the 1999 survey. The BSP drew a blank, which had a support base of 20.0 percent in the earlier survey. The support base of the BJP had also shrunke from 12.0 to 8.33 percent. The SP had made impressive inroads into in this caste by gaining the support of 25.0 percent, which was more than the double of the previous support. The Congress, which had no support in 1998, was successful in winning the favour of 12.5 percent of the electorate during the 1999 survey. But the most significant shift was witnessed in favour of the Apna Dal. In the earlier survey, only 4.0 percent had indicated their preference in favour of the party, whereas in the present survey, more than half of the respondents of this caste favoured the Apna Dal. This party is known to be a party of the Kurmis and the national president of the party himself was contesting for the second time from the Phulpur constituency. Incidentally, Sone Lal Patel had received serious injuries during the lathi charge and firing by the police on the supporters of his party at a public meeting held in the city prior to the filing of his nomination papers. The incident created anger against the police action and strong sympathy for the candidate among the Kurmis. The fact of 54.2 percent support for the Apna Dal in the present survey implied that the 52.0 percent among the Kurmis who were undecided at the time of 1998 survey had actually voted for the Apna Dal in that election. That is why in the present survey 87.5 percent stated that they did not change their party preferences

Kushwaha: The shift in preferences was higher than the sample norm in this caste. They were open in informing their preferences and, no one was found unwilling to disclose his or her choice regarding partisanship. The indecisiveness had also declined from 36 percent to 20 percent. As regards partisanship, their preferences were closer to the Kurmi caste. There had been loss for the BJP (from 27.2 to 20 0 percent) and gain for the SP (36.4 to 40.0 percent) in terms of the support base. The Congress and the BSP broke fresh grounds in this caste. Both these parties did not have any support in the previous survey. The Apna Dal was not successful in penetrating into this caste despite the fact that this caste was closest to the Kurmi caste in terms of social behaviour. The Samajwadi party was able to muster maximum support (40.0 percent) from the electorates of this caste.

It appeared that this caste had not idetified itself with any particular party. They did want to be clubbed with the Kurmi dominated party of Apna Dal, at the same time they were found disillusioned with the BJP. Hence they were keeping their options open by providing support bases to the BSP and the Congress. Yet, by and large, they continued to prefer the SP during 1999 as in the case of 1998 survey.

Vishwakarma: The proportion of electorates among the Vishwakarmas who shifted their party preferences was highest among all the castes. This proportion (18.2 percent) was more than the double of the sample norm. But the indecisiveness had declined from 50.0 to 27.3 percent. This shows that although there had been significant shift in preferences, the choices were firm and clear at the time of the survey in 1999. Nearly two thirds of this caste had indicated their preference in favour of the BJP. This was a significant gain for the BJP because in the previous survey the support base of the party was limited to merely 7.1 percent, which rose to 63.6 percent in the latter survey. The SP was able to win a small support of 9.09 percent, which was a net gain for the party, because in the earlier survey it had no support in this caste. The support bases in 1998 of the BSP (28.6 percent) and the Congress (14.3 percent) completely vanished in the present survey. The shifts in party preferences and overwhelming support for the BJP indicated that among the Vishwakarmas there was a trend of polarisation emerging in favour of the BJP during the 1999 elections.

It has been stated in chapter V that as a caste, the Vishwakarmas are rural artisans and in recent years they were not able to withstand the competition with the new technology, and their traditional vocations were facing the danger of extinction. Of late, their economic conditions had deteriorated. The penetration of new technology in the market compelled them to upgrade their traditional skills and introduce intensively the use of modern technology in their trade. It not only involved large-scale investments but linkages with various training and marketing institutions. In order to achieve these objectives they needed support from the government through various schemes in this regard. The party in power, if inclined to take steps in this direction, would always earn their favour. The BJP were in power in the State and were not likely to be dislodged in the immediate future. In this situation the Vishwakarma electorate might have favoured the BJP hoping assistance from the government.

Bind: Among the Binds there was complete absence of shift in party preferences. All the respondents of this caste stated that they still continued, to support the party which they had favoured in the previous election. The proportion of indecisiveness among them had nearly doubled. The percentage of undecided electorates among them had increased from 13.3 to 25.0 percent. Nearly two-thirds of this caste had indicated their preference in favour of the BJP. This was a significant gain for the BJP because in the earlier survey the support to the BJP was only 40.0 percent. The candidate-caste factor was responsible for this increase in support for the BJP among the Binds. The party retained its candidate Beni Madhav, belonging to the Bind caste, for the second time from the Phulpur constituency

The SP faced a serious setback by losing its support base substantially in this caste. Its share among them declined sharply from 46.7 to only 8.3 percent. As a result the BJP, which was a little behind than the SP in terms of the support base in 1998, overtook the SP and was able to win nearly eight times larger support base than the SP. No other party was able to gain support among this caste either during 1998 or in the present survey.

At the same time the proportion of undecided electorate increased. On the one hand the BJP candidate was the casteman, on the other another, caste leader Phoolan Devi, the bandit queen, was contesting from the neighboring Mirzapur-Bhadohi constituency. She was pressing for support in favour of her party, the Socialist party. The dilemma whether either to vote for the caste candidate in one's own constituency or to oblige a glamorous leader from the caste by voting for a candidate of her party belonging to a different caste. Hence a section of the Binds remained confused at the time of our survey.

Other MBCs: The shift in preferences among other numerically small MBC castes, which included Gaderia, Nai, Kumhar, Sonar, Bhujwa and Kahar, in our sample was as high as 17.2 percent, nearly double the sample norm. Obviously, the commitment for partisanship was substantially lower in this group. But the proportion of undecided electorate had declined from 32.0 to 24.1 percent, which means that the indecisiveness had declined to some extent. The BJP had lost its support base by one third of what it had during 1998 (36.0 percent). Similarly, the BSP also suffered as its entire support was wiped out. The Congress was able to gain support of a tiny section (3.5 percent) in these castes. The SP was the major gainer by winning more than half of their support.Its support was enhanced from 20.0 to 51.7 percent of the electorate among these castes. At the state level no party was identified with these castes nor was there any such effective and recognized leader from among them at the local level who could motivate the fellow castemen in favour of a particular party. This provided sufficient space for non-committedness among a section of voters in these castes.

Brahmin: The shift in party preferences among the Brahmins had been very low (2.7 percent). Nearly ninety five percent said that they still continued to support the party, which they preferred during the last election. The partisanship among Brahmins was so committed that the indecisiveness declined to the level of 6.8 from

22.1 percent. The BJP further consolidated its support from 68.4 to 83.8 percent in this caste. This consolidation compares favourably with the SP among the Yadavas and the Muslims and the BSP among the Chamars and the Pasis. The SP had never a sizeable base among them. Its share of support fell to as little as 1.4 percent from 6.3 percent. The BSP suffered the same fate here and lost even the 2.1 percent support, which it had earlier. While the SP and the BSP were losing ground the Congress significantly was able to increase its support base from a mere 1.1 percent to a noticeable proportion of 8.1 percent. Thus, the electorate of this caste was polarised in favour of the BJP, with dissenters among them opting for the Congress.

Thakur: In this caste there was no shift in preferences. The proportion of undecided electorate in it declined from 28.6 to 20.0 percent, which shows that the indecisiveness in terms of party preferences had been reduced. The BJP, which was favoured by 50.0 percent of the Thakur electorate in 1998 survey, was not able to retain its support base and was reduced to 40.0 percent in 1999. The BSP, preferred by a small section of 7.1 percent in 1998, lost its entire support base during the period between the two surveys. The net gainer had been the SP, which extended its support base from 14.3 percent to 40.0 percent, at par with the BJP. At the time of 1999 survey the Thakur electorate was equally distributed between two parties—the BJP and the SP. No other party was favoured by this caste in 1999.

The phenomenon of complete non-shifting was in contrast to the variations in terms of partisanship indicated during the two surveys. In order to explain this contradiction the responses of the electorate at the time 1998 survey would have to be looked into afresh. It appeared that a major shift in the partisanship might have occurred between the period of our survey and the polling day. About 10.0 percent out of the 50.0 percent who indicated their preference in favour of the BJP had shifted in favour of the SP at the last moment. Similarly the 7.1 percent who were supporting the BSP, in the end went in favour of the SP. From amongst the 28.6 percent undecided electorate, 8.6 percent broke away from the undecided to partisanship and made up their mind to go with the SP. This pattern of partisanship continued to prevail at the time of our survey in 1999. That is why all the Thakur respondents were indicating that they still continuedto prefer the parties which they had voted for in 1998.

Vaishya: Among this caste the proportion of electorate who had shifted from their earlier choice was higher than other castes of the upper caste group. It was 14.3 percent, nearly 70 percent higher than the sample norm. Obviously, the proportion (80.9 percent) of such electorate who did not want to shift from their earlier choice was lower than the sample norm. But, at the same time, the proportion of undecided electorate had been reduced from 25.0 to 19.0 percent, which shows that the indecisiveness had declined. The BJP was able to consolidate its support base in this caste and gained the favour of nearly two-thirds of Vaishyas, which was only 50.0 percent during the previous survey. The SP lost its base from 20.0 to 14.3 percent. The Congress suffered a marginal loss and its share in the support base was reduced to 4.8 from 5.0 percent. The BSP did not find any support among this caste either in 1998 or during 1999 survey. The reason for the shifting during the period between the two surveys was very simple. In the previous election the SP had fielded a candidate from this caste which attracted fellow castemen to favour the SP. He was replaced this time and hence the Vaishyas, who happened to be the support base for the BJP for a long time in the past, returned to their traditional fold. Thus, the candidate-caste factor played a major role in determining the choices of the Vaishya electorate.

Kayastha: In this caste there was no shift in party preferences between the period of the two surveys. The indecisiveness in this caste was completely eliminated at the time of the 1999 survey, which was 35.3 percent in 1998. There were, however, variations in their party preferences between the previous and the present survey as shown in the table. If there was no shift in the party preferences, the variations in 1999 could not have occurred. At the time of 1998 survey the BJP and the SP both were favoured by 11.8 percent each and the BSP by 41.2 percent and the remaining 35.3 percent were undecided. In the survey of 1999 the BJP was preferred by 66.7 percent and the Congress by 33.3 percent. There was no support at all for the BSP and the SP and the there was no undecided electorate also. In the face of these facts the electorate stated that they had not shifted their party preferences. Clearly there was contradiction between the two statements. It could be understood by noting that in the time gap between the dates of the survey and the polling shifts in preferences had taken place in 1998. The practice of the eleventh hour shift is not unusual in the behaviour of our electorate. In this case the entire lot of undecided electorate must have shifted in favour of the BJP. Towards the end of the election campaign when the fact that K.P. Srivastava was out of contest, a section of the Kayastha voters, must have shifted their preferences in favour of the BJP. At the same time, the section showing allegiance to the SP, having found that the caste was divided between the BJP and the BSP only, got split between the two. As a result gained two-third support in the caste and the remaining favoured the BSP. The Kayastha electorate was in favour of K.P. Srivastava not the BSP. It never owned the BSP as its party and portrayed itself as non-BJP electorate. Therefore in 1999 survey this section in the Kayastha caste, while stating that it had not changed the party preferences, it actually meant that it continued to be non-BJP voter and there was no shift in its instance in this respect. With the BSP and the SP out of favour in this caste, the non-BJP section in it favoured the Congress. In this sense there was no shift in electorates' preference

Party-wise Gains and Losses

In the light of the observations made above the gains and losses to different parties in terms of support bases might be analysed now. The caste-wise composition of support bases of different parties is presented in Table 6.7.

In the above table it is evident that the proportion of undecided voters had declined sharply from 26.4 per cent to about 13.0 percent between 1998 and 1999 survey. This decline was indicative of the elimination of indecisiveness among a sizeable proportion of the voters, which might be the product of several factors which had influenced the general environment of national as well as the local politics. It also implied that the parties had been successful in bringing more and more electorate into the electoral politics. The variations in the support bases of different parties are given below:

Bhartiya Janata Party (BJP): During the 1998 survey, the BJP earned the largest support (36.9 percent) among the electorate. In the present sample also the BJP continued to be the largest preferred party, but the size of the support base declined by about 3 percent points (from 36.9 to 33.5 percent).

In 1999, the BJP had no support among the Muslims and the Pasis. At the time of the 1998 survey the party was able to receive support of a small section among the Muslims which was merely one percent of the party's support base. In 1999, that too was lost. In case of the Pasis they formed about 7 percent of the support base of the party at the time of 1998 survey which too was completely lost at the time of 1999 survey. But, as has been observed in the analysis of caste-wise shifts, the Pasis had shifted away from the folds of the BJP by the time of the actual polling during 1998 elections itself. So in real sense there was no loss for BJP in this caste.

The Brahmins continued to be the main support base of the BJP, nearly 55 percent support came from this caste alone for the party. Earlier, it was about 40 percent. Only the Congress was the other party, which could manage some support for itself among the Brahmins. Thus, Brahmins were polarized heavily in favour of the BJP. Next to the Brahmins the Vaishyas, a community known for its support to the BJP from the days of the Jan Sangh, constituted major support base comprising nearly 12 percent of the support. The Vaishyas support doubled compared to the previous survey. Another major support for the party came from the MBCs, particularly from the Binds and the Vishwakarmas, constituting a proportion of about 7 and 6 percent receptively. These castes constituted very small proportion of the support base of the BJP in 1998 (3.4 and 0.6 per cent respectively). The Chamars and the Other Numerically Small MBCs had formed about 3.6 percent share in the support for the BJP, which was a loss of about 50 percent among them. The share of the Kayasthas, Kurmis and the Kushwahas in the support of the party remained more or less the same, nearly 1.8 percent. As compared to the 1998 survey, major loss was among the Yadavs and the Thakurs. As regards the Yadavas, in the previous survey they constituted nearly 14 percent of the support, but the major section had shifted away from the party by the time of the polling as has been observed in the shift-wise analysis. So, in real terms it was not a loss. The most significant loss was observed among the Thakurs who are a part of the Upper Caste group. They share of this caste in the support for the party was reduced from 4.5 to 1.8 percent between the two surveys.

There could be no question about the fact that the BJP was mainly supported by the upper castes. The loss suffered by it among the dominant OBCs was mode up by the gains scored in the MBCs. The setback among the SCs was a severe blow to the party, for it could not be compensated in terms of shifts of preferences among them here and there.

Samajwadi Party: Nearly all the castes of the sample, barring the Kayasthas, were providing from very small to substantial base

Table 6.9
Comparative Chart of Caste-wise Composition of Support Bases of Different Parties: 1998 & 1999

(in percent)

Castes	*Year*	*No Response*	*BJP*	*SP*	*BSP*	*Congress*	*Others*	*None*
Brahmin	1998	18.8	41.1	6.3	3.6	16.7	—	—
	1999	11.6	55.9	1.1	0.0	17.1	—	—
Thakur	1998	3.6	4.5	2.1	1.8	—	—	—
	1999	1.8	1.8	2.2	0.0			
Vaishya	1998	4.5	6.4	4.2	16.7	—	—	—
	1999	11.7	11.7	3.4	2.9			
Kayastha	1998	5.4	1.3	2.1	12.7	0.0	—	
	1999	0.0	1.8	0.0	0.0	2.9	—	
Upper Caste Hindus	1998	32.1	53.5	14.7	18.2	33.3	—	—
	1999	23.3	71.2	6.7	0.0	22.9		
Kurmi	1998	11.6	1.9	3.2	9.1	0.0	100.0	—
	1999	0.0	1.8	6.7	0.0	8.6	86.7	
Yadav	1998	4.5	14.0	31.6	16.7	—		
	1999	11.6	1.8	31.5	8.6	—		
Kushwaha	1998	3.6	1.9	4.2	0.0	0.0	—	—
	1999	4.7	1.8	4.5	2.9	2.9		
Dominant BC	1998	19.6	17.8	38.9	9.1	16.7	100.0	—
	1999	16.3	5.4	42.7	2.9	20.0	86.7	
Vishwakarma	1998	6.3	0.6	0.0	7.3	33.3	—	—
	1999	7.0	6.3	1.1	0.0	0.0		
Bind	1998	1.8	3.8	7.4	—	—	—	—
	1999	7.0	7.2	1.1				
Other MBC	1998	7.1	5.7	5.3	5.5	0.0	6.7	
	1999	16.3	3.6	16.9	0.0	2.9	3.45	
MBC	1998	15.2	10.2	12.6	12.7	33.3	6.7	
	1999	30.2	17.1	19.1	0.0	2.9	1.92	
Chamar	1998	13.4	6.4	4.2	29.1	0.0	—	
	1999	11.6	3.6	1.1	47.1	28.6	—	
Pasi	1998	7.1	7.0	2.1	23.6	0.0	—	—
	1999	7.0	0.0	1.1	50.0	5.7		
Kol	1998	1.8	3.2	4.2	7.3	0.0	—	7.14
	1999	1.8	1.8	5.6	0.0	14.2		
Dhobi	1998	—	—	—	—	—	6.7	—
	1999							
SC	1998	23.2	16.6	10.5	60.0	16.7	6.7	
	1999	20.9	5.4	7.9	97.1	48.6	1.35	
Muslims	1998	2.7	1.3	23.2	—	0.0	—	7.69
	1999	4.7	0.0	22.5		5.7		
Others	1998	6.3	0.6	0.0	—	—	—	
	1999	4.7	0.9	1.1				
All Castes	1998	100.0	100.0	100.0	100.0	100.0		
	1999	100.0	100.0	100.0	100.0	100.0		
% support to parties in total sample	1998	26.4	36.9	22.4	12.9	1.2	0.2	1.21
	1999	13.0	33.5	26.9	10.3	10.6	4.5	

for the support to the party. The largest share in support comprised the Yadavas representing about 31.5 percent. It was exactly of the same size as in the previous election survey. Next major group in the support of the party was that of the Muslims, nearly 22 percent, which was slightly lower than the previous level of 23 percent. Just as in the case of the BJP the Brahmins formed the 55 percent support, the Yadavas and the Muslims together constituted 54 percent of the over-all support to the SP. Another major group comprising numerically small MBCs in our survey provided the support of about 16.5 percent. The support by these castes in the previous election was only 5.3 percent. Thus it was a major gain for the party. The Kurmis formed another major support with an increased share of 6.7 percent. There had been no change in the size of the share of the Kushwahas which remained at around 4.5 percent. The Kols provided a support with an increased share of about 5.5 percent It was significant in the sense that the share in overall support of the Kols had increased inspite of their being a part of the Scheduled Caste group where the SP was facing losses. The share of the Vaishyas declined, yet it was 3.4 percent. There were other miniscule supports among the Brahmins, the Vishwakarmas, the Binds, the Chamars and the Pasis for the party. There was no noticable increase in the share of the Thakurs in the overall support for the Party.

On the overall basis, the party was a net gainer. It increased its share in the total electorate from 22.4 to 26.9 percent. The party consolidated its support base among the Dominant Backward Castes and the MBCs. It retained its base among the Muslims. Among the Upper Caste group it suffered heavy losses. The losses were noticeable among the SCs also.

Bahujan Samaj Party: As regards the BSP the overall support was reduced from 12.9 to 10.3 percent.The party was wiped out among the Upper Castes as well as the MBCs. In the total support received by the party the share of the Chamars and the Pasis was 47 and 50 percent respectively. The party appeared to have only the scheduled caste base in 1999 survey. The 2.6 percent point loss may not appear heavy but in terms of its support among the upper caste, the OBCs and the Muslims, the losses were serious

Congress: The gains earned by the Congress were one of the most significant feature of the 1999 elections. In the previous survey merely 2.8 percent respondents of the sample preferred it, which increased dramatically to 10.6 percent, nearly four times higher than the previous level. The proportion is marginally higher than the preferences indicated for the BSP (10.3 percent). This phenomenal rise in support base of the Congress was an indication of the re-emergence of the Congress as a viable alternative after lying in woods nearly for about a decade. This change made the electoral contest from triangular to quadrangular, which affected the behavioural pattern a large section of voters in the State.

If the caste composition of the support base of the Congress is analyzed it is found that barring three major castes—Thakurs, Binds and Vishwakarmas—all other castes included in the sample were represented in the support base of the party. In 1998 the support came only form the four castes of the sample and that too in a very small size. Among the castes supporting the Congress this time the largest proportion was of the Chamars (28.6 percent) followed by the Brahmins and the Kols, 17.1 and 14.3 respectively. Significantly, the support to the Congress came from such castes also which were heavily polarised in favour of other parties like the Yadavas, the Pasis, the Kurmis and the Muslims. The inclusion of the Muslims in the support base of the party was noteworthy because after the Ayodhya incident of 1992 the Muslims never favoured the Congress either in the Parliament or in the assembly elections in the State. If this trend of support base for the Congress is consolidated it could initiate newer forms of caste reconfiguration in the state and the Congress may gain its traditional support base of Brahmins, Muslims and the Scheduled Castes.

IV
Concluding Remarks

The 1999 survey results show that for the first time in the entire decade the electoral contest was found to be quadrangular instead of triangular, which had significant implications. The emergence of the Congress as a serious contender for power at the Centre had brought some more people, though small in number, in the electoral contest.

The competitive mobilisations born out of the instability pushed all the parties to keep continuing their mobilisation activities uninterrupted. It led to the improvement in the political participation of the electorate to some extent. Significantly the major form of mobilisation by the parties was the organisation of rallies and demonstrations, mainly at the district headquarters. During the period between 1998 survey and the present one, the public meetings were found to be losing relevance as a form of mobilisation strategy.

The political participation index developed during the 1996 parliament study in order to assess the intensity level of political participation of the voters stood valid for 1999 also with the rider that the public meetings had merged into the form of rallies and demonstrations.

To quit one party and join another for the success in elections was no more an act of political immorality in the perception of the electorate. In fact, not the party a candidate belonged to but his caste was crucial. The caste serves the two-way purpose in our socio-political system. It helps the parties as well as the candidate to reach to the voter residing in the remotest part without much difficulty. On the other hand it provides a social network through which the member residing on the periphery could approach the leaders at the centre of the network for various personal gains. So, not the policy of the party announced in the manifestoes but likely gains to accrue through the state power, was to be crucial to the electorates' behaviour.

The local issues continued to dominate the decisions for party preference which were in reality perceived as indirect personal gains. The increased competitive populism by different parties in the state had contributed to the development of such attitude.

The supervision of the Election Commission had also appeared to be weakened as the parties had devised ways and means to circumscribe the expenditure in excess of the prescribed limit.

The analysis of shift in party preferences highlighted that during the intervening period

- *(i)* commitments for partisanship had considerably enhanced among the electorates;
- *(ii)* the proportion of the 'shifters' was fairly low;
- *(iii)* the proportion of the 'undecided' declined to about half;
- *(iv)* the BJP and the BSP had suffered a loss in their support bases;
- *(v)* the Congress, the Apna Dal and the SP had increased their support bases;
- *(vi)* the most significant gain was in the case of the Congress while the gains by the Apna Dal were also noteworthy;

(vii) a small section among the electorates was found dissatisfied with the policies of the parties.

It was found in our survey that every party, barring the Congress had some castes serving as a core support for it. There were the Brahmins in case of the BJP, the Yadavas and Muslims in case of the SP and the Chamars and the Pasis for the BSP. The support for the Congress was spread over different groups and the caste within them. Around the core caste or castes the parties endeavoured hard to win support in different castes. The parties extensively used the caste-candidate factor. The survey also indicated that the process of re-configuration is not likely to end in near future.

NOTES

1. Seats Won by Pre-poll alliances:
   BJP and allies-252 (BJP-178, Samata-12, AIADMK-18, BJD-9, SAD-8, Trinmool-7, Shiv Sena-6, Lok Shakti-3, PMK-4, MDMK-3, TRC-1, JP-1, HVP-1 JD-6, TMC-3, DMK-6 TDP-12, SP-20, CPM-32, CPI-9, RSP-5, FB-2, NC-2, Secular Cong.-1).
   Congress and allies-167 (Congress-142, RJD-17, RPI-4, Muslim League-2, Kerala Congress-1, RJP-1)
   Others-21 (BSP-5, SJP-1, United Minority Front-1, Majlise Ittehad Musalmeen-1, Autonomous State Conf.-1, Haryana Lok Dal-4, Arunachal Congress (Apang)-2, Sikkim Democratic Front-1, Manipur Socialist Party-1, Independent-5).

2. **Party-wise Representation in the Vajpayee Government**

Party	*No. of MPs*	*No. of Minister*
BJP	179	25
AIADMK	18	4
Samta	12	2
RJD	9	2
Akali Dal	8	2
Shiv Sena	6	1
DMK	4	1
Lok Shakti	3	1
TRL	1	1
Arunchal Congress	2	1
Independents	4	3
Total	276	43

   Source: India Today, March 30, 1999, p. 29.

3. The survey was conducted in 12 cities—Delhi, Mumbai, Calcutta, Chennai, Bangalore, Hyderabad, Ahmedabad, Lucknow, Jaipur, Patna, Bhopal and Cuttack—and interviewed 1635 people in the 18 plus age group on May 13, 1998 (India Today, May 25 1998, p. 25).

4. **Area under onion crop in different states**

State	*% of total*
Maharastra	20.0
Orrisa	14.8
Uttar Pradesh	12.2
Karnataka	11.5
Gujrat	8.2
Total	66.7

5. According to the Agriculture Ministry, normally 20 percent of the ratio crop (harvested in May-June) was affected involving a production loss of 4 lack tonnes.
6. **Retail Price of Onion (Delhi)**

Period	*Price Rs./Kg.*
11 June 1998	6.00
31 July 1998	16.00
14 August 1998	26.00
31 August 1998	22.00
17 September 1998	33.00
3 October 1998	40.00
7 October 1998	46.00
30 October 1998	60.00

7. **Results of Vidhan Sabha Election 1999 held in Four States**

State (Total Seats)	*Congress*	*BJP*	*BSP*	*Others*
Delhi (70)	51	15	—	3
Madhya Pradesh (320)	172	119	11	18
Rajasthan (200)	150	33	2	12
Mizoram (40)	6	—	—	34
Total (630)	379	167	13	67

8. On September 22-23 night 1998, three names were going raped and their unison was looked by located at Nanpada in Jhabua district of Madhya Pradesh. Four days later on September 26 1998 broadest strike at a Cathoira unisseon at Jamali, a few kelometers from Nanpada. On September 27, 1998 a mission in Bhopal was attacked by resident Bhopali Janata Crlmy (Inda Today, October 13, 1998, p. 31).

   On January 23-23 night in Manoharpur village of Orrisa's Keonjher district Australian born Christian missionary Graham Stewart Staines (58) and his two sons Philip (10) and Timothy (7) were burnt to death, allegedly by a mob of villagers led by a Bajrang Dal activist Dara Singh.
9. **Dicipline Measures;** *(i)* Cut in the out-of-pocket allowance of ministers under wheel a minister can claim upto Rs. 1.5 lakh a month without submitting vouchers; *(ii)* Withdrawal of ministers' free rail coupons worth Rs. 82,000.00; *(iii)* Ban on police escorts in the state capital Lucknow; *(iv)* Restriction on air travel for ministers and bureaucrats; *(v)* Ban on foreign trips for ministers and senior officers; *(vi)* No leave enchantment except in the case of class III and IV employees; *(vii)* Voluntary surrender of 50 percent of ministerial salary and allowances till March 1999; *(viii)* Bowes and increased DA to go into employees' provident fund intend of cash payment (India Today, December 23, 1998, 39).

10. On November 6, 1998 Kalyan Singh unveiled and 12th statue of Maharana Pratap at Hazratganj, Lucknow, A week earlier be inaugurated a life-size statue of Veerangna Uda Devi who had killed 35 British soldier at the same spot in 1857, He also assured the Maharaja Bijli Pasi Trust will be established. He honored the Amausi Airport officer Sardar Vallabh Bhai Patel. Similarly statues of Maharani Avanti Bai, Bhama Shah, Rabindra Nath Tagore and Rani Luxmibai were erected; (India Toady November 302 1998, 37-98.
11. In the past six-month alone, more than 40 traders have been targeted by extortionists. Four of them have been killed, over half a dozes injured, five kidnapped and 13 others looked at gunpoint. In most of the cases the businessmen preferred to pay up rather than report the matter to the police (India Today, September 7, 1998, 30).
12. A total of 27,183 licensee hand already been issued in Lucknow and some 18000 applications were pending with the district administration (India Today, September 7, 1998, 30).
13. India Today reported, "This is perhaps the first time in the country that the police, besieged by a spurt in incidents of kidnapping, extortion and looking at gunpoint, is imparting training in five areas to citizens." (India Today, September 7, 1998, 30).
14. The proportion of shifters was 17 percent between 1962 and 1967 and 19 percent between the 1967 and 1969 elections (Sheth 1975; 7).

7

Conclusions

The analyses on the changing patterns of the electorates' behavior have highlighted some important trends in the socio-economic and political environment of the state, which may be utilized as useful inputs for the formulation of public policies. Since the book covers three Lok Sabha elections and the 1996 State Assembly election spread over a period of four years it provides an opportunity to observe the dynamics of certain institutions and processes which determine the nature of the governance and development in the State during the nineties.

Caste as the Key Determinant of Voting

During the elections under study it was observed that the social relations and institutions based on caste dominated the political scene in UP as compared to the political parties and ideologies. The role of caste had never been so clear, vocal and effective as in the elections held in the nineties. Acquiring the status of a powerful political force by a traditional social institution for electoral mobilisations was a significant socio-political development of this period. Voting along the caste lines had become an acceptable political reality at all levels. From the local bodies to the State Assembly and the Lok Sabha elections the caste-based voting was all pervasive.

The transformation of caste into this political form has been termed as the politicization of caste (Kothari). It had been viewed as a process that brought the marginalised section hitherto lying on the periphery into the centre stage. It has also been observed as an 'emancipatory process' in favour of the exploited castes (Alam). The overwhelming success of the parties representing the OBCs and SCs in the 1993 elections was seen as the 'second democratic upsurge' (Yadav). The findings of our studies have, however, demonstrated that to glorify the role of castes or caste-based parties in this manner is misleading. The ground level realities explicitly expose that the caste based politics and mobilisations were the handiwork of a class which is present in every caste and is successfully using the social institutions for concentrating the economic and political power in its favour.

(a) Group Behaviour

To vote along the caste lines is an expression of group behaviour. It belied the assumption that as the democracy grew parochial identities like castes and tribes would automatically vanish away. The caste-based groups were not like trade unions inclusive of people from different social groups demanding the fulfillment of their common demands. Their aspirations and demands were related only to a particular caste.

The group motivates its members to vote. During the surveys conducted it was observed that a large number of electorate was not aware of the fact that in the coming few days elections were to be held, even though the elections had been notified. It emerged in our survey that the majority of the electorates was illiterate and poor and was out of reach of the media. The participation of such electors in the political activities organised by various political parties before or after the elections was negligible. The political parties had no direct access to such electorate. In addition, the common electorate looked upon the political parties and their leaders with contempt. Yet, at the time of elections, they were found enthusiastically participating in the polls and ran after these very parties and leaders. The survey results revealed in no uncertain terms that the electorate, which was indifferent towards elections, ultimately did vote. It was found that the electorate with the notion *kou nrip hoye hame ka hani* was motivated to reach the polling booth and participate enthusiastically by his family at micro level and by caste at macro level. This attitude of participation in cooperation with the community was the expression of group solidarity based on the authority of caste.

While voting along the caste lines an individual voter surrendered his right to vote in favour of the decision of the group. It might appear to be a rational choice for he was aware that he could not influence the final result by his single vote, but by joining a larger group his single vote could contribute in getting the poll results on the lines which could be beneficial for him too. In this endeavour he would try to situate himself as close as possible to the group decision.

(b) Caste-Based Social Network

How does a caste motivate its members to vote for a particular candidate or the party? Panini has observed that each caste has a person-based social network which controls insiders' information about economic opportunities, transmits skills and provides varied types of human and material support. The membership of a caste makes a person part of this person-based social network (Panini 1996; 39). Thus, the moment an individual was born in a caste he would get linked with its social network and would become beneficiary in numerous ways effortlessly. Therefore the social network of a caste could become an important social resource for its member. While voting along the caste lines the voter would surrender his individual bargaining power in the expectation that in future the social network available with the caste would serve him as a socio-economic resource.

The structure of these social networks corresponds to the structure of an atom. In the centre there is a nucleus which is surrounded by numerous orbits. The prosperous and dominant members of the caste constitute the nucleus and they hold the key positions of this network. They are privileged with education, share in services, business and land holdings etc. The remaining members of the caste are situated at different points on different orbits around the nucleus. The distance from the nucleus is reflective of the relative economic strength of the member concerned. The most disadvantaged sections of the caste are located on the periphery. Thus, it is clear that the castes are not homogenous and are stratified.

The size of the nucleus and the distribution of electorate on the surrounding orbits would determine the form of the social network of a particular caste. In the study of 1996 Lok Sabha elections an attempt has been made to distinguish such stratification in terms of caste-groups with the help of an Achievement Status Index (ASI). On the basis of that index all the four major caste-groups were classified into three status categories namely; high, medium and low. That distribution could be used to understand the structure of social networks. However, there would be a difference. In terms of achievement status the stratification is vertical whereas in the case of social networks the distribution is horizontal. The electorate with high achievement status represents the nucleus while the electorate belonging to medium status form the inner orbit and the outer orbit symbolizes the lower status electorate. Although the said achievement status index was limited to four major caste-groups only, it could be indicative of the patterns of social networks of the independent castes also that were included in the caste-group.

In the over-all sample slightly more than half belonged to the lower strata, nearly 38 percent were in category of medium and only about 12 percent of the electorate were found in the high strata. Thus the combined size of the nuclei of all the prevailing networks stood around 12 percent of the total electorate. The inner orbit comprised of the 38 percent while more than half were situated on the outer orbit. This configuration could be denoted as (12, 38, 50). The first digit in the bracket represents the size of the nucleus in terms of percent distribution of higher strata electorate while the second and third digits are the proportions of medium and lower strata electorate respectively. With these notations the configurations of the structure of networks of different caste-groups could also be illustrated. Among the SCs the configuration was (5, 20, 75), in case of OBCs it was (6, 37, 57), among the Muslims (17, 39, 42) and for the upper castes (23, 53, 24).

The above configuration of structures of social networks indicated certain features. The smaller size of nucleus among the SCs and OBCs suggested that the conflicts among them would be less and thus the number of social networks would also be less. In case of the Muslims the relatively large size of the nucleus suggested that there would be conflicts larger in numbers that would encourage multiplicity of networks. The configuration among the upper castes was a clear case of functioning of multiple networks with considerable amount of conflicts. Another implication was the benefits of state patronage were cornered by a few in case of the SCs and the OBCs while in case of the Muslims and the upper castes they were shared among larger proportion.

The principal motive to continue as a member on the orbits around the nucleus of a particular caste-based social network was basically the occurrence of personal gains in present or the possibility of likely gains in future. Most of the gains appeared in the form of state patronage. So every caste-based social network necessarily linked itself with one party or the other at the time of elections. In all situations the members of the nucleus earned the highest rewards in various forms in case the candidate supported by the caste-based social network got into power while others are also benefited according to their positions and roles. So the policies and programmes of the parties announced in their manifestoes did not determine the electorates' behaviour but the likely gains to accrue in the process of distribution of the favours through the state patronage was crucial in this regard.

It would be wrong to come to the conclusion that castes have an all accepted social network. The clash of personal interests among the members of a nucleus results in the emergence of alternative networks. Weaker castes would establish fewer networks whereas the number of networks among influential castes would be larger. The multiple networks often collide with each other for acquiring certain favours and benefits. If the conflict is not resolved amicably some of the networks may go to the extent of joining hands with the networks of other castes. In politics such changes could be visualised as shift in preferences resulting in the re-configuration of castes. In all these the principal gainer would always be the nucleus of networks.

(c) The Nucleus and the Party Politics

Some members of the nucleus of the caste-based social network functioned like caste leaders in the political fields. The networks operated under the leadership of these caste leaders. Sometimes they were elected through formal institutional arrangements but mostly they acquired their position by informal channels. The influence of these caste leaders evolved in three phases. The first phase was the period when the Congress was in dominance. During that period the caste leaders, howsoever they might have been influential, their direct intervention in the political realms was negligible. In those days, in order to gain political prestige or identity, they had to depend on some party or the other. They were functioning as the agents of the political parties or leaders. They were communicators of the party's programmes and the leader's ideas among the masses. For this purpose they used the prevalent notions and symbols and made the messages acceptable. They worked as media at the grass root levels between the electorate and the party. These caste leaders performed the important function of motivating their caste voters for or against a party at the time of elections. In the second phase the Congress declined at the national level and fragmented into a number of regional Congress parties. Other political parties also met the same fate one after the other. This situation provided space for the emergence of numerous state level parties The disintegration of parties was so frequent that the identity of political parties itself ceased. Gradually the opportunism of the party leaders ruined their image among the masses and their popular base shrank day by day. The result was that by the beginning of the decade of eighties the political leaders lost whatever influence they had. Consequently their dependence on the caste leaders increased more and more in order to carry voters with them. The dependence of various political parties upon these caste leaders, apart from the Lok Sabha and State Assembly elections, was clearly visible at other elections also like university or college students union elections, teachers association elections, village panchayats and co-operative elections etc. In order to expand their base and influence the political parties, directly or indirectly, promoted these caste leaders in a number of ways. On the other hand the caste leaders, conscious of their own importance and utility in the elections, succeeded in acquiring important positions in party organisations at every level. The third phase began with the nineties. In this phase the caste leaders had acquired a position from where they could split a party at any moment and join another, carrying their caste followers along with them or even launch a new party of their own. These caste leaders were found so much emboldened during this phase that they did not hesitate in quitting even the ruling party and were able to float a new party throwing challenge to the party in power. In 1989 Mulayam Singh Yadav quit the then Janata Dal that was leading the government in the Centre as well as the State. In 1994 Sone Lal Patel left the Samajwadi Party which was leading the government in the State at that time and formed a new party named Apna Dal. Similarly, when the central leadership of the BJP decided to change its Chief Minister in UP in 1999, Kalyan Singh left the party and floated a new party Rashtriya Kranti Dal. The Rashtriya Lok Dal of Ajit Singh was also another example of this phenomenon. All these leaders depended mainly on their own caste. These leaders and their parties did not have influence in the entire state. Rather, it was limited to some districts or region depending upon the concentration of the caste they were representing. A qualitative change was noticeable in the electoral politics of UP during this period. These caste leaders had no pretensions of any political or national viewpoint. This brought about a situation in which even at the time of elections political issues were missing in popular gossips at ground level. The implications of questions like liberalisation, multinational companies, planned development and national security were of course discussed in the press. However, these subjects could not acquire importance at the popular level. In the absence of discussions on such subjects the caste leaders very smoothly pushed in the regional and caste pride as major issues. It was natural also, for the entire political training and culture of the caste leaders had developed in terms of caste problems. Whenever the caste leader would initiate any discussion the question of caste with regard to the comparative superiority or deprivation would occupy the prime place.

Caste Conferences: As has been discussed earlier, caste leaders were placed on top positions of the social network of their caste. To mobilize their castemen in their favour they organized caste conferences at different levels, particularly at the time of elections. All these conferences a priori were cultural expressions of the social network of the castes concerned, but at these conferences the general voter of the caste was offered the signal of economic and personal gains. The attendance and the impact of the appeal in the conference were considered as a yardstick to assess the influence of the caste leaders.

Dominant Neo-Rich

In the preceding section the structure of caste-based social networks and the role of their nuclei in terms of caste leaders have been discussed. In economic sphere the emergence of the neo-rich is the expression of these nuclei. The neo-rich are a class inclusive of different castes. With the strength of social network behind them the nuclei very cleverly serve their economic interests through the patronage of state power. The processes and institutions that are related with the prevailing democratic system, developmental planning and public policies have been capitalised by this class in its own favour. The attitude and behaviour of this neo-rich class has transformed the nature and character of political culture and mobilastion strategies in the state. The characteristics of this class have been discussed under the following three heads:

(a) Concentration of Economic Power

The emergence and strengthening of the neo-rich as a class is better reflected in the rural areas. It includes mostly the big, medium and upcoming small farmers. In the post-Green Revolution phase these farmers benefited most from the increased productivity by introducing new farm technologies. Their agricultural operation was predominantly mechanized. They produceed marketable surplus in agriculture. By acquiring economic prosperity they became the dominant section in rural areas. Consequently a strong and assertive lobby of surplus producing farmers emerged in the State. Militant farmers' movements during the eighties under the Bhartiya Kisan Union were the expression of this lobby. On several occasions, the Central and the State governments were forced by this lobby to enhance the procurement prices of foodgrains and the support prices of sugarcane. This lobby also exerted pressure on the governments for not increasing the power tariff, irrigation charges or diesel prices in spite of the unbearable burden of subsidies. This class of farmers appropriated most of the gains resulting from the programmes of rural or community development. These surplus-producing prosperous farmers also cornered large chunks of bank and co-operative loans and managed successfully to get exempted from its recovery, partially or fully. This emboldened class manipulated maximum contracts relating to various public works in rural areas, which gave another source of income to them. They owned big or small non-farm rural businesses. Various kinds of agencies like tractors and agriculture implements, fertilisers, seeds and pesticides, bicycles, building material, tyres, diesel/petrol, etc. were obtained by this class. Besides, non-farm rural industrial units like brick kiln, rice mill, cold storage, food preservation etc. were also under the ownership of this class. This class shared a large proportion in the growing trade of natural resources available in rural areas like timber and major or minor minerals. Most of the highly educated persons in the rural areas came from this section and they employed in government and organized private sector. They also ran private schools and colleges in rural areas. They had close links with the government machinery at all levels. In course of time this class became so strong that in connivance with the development bureaucracy they successfully managed to lay hands on substantial amount of funds allocated for poverty alleviation programmes. In recent years in the name of decentralised planning the funds that were being allotted to village panchayats had also been cornered by this class. This neo-rich class was the forebearer of competitive caste politics, which served their economic interests. Since they commanded the top positions and formed the nuclei among their caste-based social networks they were capable of mobilising their castemen by creating illusions of numerous gains.

The dominant neo-rich class constituted 13.5 percent of the total rural households in the state. The total value of all the assets including land and buildings in rural areas of Uttar Pradesh has been estimated at around Rs. 262 thousand crores, out of which more than half is controlled by this class. The average value of assets owned by them has been estimated at Rs. 5.32 lakhs per household. Nearly 57 percent land, about 70 percent of all agricultural machinery, nearly 57 percent of all transport equipment and 36 percent of buildings and durable household goods are under their possession. They own about 96 percent of tractors and almost all the tractor trolleys in rural areas. The above pattern of assets distribution has significant implication. The assets which determine the mechanisation of agriculture are mostly controlled by this class and simultaneously the transport sector which includes trucks, buses and light motor vehicles is also predominantly controlled by them. These assets are income-generating assets and the hiring charges accruing from such assets provide continuous flow of income. The ownership of nearly all tractor trolleys indicates that lucrative non-form occupations are fully dominated by this group. These occupations include contract works under various development agencies like road building, irrigation, construction, transportation of forest products, minerals, farm products etc. as well as running the brick kilns The distribution of buildings and durable household goods reveals that the prosperity visible in the rural markets or in the form of pucca houses in the countryside is reflective of the economic ascendancy of only a few households. The subject has been discussed at length in chapter II.

The neo-rich can be further divided into two categories on the basis of dominance in state politics. In this regard nineties can be considered as a cut off point. It is noteworthy that the neo-rich of nineties were more subtle, more urbane and more aggressive than the neo-rich of the seventies and eighties mostly concentrated in the rural areas. The gains of the earlier neo-rich were mainly from new technology in agriculture, higher prices for farm produce, contracts in social forestry, rural road construction, canal and irrigation related works and maintenance of public buildings in rural areas. But the factors responsible for the emergence of the neo-rich in the nineties were entirely different. The benefits accruing to them in economic fields were closely linked with the political connections at higher levels. The dominant neo-rich of the nineties are the main actors of politics and they influenced the voting decision of the masses during the elections. They could be seen as active players between politics, administration and business. They treated politics as a tool for advancing their interests in trade and business. The phenomenon could be termed as commercialisation of politics. This class was using the state apparatus for protecting and promoting its economic interests. They constituted the base of leadership of different political parties and the legislatures and even ministers emerged out of them. The rivalry in commercial fields got reflected in politics and thus any re-configuration of social forces must be viewed in this light.

(b) The Neo-Rich and the Rural Poor

It was obvious that when the process of concentration of assets was underway the redistribution of resources in favour of the poor would not pick up and the policies aimed at restructuring of the economy would also not yield results. The benefits of the programmes of poverty alleviation would not reach the target population. Amidst these constraints several new occupations emerged in the state's economy, which were providing employment opportunities in non-agricultural sector. This phenomenon changed the form of patron-client relationship of rural labourers. The availability of work in the non-agricultural sector was closely linked with the relationship between the rural poor and the neo-rich class because they were now the net employers of rural labourers in farm and non-farm activities in the rural areas. This was true for the government sponsored schemes also because there was strong nexus between the development bureaucracy and the dominant neo-rich. There was another reason which promoted dependency relationship. The public institutions supposed to serve in various forms for the welfare of people have failed to deliver the services. They too functioned along with the nexus with dominant neo-rich. So, if a person even though entitled to receive benefits, wanted the help of police or relief from the police, land records from the lekhpal, scholarships for children, benefits from various rural development programmes or even to get included in the list of Below Poverty Line families, he would have to depend on his links with the local dominant neo-rich. Here it is noteworthy that the neo- rich of the beneficiary's own caste could easily be accessible as compared to the neo-rich of other castes. This linkage also strengthened the dependency relationship between the poor and the dominant neo-rich.

(c) The Neo-Rich and the Self-employed

The impact of liberalization and privatization in economic policies was now clearly visible. As a result of liberalization private enterprises grew at a faster pace. In recent years unorganized self-employment had also grown speedily. It was found that the employment opportunities created due to growth of this sector could be availed through caste networks. At the same time if an individual established his own enterprise he would need a minimum level of social support from the days of its inception until it became economically viable. Initially the entrepreneur would obtain this support from his castemen. In this way the section of the castemen with a poor level of living got naturally linked with the dominant and prosperous section of the caste in the form of prospective economic security. In this way the rich section or not so rich of the voters, engaged in running an enterprise, small or big, in organized on unorganized sector, legal or illegal, decide upon their votes keeping these facts in view. This fact is valid in both the urban and the rural areas. This tendency prevalent among the richer section of a caste became the factor of mobilization of votes. It can be termed as commercialization of politics, which had asserted itself in recent years. The political activities ceased to serve as a standard form of democracy; they served as a tool to expand and diversify the enterprise (commercial activity). Politics loses form as an ideal. If this tendency continues, the political power, in league with economic power, will become handmaid of a few dominant rich sections of the society.

(d) The Neo-Rich and the Election Campaign

It has been found that in the elections the political parties had been placing very little emphasis on mass contacts in their election campaigns. There was very little communication between the parties and the common electorate. In fact, the candidates or the parties preferred to contact neo-rich only instead of the common voters. They called meetings at the residences of the neo-rich families in which local level caste leaders participated and were made responsible to manage the support of their network in favour of a particular candidate. The trade and professions of the leading supporters of the candidates set up by different political parties could provide a good clue to understand the close relationship between certain occupations and election campaign organisers. It was found in our survey that factory owners, transporters, owners of petrol filling stations and gas agencies, liquor contractors, dealers of cold drink agencies, builders and estate property dealers, contractors, proprietors of nursing homes, coaching institutes, wholesale traders, leading advocates and university professors were the chief campaigners for the BJP and the SP. The Congress enjoyed the support of the industrialists, transporters, leading advocates, railway contractors while transporters, proprietors of nursing homes, owners of gas agencies and the contractors were seen to support of the BSP. Thus the campaign organisers and financiers of all the parties came from the same class which enjoyed the patronage of the state apparatus and therefore had a stake to see a particular candidate succeed. None of them had any ideology. Most of them had promoted the cause of different political parties at different times. This class treated politics and elections as a very potent weapon to serve its economic interest. The political competitiveness displayed during elections exhibited their commercial competitiveness.

Political Parties

Mobilisation Strategies

In Uttar Pradesh caste mobilisations dominated the electoral politics during the entire decade of nineties. The analysis of electorates' behaviour over the period would indicate that the political parties in the state were engaged in experimenting various caste re-configurations. On the basis of mobilisation strategies the period of nineties could be divided into two phases, the pre-1996 and the post-1996. In the first phase the castes were combined on the basis of four major caste groups represented as the Scheduled Castes, Other Backward Castes, Upper Castes and the Muslims. The assertion of the SCs against the manuvad under the leadership of the BSP was a significant feature of the mobilasation in pre-1996 phase. The success of Mandal agitation which gave reservation to OBCs in the central services and was utilised as a symbol for consolidating the backward castes was another feature of mobilisation strategies during this phase which strengthened the SP. The third strategy centered on the Ram Mandir issue gave boost to the consolidation of the upper caste electorate and the BJP emerged as a substantial gainer. The parties were predominantly depending upon inclusion and exclusion strategies in terms of caste groups.

When the elections to the 1996 Lok Sabha were held the BJP gained in U.P., but in the State Assembly elections held six months later it proved to be a repeat of 1993 results. That meant the prevailing caste alliances of different parties had reached the plateau. In the following elections the caste equations were not repeated. Inter-caste and intra-caste groupings had displayed the tendencies of disintegration. Although the political parties continued to be formally recognised by their earlier support bases i.e. the BJP as the upper caste party, the SP as the party of the OBCs and the BSP that of the SCs, all of them failed to retain the support of all the castes in the groups which they were representing. Such a situation had arisen because while in power the parties could not distribute the state patronage even handedly among all the castes of the supporting caste group. Incidentally, all the parties had been in the government in the state at one time or the other during the nineties. This led to the possibilities for other parties to win away sections of the dissatisfied castes. But all the three parties succeeded in retaining the core castes with them—the BJP retained the Brahmin, the SP could keep the Yadavas and the Muslims and the BSP continued to enjoy the Chamar support. Keeping the support of the core caste with them, these parties had endeavoured to fetch the support of castes from amongst the other caste groups. The result was that all the parties set up candidates from all the castes irrespective of the fact as to which caste group they belonged to earlier. Thus it had been the phase of experimentation in changing caste re-configurations election by election. The formations under the banner of the SCs, the OBCs and the Upper Castes tended to disintegrate.

Autocratic Behaviour of the Leaders

Another feature of the decade was the emergence of three leaders—Kalyan Singh, Mulayam Singh, and Mayawati of the BJP, SP and BSP respectively. Curiously, all the three had autocratic personality traits. Within their parties, atleast in case of Mulayam Singh and Mayawati, the word uttered by them was the law. Dissenters had to be suppressed and divergence of opinion was not to be tolerated. The culture of blind support to the leader prevailed. Therefore there was no need of properly elected committees at different levels in the SP and the BSP .The position of the BJP was slightly different. There were dissenters in it and they could and did appeal against autocratic behaviour of Kalyan Singh in the functioning of the government. The central leadership of the party pulled him up. Kalyan Singh was not to be deterred by such interventions. He was not accommodative in the party or the governmental matters. He could accommodate with coalition partners but not the dissenters in his own party. So much so that when the top leadership of the party offered him to join the government at the centre and vacate the chief ministership for some one else, he refused to oblige. He threatened that the party would break up and was suspected of sabotage in the 1999 Lok Sabha elections in the state. When ultimately he had to go, he broke the BJP in UP and formed a new party Rashtriya Kranti Dal.

Regimentation of Support Base

These three leaders were able to exploit the social networks of different castes constituting their support base. By using identity symbols they not only consolidated their caste support but they preferred to mobilise their support on regimental patterns. This meant the followers should think in accordance with the thoughts of their leader, the followers did not have the right to differ, the followers must always be ready to obey the orders of their leaders, all the followers must behave in a similar way. To develop their support base in regimented form these leaders adopted 'we' and 'they' approach in their rhetoric. 'We' must keep ourselves organised (that too under their leadership) otherwise 'they' will capture the power and 'we' all would be penalised. A typical form of en-masses fear psychosis was created and sustained by repeated crying in mobilisation campaigns during the intervening periods.

The regimentation strategy worked gainfully .All the failures of the leaders got an acceptable cover that the leader was committed to implement the programmes in their favour but 'they' created hurdles. So unless 'our leader' got an absolute majority he would have to depend on 'them' and hence 'we' must get ourselves more organised and vote in full strength in support of 'our' party. This thinking forced the support base of the three leaders not to deviate. All the three support bases were of the opinion that in case the leader of the rival group captured the power they would be on the losers' side. No group was ready to believe that the leader from any other two groups would take care of them or the whole society. This caused the stalemate in state politics for the last one decade.

The Environment

It is necessary to raise the issue of the socio-political environment in which elections were held in the state during the period under study. Some of the issues raised are of recent developments and have passed unnoticed in the context of electoral behaviour.

(a) Unresolved Local Problems

In all our surveys the electorate had placed the local issues on top among factors that determined their vote. Since the local problems had not been attended to over the years the reactions of the electorate had varied from indifference to violence. A large number was dissatisfied and grumbled yet participated in the polls under the influence of social network of the caste.

It was found that due to the unending neglect of the local problems by the government and administration a substantial number of eligible electors did not get enthused to vote. Since there was no alternative available, a good number of them became indifferent. Some among them did not just stay away from the elections, rather they gave vent to their dissatisfaction by boycotting the elections. They exerted pressure for the resolution of their local problems through collective boycotts. The non-resolution of the problems generating anger sometimes led to the gherao of and slogan shouting against the leaders at the time of elections. This group placed trust in power of the masses and was more active and violent. The youth constituted larger proportion among them. Therefore, the main reason for indifference, non-cooperation or anger leading to non-participation in voting was the non-fulfillment of basic amenities.

(b) Decline of the Public Institutions

In a welfare state, the government is seen as the provider of the public health, education, drinking water, sanitation, electricity, transport services, administration of justice apart from the security to life and property. Over the years the institutions created for the purposes mentioned above were on the decline due to unchecked corruption, mismanagement and political interference. There was a near collapse of the public delivery system.

Local self-governments were unable to provide drinking water and sanitation, public health services, maintenance of streets and drainage systems. State governments failed to ensure law and order, justice, corruption free effective administration and uninterrupted electric supply. Those who could afford had resorted to alternate arrangements at individual or collective level. Resorting to private tube-wells and boosters for drinking water, generators for electric supply, private nursing homes side by side the government hospitals, chartered transport service parallel to the public transport system, coaching centers in place of non-performing formal educational institutions and above all private security networks substituting the police signified the decline in the system of public institutions.

A general impression was created in public mind that no services could be obtained in public institutions without paying bribes. Frustrations built up and protests took place by mobs against the government functionaries. One who would be aggressive and could incite the mob for violence became the leader and hero. The mob would destroy public property without any hesitation. At that time a complete anarchy would prevail. After the violent protests the leaders would negotiate and settle the problem. They would now be treated as public spokesmen.

(c) Criminalisation

It is to be noted that the Election Commission took a very strong view to combat criminalisation in politics and suggested that the political parties should avoid selecting candidates with criminal records. Political parties also agreed with the suggestion. However, in practice, it was noticed that in their intense desire to win the election at 'any cost' and by 'any means' they resorted to field candidates with criminal records. All the parties, without exception, set up such candidates. In election campaigns the parties were then compelled to glorify them. At some places there were criminals who entered the electoral contest successfully while in jail. Whether they won or lost, they acquired a status of respectability. The increasing tendency among political parties to put up candidates with criminal records was reflective of the fact that such candidates enjoyed sizeable support of their caste electorate. The results also testified to these assumptions. After all, the candidates with criminal records could win a seat only if the majority of valid votes were in his favour. The argument that criminals won the elections by booth capturing alone was not enough. The electorate legitimised the leadership of a criminal by casting votes in his favour because he was their casteman.

It would not be inappropriate to correlate the legitimisation of criminal background leadership with the failure of the public institutions. For example, the police force failed to ensure the maintenance of law and order and protection of life, property and 'izzat' of the peace loving and law-abiding citizens. People did not have any alternative but to turn towards the criminal background leader and by whose intervention they got some immediate relief. Similarly, there was a perception that the judiciary could not ensure justice because justice delayed is justice denied and more so the prevailing corruption had made the situation worse. But if a criminal 'dada' got involved, the aggrieved party would certainly get his grievances redressed. A powerful criminal ensured proper treatment of poor people in the hospitals, admissions in schools, relief from 'goonda' tax in the market, movement of women in public places without fear, relief from harassment by the inspectors of various departments and even appointments in public and private institutions. This environment provided opportunity to criminal to gain respectability in the society and support of his caste electorate during the polls. With this 'robinhood' image the criminal turned leader would become an important element of the nucleus of his caste-based social network and in all the cases the network supported him. This phenomenon established the fact that the nuclei of the social networks which was identified with the dominant neo-rich was closely associated with the criminal background leadership. The neo-rich needed them. This trend had been on increase during last few years. The instability of governments and failure of system had encouraged this trend further. It had led to a situation in which such criminals backed by the social network of the caste had come to occupy the ministerial berths in the state government apart from other positions of power through elections at numerous levels.

To sum up, it can be said that in Uttar Pradesh, during the period of the nineties there has emerged a strong class of dominant neo-rich which is leading the caste-based social network. The class representing the nucleus of the social network is the key player of competitive politics during elections. The economic as well as political powers, both are progressively being concentrated in the hands of this class. Politics is being utilised as a tool to serve their economic interest. This class does not have any political commitment for any political party. It can change the party any moment if its personal economic agenda requires so. This class overwhelmingly represents the leadership at all levels of different political parties in the state. Leaders emerging from this class are assertive and aggressive in its nature. They lack the accommodative attitude the which is basic value for the success of a democratic system. It is due to this reason that they have converted their support bases into regimented formations. The leaders of the same class are also leading the ongoing process of reconfiguration of caste groups. Thus, the caste-based mobilastions and voting behaviour are in no way the 'democratic upsurge' or 'emancipatory processes'. Instead it reflects the strengthening of oligarchic tendencies in the state.

APPENDICES

Appendix - I

GB Pant Social Science Institute, Jhusi, Allahabad Parliament Election—1996

Research Study Questionnaire

(A) 1. Parliament Constituency————————

2. Assembly Segment————————

(B) 3. Elector's Name

4. Address

5. Age

6. Gender

7. Education

8. Religion

9. Caste

10. Marital Status

11. Occupation

(C) 1. Are you aware that the Parliament elections are to be held after some days? Yes/No

2. On what date voting will take place in your area? Yes/No

3. Will you cast your vote? Yes/No

3.(a) If yes, why?

4. How many times you have cast your vote in the previously held elections?

5. Are you a member or sympathiser of any political party? Yes/No

5 (a) if yes, what are the forms of participation in the activities of your party
Participation in public meetings
Participation in rallies/demonstration

Participation as election campaign worker
Any other

6. Do you have interest in acquiring information relating to the activities organised by different political parties during elections? Yes/No
   if yes, mention the medium
   Newspaper
   Radio
   TV
   Market gossips
   Family members/ Neighbours
7. Do you have read the manifesto of any party? Yes/No

7 (a) if yes, of which party?

8. To which of the following you will attach importance while deciding your vote?

Price rise	Law and order
Unemployment	Kashmir issue
Regional development	Economic liberalisation
Social justice	Multinational companies
Stable government	National security
Traditions	Any other

9. Do you think that in this election votes will be caste along the caste lines? Yes/No
10. Are the voters in your constituency pressurised in any way at the time of vote? Yes/No

10(a) if yes, in what way?

11. In which way the political parties are trying to influence the voters?
    Use of money
    Use of caste/religion
    Use of muscle power
    Poster/banneer
    By public meetings
    By mass contact
12. Did any candidate or his representative visit you seeking your vote? Yes/No

12(a) if yes, who visited you and how many times?

13. While voting which among the following is given greater weightage:
    Party/Candidate

14. Do you know any candidate personally?
14(a) if yes, how did you come to know him and since when?
15. Should in your opinion independent candidates be allowed to contest elections? Yes/No
15(a) if yes, why?
16. Is there any chance of success in the election of any independent candidate? Yes/No
16(a) if yes, from which constituency?
17. If voting took place today who will win?
18. In your constituency the percentage of vote cast is low. In your opinion what steps could be taken to improve it?
    More vigorous campaign by the political parties
    Polling stations at convenient places
    Better security arrangements
    Imposition of fines for non-participation in the elections
19. Was any eligible voter of your family excluded from the voters' list? Yes/No
19(a) if yes, why?
    For want of age certificate
    Carelessness on the part of the voter
    Inefficiency on the part of the election officials
20. Do you think that the present election campaign is in any way different than the earlier ones? Yes/No
20(a) if yes, is it desireable?

Date
Place

Signature of the Investigator

Appendix - II

GB Pant Social Science Institute, Jhusi, Allahabad
Uttar Pradesh Assembly Election—1996

Research Study
Questionnaire

PART-I
Confidence Building

The Institute is conducting a study relating to the ensuing state assembly elections. We have putforth some queries related with this election to the voters like you. We would be grateful for your cooperation in this regard. The information so obtained would be utilized for the research purposes only.

Would you offer your cooperation in this study? Yes/No

If no, can you state the reason?

PART-II
Opinion-Attitude Scales

1. Are you aware that the state assembly elections are to be held after some days? Yes/No
2. When will the voting take place in your area? Yes/No
   If yes, Day——————— Date———————
3. Will you cast your vote?
   Certainly/ May go/ Uncertain/ May not go/ Certainly not
4. Will you state the reason for doing so?
5. How many times you have cast your vote in the previously held elections?
   0 1 2 3 4 5 6 7 8 9 10 or more
   Never/ Occasionally/ Never

6. How much do you participate in the following political activities:

	Always	*Occasionally*	*Neither much nor less*	*Very Less*	*Never*
Public Meeting					
Rallies/Demonstration					
Party Meetings					
Electioneering					
Financial Contributions					
Identification/ Affinity with any political party					

7. How much information regarding elections you have received from following media?

	Very much	*Few*	*Very less*	*None*
Family Members/ Local Leaders				
Newspapers				
Radio/ TV				
Interactions in Markets/ Hats				
Public Meetings				
Any Other				

8 How many election manifestoes of different political parties you are. aware of?

0 1 2 3 or more

9. How did you get to know about the ideas and programmes of the candidates and the parties?

Through—

—Manifestoes

—Excerpts published in the newspapers

—Public speeches

—Discussion with family members/ friends

—Posters

—Slogan shouting

—Pronouncements broadcast on loudspeakers

—TV/ Radio broadcast

Not aware at all

10. There are several grounds upon which the votes are cast How do you view the following in this respect:

	To a great extent	*Uncertain*	*Not at all*
Local Problems			
Ideology of the Parties			
Candidates' Image			
Personal Relations with a particular Candidate			
Caste or Religious Affinity			
Monetary and Other Benefits			
Any Other			

11. To what extent the parties or candidates are employing the following to woo the voters?

	Too much	*Average*	*Not at all*
Money			
Caste/Religion			
Muscle power			
Posters/Banners/Loudspeakers			
Public Meetings			
Mass Contacts			
Any other			

12. What is your opinion on the following statements:

	Absolutely Correct	*Correct*	*Can't say*	*Wrong*	*Absolutely Wrong*
Elections are the means for the formation of a democratic government					
The parties exist for the service of the people					
The parties are now identified with the castes					
The leaders have become selfish/greedy					
The political leaders are no more accountable to the society					
The influence of criminals is on rise					
A single vote of yours would hardly matter					

Elections under terror and fear are meaningless

Trust in the election process is on decline

To wait in the queue for a long time at the polling booth is painful

To cover the distance to reach the polling station is tiresome

The decline in the political culture of the country can be checked only through elections

Every single vote is invaluable

33% reservation of seats for women in the State Assemblies/ the Loksabha is fair

---

13. How much confidence do you repose in the present electoral system?
    Very much/ Much/ Little/ Very little/ Not at all

PART-III
Background Data

1. Assemly Segment
2. Respondent's Sl. no. in the electoral roll
3. Respondent's Name
4. Address
5. Age
6. Gender
7. Educational Status
8. Marital Status
9. Religion
10. Caste
11. Occupation

The number of people present at the time of interview

Signature of the Investigator — Place

Date — Time

GB Pant Social Science Institute, Jhusi, Allahabad
Parliament Elections—1998

Research Study
Questionnaire

PART-I
Confidence Building

The Institute is conducting a study relating to the ensuing state assembly elections. We have putforth some queries related with this election to the voters like you. We would be grateful for your cooperation in this regard. The information so obtained would be utilized for the research purposes only.
Would you offer your cooperation in this study? Yes/No
If no, can you state the reason?

PART-II
Opinion-Attitude Scales

1. Are you aware that the state assembly elections are to be held after some days? Yes/No
2. When will the voting take place in your area? Yes/No
   If yes, Day———— Date————
3. Will you cast your vote?
   Certainly/ May go/ Uncertain/ May not go/ Certainly not
4. Will you state the reason for doing so?
   It is my right
   Exercising this right will benefit my family and me
   By our vote our party will be successful and a government in our favour may be formed
   All are going to vote therefore we will also vote

We will go to vote if transport is provided
May be out of station on the polling day
If on duty, then may not vote
Will not go to vote for health reasons
Will not go to vote, it involves inconvenience
Arrangements are not good
Elections are useless, after winning the elections no one bothers about us
It is useless to vote
It will not matter in any way if I don't vote

5. Did you vote in the elections held earlier?
   Always/ Sometimes/Never
6. You are aware of the election manifestoes of how many political parties?
   0 1 2 3 4 or more
7. How much do you participate in the following political activities:

	Always	*Occasionally*	*Neither much nor less*	*Very Less*	*Never*
Public Meeting					
Rallies/Demonstration					
Party Meetings					
Election Campaign					
Monetary Contributions					
Identification/ Affinity with any political party					

8. How much information regarding elections you have received from the following media?

	Very much	*few*	*Very less*	*None*
Family Members/ Acquaintances				
Local Leaders				
Newspapers				
Radio/TV				
Interactions in Markets/ Hats				
Public Meetings				
Any Other				

9. How did you get to know about the ideas and programmes of the candidates and the parties?
Through—
—Manifestoes
—Excerpts published in the newspapers
—Public speeches
—Discussion with family members/ friends
—Posters
—Slogan shouting
—Announcements on loudspeakers
—TV/ Radio broadcasts
Not aware at all

10. There are several grounds upon which the votes are cast How do you view the following in this respect:

	To a great extent	*Uncertain*	*Not at all*
Local Problems/ development of the locality			
Ideology of the Parties			
Candidate's Image			
Personal Relations with a particular Candidate			
Caste or Religious Affinity			
Monetary and Other Benefits			
Any Other			

11. To what extent the parties or candidates are employing the following to woo the voters?

	Too much	*Average*	*Not at all*
Money			
Caste/Religion			
Muscle power			
Posters/Banners/Loudspeakers			
Public Meetings			
Mass Contacts			
Any other			

12. What is your opinion on the following statements:

	Absolutely Correct	*Correct*	*Can't say*	*Wrong*	*Absolutely Wrong*
Elections are the means for the formation of a democratic government					
The parties exist for the service of the people					
The parties are now identified with the castes					
The leaders have become selfish/greedy					
The political leaders are no more accountable to the society					
The influence of criminals is on rise					
A single vote of ours would hardly matter					
Elections under terror and fear are meaningless					
Trust in the electoral system is on decline					
To wait in the queue for a long time at the polling booth is painful					
To cover the distance to reach the polling station is tiresome					
The decline in the political culture of the country can be checked only through elections					
Every single vote is invaluable					
33% reservation of seats for women in the State Assemblies/ the Loksabha is fair					
Frequent elections are burden on people					
Elections involve people's power					
No candidate returns after the elections in our midst					
People are voting along the caste lines					
The powerful asks for vote under threat					
The practice of bogus voting continues					
We are happy with our candidate whom we voted for on the last occasion					

13. What do you expect from the party of your choice?

	Very much	*Much*	*Can't say*	*little*	*Very little*
Would benefit you and your family					
Would develop your village					
Would benefit your caste					
Any other					

14. It is said that a sharp decline is taking place in the political system. In this regard what is your opinion about the role of the following:

	Definitely	*Alright*	*Can't say*	*No*	*Not at all*
The rising influence of casteism/communalism					
Rising Influence of criminals in elections					
Lack of ideology in the political parties					
Corruption among top leadership					
Lack of political awaraeness among voters					
Greed for power among the political parties					
Appeasement of particular religious or caste groups					

15. If voting takes place today what would, in your opinion, be the chances of success of different parties in your area?

	Very high	*High*	*In contest*	*Low*	*Very low*
BSP					
United Front					
BJP					
Congress					
Others					

16. Before going to vote every voter take a decision about his vote. You must have also decided about your vote. We would not ask you about whom you have decided to vote for. However, if the opponent of that candidate helps you in the following, how many chances are there for shift in your vote in his favour?

	Very much	*Much*	*Can't say*	*Little*	*Very little*
Gets a loan sanction for your business					
Gets a loan sanction for house building					
Gets your old age pension sanction					
Gets your son employed					
Pressure exerted by someone who had helped you in arranging the marriage of your daughter					
Gets you free from the police harassment					
Has helped you in getting the possession of the patta land					
Has got a hand pump installed in your neighbourhood					
Has got kharanza laid in your locality					
Has got electric line for your locality					
Has got a school open in your village					
Has got a dispensary opened in your village					

17. Which is the party of your choice in the present phase?
18. Do you know who gets the elections conducted?
    Government/President/Prime minister/Election Commission/District Magistrate
19. Have you received your voter identity card? Yes/No
20. Suppose you have made up your mind to vote for a candidate to vote for a candidate who has no chance of success. How much possibility would be there for change in your decision in view of this?
    Very Much/ Much / Uncertain / Little / Very little

PART-III
Background Data

1. Assemly Segment
2. Respondent's Sl. no. in the electoral roll
3. Respondent's Name
4. Address
5. Age
6. Gender
7. Educational Status
8. Marital Status
9. Religion
10. Caste
11. Occupation
12. Land ownership
13. Approx. Monthly Income

The number of people present at the time of interview

Signature of the Investigator — Place
Date — Time

Appendix - IV

GB Pant Social Science Institute, Jhusi, Allahabad
Parliament Elections—1999

Research Study
Questionnaire

PART-I
Confidence Building

The Institute is conducting a study relating to the ensuing state assembly elections. We have putforth some queries related with this election to the voters like you. We would be grateful for your cooperation in this regard. The information so obtained would be utilized for the research purposes only.

Would you offer your cooperation in this study? Yes/No

If no, can you state the reason?

PART-II
Opinion-Attitude Scales

1. Are you aware that the state assembly elections are to be held after some days? Yes/No
2. When will the voting take place in your area?
   If yes, Day———— Date————
3. Will you cast your vote?
   Certainly/ May go/ Uncertain/ May not go/ Certainly not
4. Will you state the reason for doing so?
   It is my right
   Exercising this right will benefit my family and me
   By our vote our party will be successful and a government in our favour may be formed

All are going to vote therefore we will also vote
We will go to vote if transport is provided
May be out of station on the polling day
If on duty, then may not vote
Will not go to vote for health reasons
Will not go to vote, it involves inconvenience
Arrangements are not good
Elections are useless, after winning the elections no one bothers about us
It is useless to vote
It will not matter in any way if I don't vote

5. Did you vote in the elections held earlier?
   Always/ Sometimes/Never
6. You are aware of the election manifestoes of how many political parties?
   0 1 2 3 4 or more
7. How much do you participate in the following political activities:

	Always	*Occasionally*	*Neither much nor less*	*Very Less*	*Never*
Public Meeting					
Rallies/Demonstration					
Party Meetings					
Election Campaign					
Monetary Contributions					
Identification/ Affinity with any political party					

8. How much information regarding elections you have received from the following media?

	Very much	*few*	*Very less*	*None*
Family Members				
Acquaintances				
Local Leaders				
Newspapers				
Radio/TV				
Interactions in Markets/ Hats				
Public Meetings				
Any Other				

9. How did you get to know about the ideas and programmes of the candidates and the parties?
Through—
—Manifestoes
—Excerpts published in the newspapers
—Public speeches
—Discussion with family members/ friends
—Posters
—Slogan shouting
—Announcements on loudspeakers
—Radio broadcasts
—Viewed on TV
Not aware at all

10. There are several grounds upon which the votes are cast How do you view the following in this respect:

	To a great extent	*Uncertain*	*Not at all*
Local Problems/ development of the locality			
Ideology of the Parties			
Personal Relations with a particular Candidate			
Caste or Religious Affinity			
Monetary and Other Benefits			
Personal or family benefits			
Any Other			

11. To what extent the parties or candidates are employing the following to woo the voters?

	Too much	*Average*	*Not at all*
Money			
Caste/Religion			
Muscle power			
Posters/Banners/ Loudspeakers			
Public Meetings			
Mass Contacts			
TV/Video			
Any other			

12. What is your opinion on the following statements:

	Absolutely Correct	*Correct*	*Can't say*	*Wrong*	*Absolutely Wrong*
Elections are the means for the formation of a democratic government					
The parties exist for the service of the people					
The parties are now identified with the castes					
The leaders have become selfish/greedy					
The political leaders are no more accountable to the society					
The influence of criminals is on rise					
A single vote of ours would hardly matter					
Elections under terror and fear are meaningless					
Trust in the electoral system is on decline					
To cover the distance to reach the polling station is tiresome					
The decline in the political culture of the country can be checked only through elections					
Every single vote is invaluable					
33% reservation of seats for women in the State Assemblies/ the Lok Sabha is fair					
Frequent elections are burden on people					
Elections involve people's power					
No candidate returns after the elections in our midst					
People are voting along the caste lines					
The powerful asks for vote under threat					
The practice of bogus voting continues					
We are happy with our candidate whom we voted for on the last occasion					

13. What do you expect from the party of your choice?

	Very much	*Much*	*Can't say*	*little*	*Very little*
Would benefit you and your family					
Would develop your village					
Would benefit your caste					
Provide a stable government					
Provide trustworthy and transparent government					
Strengthen law and order					
Control corruption					
Guarantee the security of the country					
Guarantee reservation for the Scheduled Castes					
Promote Social justice					
More empowerment to village panchayats					
Any other					

14. Do you feel still attached to the party for which you voted at the time of last election? Yes / No

15. It is said that a sharp decline is taking place in the political system. In this regard what is your opinion about the role of the following:

	Definitely	*Alright*	*Can't say*	*No*	*Not at all*
Rising influence of casteism/communalism					
Rising Influence of criminals in elections					
Rising influence of money					
Lack of ideology in the political parties					
Corruption among top leadership					
Lack of political awaraeness among voters					
Greed for power among the political parties					
Appeasement of particular religious or caste groups					

16. If voting takes place today what would, in your opinion, be the chances of success of different parties in your area?

	Very high	*High*	*In contest*	*Low*	*Very low*
BSP					
United Front					
BJP					
Congress					
Others					

17. Before going to vote every voter take a decision about his vote. You must have also decided about your vote. We would not ask you about whom you have decided to vote for. However, if the opponent of that candidate helps you in the following, how many chances are there for shift in your vote in his favour?

	Very much	*Much*	*Can't say*	*Little*	*Very little*
Gets a loan sanction for your business					
Gets a loan sanction for house building					
Gets your old age pension sanction					
Gets your son employed					
Pressure exerted by someone who had helped you in arranging the marriage of your daughter					
Gets you free from the police harassment					
Has helped you in getting the possession of the patta land					
Has got a hand pump installed in your neighbourhood					
Has got kharanza laid in your locality					
Has got electric line for your locality					
Has got a school open in your village					
Has got a dispensary opened in your village					

18. Which is the party of your choice in the present phase?.
19. Have you received your voter identity card? Yes/No
20. Suppose you have made up your mind to vote for a candidate to vote for a candidate who has no chance of success.
    How much possibility would be there for change in your decision in view of this?
    Very Much/ Much / Uncertain / Little / Very littke

PART-III

Background Data

1. Assemly Segment
2. Respondent's Sl. no. in the electoral roll
3. Respondent's Name
4. Address
5. Age
6. Gender
7. Educational Status
8. Marital Status
9. Religion
10. Caste
11. Occupation
12. Land ownership
13. Approx. Monthly Income

The number of people present at the time of interview

Signature of the Investigator Place

Date Time

Appendix - V

Representation of the People Act, 1951

PART - VII
Corrupt Practices and Electoral Offences

Chapter - I

123. Corrupt Practices.—The following shall be demed to be corrupt practices for the purposes of this Act:—

(1) "Bribery", that is to say—

(A) any gift, offer or promise by a candidate or his agent or by any other person with the consent of a candidate or his election agent of any gratification, to any person whomsoever, with the object, directly or indirectly of inducing—

- *(a)* a person to stand or not to stand as, or to withdraw or not to withdraw from being a candidate at an election, or
- *(b)* an elector to vote or refrain from voting at an election, or as a reward to—
  - *(i)* a person for having so stood or not stood, or for having withdrawn or not having withdrawn his candidature; or
  - *(ii)* an elector for having voted or refrained from voting;

(B) the receipt of, or agreement to receive, any gratification, whether as a motive or a reward—

- *(a)* by a person for standing or not standing as, or for withdrawing or not withdrawing from being, a candudate; or
- *(b)* by any person whomsoever for himself or any other person for voting or refraining from voting, or inducing or attempting to induce any elector to vote or refrain from

voting, or any candidate to withdraw or not to withdraw his candidature.

Explanation.—For the purposes of this clause the term "gratification" is not restricted to pecunmiary gratifications or gratifications estimable in money and it includes all forms of entertainment and all forms of employment for reward but it does not include the payment of any expenses bona fide incurred at, or for the purpose of, any election and duly entered in the account expenses referred to in Section 78.

(2) Undue influence, that is to say, any direct or indirect interference or attempt to interfere on the part of the candidate or his agent, or of any other person with the consent of the candidate or his election agent, with the free exercise of any electoral right:

Provided that—

(a) without prejudice to the generality of the provision of this clause any such person as is referred to therein who—

(i) threatens any candidate or any elector, or any person in whom a candidate or an elector is interested, with injury of any kind including social ostracism and excommunication or expulsion from any caste or community; or

(ii) induces or attempts to induce a candidate or an elector to believe that he, or any person in whom he is interested, will become or will be rendered an object of divine displeasure or spritual censure,

shall be deemed to interfere with the free exercise of the electoral right of such candidate or elector within the meaning of this clause;

(b) a declaration of public policy, or a promise of public action, or the mere exercise of a legal right without intent to interfere with an electoral right, shall not be deemed to be interference within the meaning of this clause.

(3) The appeal by a candidate or his agent or by any other person with the consent of a candidate or his election agent to vote or refrain from voting for any person on the ground of his religion, race, caste, community or language or the use of, or appeal to religious symbols or the use of, or appeal to, national symbols, such as the national flag or the national emblem, for the furtherance of the prospects of the election of that candidate or for prejudicially affecting the election of any candidate:

[1][Provided that no symbol allotted under this Act to a candidate shall be demed to be a religious symbol or a national symbol for the purposes of this clause.]

(3-A) The promotion of, or attempt to promote, feelings of enmity or hatred between different classes of the citizens of India on grounds of religion, race, caste, community, or language, by a candidate or his agent or any other person with the consent of a candidate or his election agent for the furtherance of the prospects of the election of that candidate or for prejudicially affecting the election of any candidate.

(4) The publication by a candidate or his agent or by any other person with the consent of a candidate or his election agent, of any statement of fact which is false, and which he either believes to be false or does not believe to be true, in relation to the personal character or conduct of any candidate, or in relation to the candidature, or withdrawal, of any candidate, being a statement reasonably calculated to prejudice the prospects of that candidate" election.

(5) The hiring or procuring, whether on payment or otherwise, of any vehicle or vessel by a candidate or his agent or by any other person with the consent of a candidate or his election agent, or the use of such vehicle or vessel for the free conveyance of any elector (other than the candidate himself, the members of his family or his agent) to or from any polling station provided under Section 25 or a place fixed under sub-section 29 for the poll:

Provided that the hiring of a vehicle or vessel by an elector or by several electors at their joint costs for the purpose of conveying him or them to and from any such polling station or place fixed for the poll shall not be deemed to be a corrupt practice under this clause if the vehicle or vessel so hired is a vehicle or vessel not propelled by mechanical power:

Provided further that the use of any public transport vehicle or vessel or any tramcar or railway carriage by any elector at his own cost for the purpose of going to or coming from any such polling station or place fixed for the poll shall not be deemed to be a corrupt practice under this clause.

Explanation.—In this clause, the expression "vehicle" means any vehicle used or capable of being used for the purpose of road transport, whether propelled by mechanical power or otherwise and whether used for drawing other vehicles or otherwise.

(6) The incurring or authorising of expenditure in contravention of Section 77.

(7) The obtaining or procuring or abetting or attempting to obtain or procure by a candidate or his agent or, by any other person with the consent of a candidate or his election agent, any assistance (other than the giving of vote) for the furtherance of the prospects of that candidate's election, from any person in the service of the Government and belonging to any of the following classes, namely:—

(a) gazetted officers;

(b) stipendiary judges and magistrates;

(c) members of the armed forces of the Union;

(d) members of the police forces;

(e) excise officers;

(f) revenue officers other than village revenue officers known as lambardars, malguzars, patels, deshmukhs or by any other name, whose duty is to collect land revenue and who are remunerated by a share of, or commission on, the amount of land revenue collected by them but who do not discharge any police functions; and

(g) such other class of persons in the service of the Government as may be prescribed:

[2][(8) Booth capturing by a candidate or his agent or other persons.]

Explanation.—(1) In this section the expression "agent" includes an election agent, a polling agent and any person who is held to have acted as an agent in connection with the election with the consent of the candidate.

(2) For the purposes of clause (7), a person shall be deemed to assist in the furtherance of the prospects of a candidate's election if he acts as an election agent of that candidate.

125. Promoting enmity between classes in connection with election.—Any person who in connection with an election under this Act promotes or attempts to promote on grounds of religion, race, caste, community or language, feelings of enmity or hatred, between different classes of the citizens of India shall be punishable with imprisonment for a term which may extent to three years, or with fine, or with both.

[3][126. **Prohibition of public meetings during period of forty-eight hours ending with four fixed for conclusion of poll.**—(1) No person shall—

(*a*) convene, hold, attend, join or address any public meeting or procession in connection with an election; or

(*b*) display to the public any election matter by means of cinematograph, television or other similar apparatus; or

(*c*) propagate any election matter to the public by holding, or by arranging the holding of, any musical concert or any theatrical performance or any other entertainment or amusement with a view to attracting the members of the public thereto,

in any polling area during the period of forty-eight hours ending with the hour fixed for the conclusion of the poll for any election in that polling area.

(2) Any person who contravenes the provisions of sub-section (1) shall be punishable with imprisonment for a term which may extend to two years, or with fine, or with both.

(3) In this section, the expression "election matter" means any matter intended or calculated to influence or affect the result of election.

126. Promoting enmity between classes in connection with election.— Any person who in connection with an election under this Act promotes or attempts to promote on grounds of religion, race, caste, community or language, feelings of enmity or hatred, between different classes of the citizens of India shall be punishable with imprisonment for a term which may extent to three years, or with fine, or with both.

[4][126. **Prohibition of public meetings during period of forty-eight hours ending with four fixed for conclusion of poll.**—(1) No person shall—

(*a*) convene, hold, attend, join or address any public meeting or procession in connection with an election; or

(*b*) display to the public any election matter by means of cinematograph, television or other similar apparatus; or

(*c*) propagate any election matter to the public by holding, or by arranging the holding of, any musical concert or any theatrical performance or any other entertainment or amusement with a view to attracting the members of the public thereto, in any polling area during the period of forty-eight hours ending with the hour fixed for the conclusion of the poll for any election in that polling area.

(2) Any person who contravenes the provisions of sub-section (1) shall be punishable with imprisonment for a term which may extend to two years, or with fine, or with both.

(3) In this section, the expression "election matter" means any matter intended or calculated to influence or affect the result of election.

127. Disturbances at election meetings.—(1) Any person who at a public meeting to which this section applies acts, or incites others to act, in a disorderly manner for the purpose of preventing the transaction of the business for which the meeting was called together, [5][shall be punishable with imprisonment for a term which may extend to [six months][6] or with fine which may extend to [two thousand][7] rupees, or with both].

[8][(1-A) An offence punishable under sub-section (1) shall be cognizable.]

(2) This section applies to any public meeting of a political character held in any constituency between the date of the issue of a notification under this Act calling upon the constituency to elect a member or members and the date on which such election is held.

(3) If any police officer reasonably suspects any person of committing an offence under sub-section (1), he may, if requested so to do by the chairman of the meeting, require that person to declare to him immediately his name and address and, if that person refuses or fails so to declare his name and address, or if the police officer reasonably suspects him of giving a false name or address, the police officer may arrest him without warrant.

127-A. Restrictions on the printing of pamphlets, posters, etc. (1) No person shall print or publish, or cause to be printed or published, any election pamphlet or poster which does not bear on its face the names and addresses of the printer and the publisher thereof.

(2) No person shall print or cause to be printed any election pamphlet or poster—

(a) unless a declaration as to the identity of the publisher thereof, signed by him and attested by two persons to whom he is personally known, is delivered by him to the printer in duplicate; and

(*b*) unless, within a reasonable time after the printing of the document, one copy of the declaration is sent by the printer, together with one copy of the document—

(*i*) where it is printed in the capital of the State, to the Chief Electoral Officer; and

(*ii*) in any other case, to the district magistrate of the district in which it is printed.

(3) For the purposes of this section,—

(*a*) any process for multiplying copies of a document, other than copying it by hand, shall be deemed to be printing and the expression "printer" shall be construed accordingly; and

(*b*) "election pamphlet or poster" means any printed pamphlet, handbill or other document distributed for the purpose of promoting or prejudicing the election of a candidate or group of candidates or any placard or poster having reference to an election, but does not include any handbill, placard or poster merely announcing the date, time, place and other particulars of an election meeting or routine instructions to election agents or workers.

(4) Any person who contravenes any of the provisions of sub-section (1) or sub-section (2) shall be punishable with imprisonment for a term which may extend to six months, or with fine which may extend to two thousand rupees, or with both.

128. Maintenance of secrecy of voting.—(1) Every officer, clerk, agent or other person who performs any duty in connection with the recording or counting of votes at an election shall maintain, and aid ion maintaining, the secrecy of the voting and shall not (except for some purpose authorised by or under any law) communicate to any person any information calculated to violate such secrecy.

(2) Any person who contravenes the provisions of sub-section (1) shall be punishable with imprisonment for a term which may extend to three months or with fine or with both.

129. Officers, etc., at elections not to act for candidates or to influence voting.—(1) No person who is a district election officer or a returning officer, or an assistant returning officer, or a presiding or polling officer at an election, or an officer or clerk appointed by the returning officer or the presiding officer to perform any duty in connection with an election shall in the conduct or the management of the election do any act (other than the giving of vote) for the furtherance of the prospects of the election of a candidate.

(2) No such person as aforesaid, and no member of a police force, shall endeavour—

(a) to persuade any person to give his vote at an election, or

(b) to dissuade any person from giving his vote at an election, or

(c) to influence the voting of any person at an election in any manner.

(3) Any person who contravenes the provisions of sub-section (1) or sub-section (2) shall be punishable with imprisonment which may extend to six months or with fine or with both.

(4) An offence punishable under sub-section (3) shall be cognizable.

130. Prohibition of canvassing in or near polling stations.—(1) No person shall, on the date or dates on which a poll is taken at any polling station, commit any of the following acts within the polling station or in any public or private place within a distance of one hundred metres of the polling station, namely:

(a) canvassing for votes; or

(b) soliciting the vote of any elector; or

(c) persuading any elector not to vote for any particular candidate; or

(d) persuading any elector not to vote at the election; or

(e) exhibiting any notice or sign (other than an official notice) relating to the election.

(2) Any person who contravenes the provisions of sub-section (1) shall be punishable with fine which may extend to two hundred and fifty rupees.

(3) An offence punishable under this section shall be cognizable.

131. Penalty for disorderly conduct in or near polling station.—(1) No person shall, on the date or dates on which a poll is taken at any polling station,—

(a) use or operate within or at the entrance of the polling station, or in any public or private place in the neighbourhood thereof, any apparatus for amplifying or reproducing the human voice, such as a megaphone or a loudspeaker, or

(*b*) shout, or otherwise act in a disorderly manner, within or at the entrance of the polling station or in any public or private place in the neighbourhood thereof.

so as to cause annoyance to any person visiting the polling station for the poll, or so as to interfere with the work of the officers and other persons on duty at the polling station.

(2) Any person who contravenes, or willfully aids or abets the contravention of, the provisions of sub-section (1) shall be punishable with imprisonment which may extend to three months or with fine or with both.

(3) If the presiding officer of a polling station has reason to believe that any person is committing or has committed an offence punishable under this section, he may direct any police officer to arrest such person, and thereupon the police officer shall arrest him.

(4) Any police officer may take such steps, and use such force, as may be reasonably necessary for preventing any contravention of the provisions of sub-section (1), and may seize any apparatus used for such contravention.

132. Penalty for misconduct at the polling station.—(1) Any person who during the hours fixed for the poll at any polling station misconducts himself or fails to obey the lawful directions of the presiding officer may be removed from the polling station by the presiding officer or by any police officer on duty or by any person authorised in this behalf by such presiding officer.

(2) The powers conferred by sub-section (1) shall not be exercised so as to prevent any elector who is otherwise entitled to vote at a polling station from having an opportunity of voting at that station.

(3) If any person who has been so removed from a polling station re-enters the polling station without the permission of the presiding officer, he shall be punishable with imprisonment for a term which may extend to three months, or with fine, or with both.

(4) An offence punishable under sub-section (3) shall be cognizable.

[9][**132-A. Penalty for failure to observe procedure for voting.**—If any elector to whom a ballot paper has been issued, refuses to observe the procedure prescribed for voting the ballot paper issued to him shall be liable for cancellation.]

[10][133. **Penalty for illegal hiring or procuring of conveyance at elections.**—If any person is guilty of any such corrupt practice as is specified in clause (5) of Section 123 at or in connection with an election, he shall be punishable with imprisonment which may extend to three months and with fine.]

134. **Breaches of official duty in connection with elections.**—(1) If any person to whom this section applies is without reasonable cause guilty of any act or omission in breach of his official duty, he shall be punishable with fine which may extend to five hundred rupees.

(1-A) An offence punishable under sub-section (1) shall be cognizable.

(2) No suit or other legal proceedings shall lie against any such person for damages in respect of any such act or omission as aforesaid.

(3) The persons to whom this section applies are the district election officers, returning officers, assistant returning officers, presiding officers, polling officers and any other person appointed to perform any duty in connection with the receipt of nominations or withdrawal of candidatures, or the recording or counting of votes at an election; and the exression "official duty" shall for the purposes of this section be construed accordingly, but shall not include duties imposed otherwise than by or under this Act.

134-A. **Penalty for Government servants for acting as election agent, polling agent or counting agent.**—If any person in the service of the Government acts as an election agent or a polling agent or a counting agent of a candidate at an election, he shall be punishable with imprisonment for a term which may extend to three months, or with fine, or with both.

[11][134-B. **Prohibition of going armed to or near a polling station.**—

(1) No person, other than the Returning Officer, the Presiding Officer, any Police Officer and any other person appointed to maintain peace and order, at a polling station who is on duty at the polling station, shall, on a polling day, go armed with arms, as defined in the Arms Act, 1959 (54 of 1959), of any kind within the neighbourhood of a polling station.

(2) If any person contravenes the provisions of sub-section (1), he shall be punishable with imprisonment for a term, which may extend to two years, or with fine, or with both.

(3) Notwithstanding anything contained in the Arms Act, 1959 (54 of 1959), where a person is convicted of an offence under this section, the arms as defined in the said Act found in his possession shall be liable to confiscation and the licence granted in relation to such arms shall be deemed to have been revoked under Section 17 of that Act.

(4) An offence punishable under sub-section (2) shall be cognisable.]

135. Removal of ballot papers from polling station to be an offence.—(1) Any person who at any election[12] [unauthorisedly] takes, or attempts to take, a ballot paper out of a polling station, or wilfully aids or abets the doing of any such act, shall be punishable with imprisonment for a term which may extend to one year or with fine which may extend to five hundred rupees or with both.

(2) If the presiding officer of a polling station has reason to believe that any person is committing or has committed an offence punishable under sub-section (1), such officer may, before such person leaves the polling station, arrest or direct a police officer to arrest such person and may search such person or cause him to be searched by a police officer;

Provided that when it is necessary to cause a woman to be searched, the search shall be made by another woman with strict regard to decency.

(3) Any ballot paper found upon the person arrested on search shall be made over for safe custody to a police officer by the presiding officer, or when the search is made by a police officer, shall be kept by such officer in safe custody.

(4) An Offence punishable under sub-section (1) shall be cognisable.

[13][**135A. Offence of booth capturing.**—[(1)][14] Whoever commits an offence of booth capturing shall be punishable with imprisonment for a term which [15][shall not be less than one year but which may extend to three years and with fine, and where such offence is committed by a person in the service of the Government, he shall be punishable with imprisonment for a term which shall not be less than three years but which may extend to five years and with fine.]

Explanation.—For the purposes of [16][this sub-section and Section 20-B], "booth capturing" includes, among other things, all or any of the following activities, namely:–

(a) seizure of a polling station or a place fixed for the poll by any person or persons making polling authorities surrender the ballot papers or voting machines and doing of any other act which affects the orderly conduct of elections;

(b) taking possession of a polling station or a place fixed for the poll by any person or persons and allowing only his or their own supporters to exercise their right to vote and [17][prevent others from free exercise of their right to vote];

(c) [18][coercing or intimidating or threatening directly or indirectly any elector and preventing him from going to the polling station or a place fixed for the poll to cast his vote;

(d) seizure of a place for counting of votes by any person or persons, making the counting authorities surrender the ballot papers or voting machines and the doing of anything which affects the orderly counting of votes;

(e) doing by any person in the service of Government, of all or any of the aforesaid activities or aiding or conniving at, any such activity in the furtherance of the prospects of the election of a candidate.]

[19][(2) An offence punishable under sub-section (1) shall be cognisable].

[20][135-B. Grant of paid holiday to employees on the day of poll.—

(1) Every person employed in any business, trade, industrial undertaking or any other establishment and entitled to vote at an election to the House of the People or the Legislative Assembly of a State shall, on the poll, be granted a holiday.

(2) No deduction or abatement of the wages of any such person shall be made on account of a holiday having been granted in accordance with sub-section (1) and if such person is employed on the basis that he would not ordinarily receive wages for such a day, he shall nonetheless be paid for such day the wages he would have drawn had not a holiday been granted to him on that day.

(3) If an employer contravenes the provisions of sub-section (1) or sub-section (2), then such employer shall be punishable with fine which may extend to five hundred rupees.

(4) This section shall not apply to any elector whose absence may cause danger or substantial loss in respect of the employment in which he is engaged.

135-C. Liquor not to be sold given or distributed on polling day.—

(1) No spirituous, fermented or intoxicating liquors or other substances of a like nature shall be sold, given or distributed at a hotel, eating house, tavern, shop or any other place, public or private, within a polling area during the period of forty-eight hours ending with the hour fixed for the conclusion of the poll for any election in that polling area.

(2) Any person who contravenes the provisions of sub-section (1), shall be punishable with imprisonment for a term which may extend to six months, or with fine, which may extend to two thousand rupees, or with both.

(3) Where a person is convicted on an offence under this section, the spirituous, fermented or intoxicating liquors or other substances of a like nature found in his possession shall be liable to confiscation and the same shall be disposed of in such manner as may be prescribed.]

136. Other Offences and penalties therefor.—(1) A person shall be guilty of an electoral offence if any election he—

(a) fraudulently defaces or fraudulently destroys any nomination paper; or

(b) fraudulently defaces, destroys or removes any list, notice or other document affixed by or under the authority of a returning officer; or

(c) fraudulently defaces or fraudulently destroys any ballot paper or the official mark on any ballot paper or any declaration of identity or official envelope used in connection with voting by postal ballot; or

(d) without due authority supplies any ballot paper to any person or receives any ballot paper from any person or is in possession of any ballot paper; or

(e) fraudulently puts into any ballot box anything other than the ballot paper which he is authorised by law to put in; or

(f) without due authority destroys, takes, opens or otherwise interferes with any ballot box or ballot papers then in use for the purposes of the election; or

(g) fraudulently or without due authority, as the case may be, attempts to do any of the foregoing acts or wilfully aids or abets the doing of any such acts.

(2) Any person guilty of an electoral offence under this section shall, —

(a) if he is a returning officer or an assistant returning officer or a presiding officer at a polling station or any other officer or clerk employed on official duty in connection with the election, be punishable with imprisonment for a term which may extend to two years or with fine or with both;

(b) if he is any other person, be punishable with imprisonment for a term which may extend to six months or with fine or with both.

(3) For the purposes of this section, a person shall be deemed to be on official duty if his duty is to take part in the conduct of an election or part of an election including the counting of votes or to be responsible after an election for the used ballot papers and other documents in connection with such election, but the expression "official duty" shall not include any duty imposed otherwise than by or under this Act.

(4) An offence punishable under sub-section (2) shall be cognisable.

137. Prosecution regarding certain offences.—[Rep. by the Representation of the People (Amendment) Act, 1966 (47 of 1966), S. 61.]

138. Amendment of Act 5 of 1898.—[Rep. by the Repealing and Amending Act, 1957 (36 of 1957), S. 2 and the First Schedule.]

NOTES

1. Ins. by Act 40 of 1975, S. 8 (retrospectively).
2. Ins. by Act 1 of 1989, S.13 (w.e.f. 15-3-1989).
3. Subs. by Act 21 of 1996, S. 10 (w.e.f. 1-8-1996).
4. Subs. by Act 21 of 1996, S. 10 (w.e.f. 1-8-1996).
5. Subs. by Act 1 of 1989, S. 14, for certain words (w.e.f. 15-3-1989).
6. Subs. for "three months" by Act 21 of 1996, S. 11 (w.e.f. 1-8-1996).
7. Subs. for "one thousand" by Act 21 of 1996, S. 11 (w.e.f. 1-8-1996).
8. Ins. by Act 21 of 1996, S. 11 (w.e.f. 1-8-1996).
9. Ins. by Act 4 of 1986, S. 2 and Sch. (w.e.f. 15-5-1986).
10. Subs. by Act 21 of 1996, S. 12 (w.e.f. 1-8-1996).
11. Ins. by Act 21 of 1996, S. 13 (w.e.f. 1-8-1996).
12. Subs. for "fraudulently" by Act 21 of 1996, S. 14 (w.e.f. 1-8-1996).
13. Ins. by Act 1 of 1989, S. 15 (w.e.f. 15-3-1989).

14. Renumbered by Act 21 of 1996, S. 15 (w.e.f. 1-8-1996).
15. Renumbered by Act 21 of 1996, S. 15 (w.e.f. 1-8-1996).
16. Subs. for "this section" by Act 21 of 1996, S. 15 (w.e.f. 1-8-1996).
17. Subs. by Act 21 of 1996, S. 15 (w.e.f. 1-8-1996).
18. Subs. for "threatening" by Act 21 of 1996, S. 15 (w.e.f. 1-8-1996).
19. Ins. by Act 21 of 1996, S.15 (w.e.f. 1-8-1996).
20. Ss. 135B and 135C ins. by Act 21 of 1996, S. 16 (.w.e.f. 1-8-1996).

Bibliography

Documents and Reports:

District Gazateer Allahabad (1968), Uttar Pradesh District Gazateers, Allahabad, Deparment of District Gazateers, Lucknow.

Election Planning (1996), Parliament Election, 1996, District Election Office, Allahabad.

Election Planning (1996), Uttar Pradesh Assembly Election, 1996, District Election Office, Allahabad.

Government of India, Ministry of Labour (1981), *Rural Labour Enquiry 1974-75; Final Report on Wages and Earnings,* Labour Bureau, Shimla.

Government of India, Ministry of Labour (1994), *Rural Labour Enquiry 1987-88; Report on Wages and Earnings of Rural Labour Households,* Labour Bureau, Shimla.

Government of Uttar Pradesh (1995), *Annual Plan, 1995-96,* State Planning Commission, Lucknow.

Government of Uttar Pradesh (1996), *Backwardness of Uttar Pradesh—Some Reasons,* State Planning Commission, Lucknow.

Government of Uttar Pradesh (1997), *Draft Ninth Five Year Plan (1997-2000) Vols. I & II,* State Planning Commission, Lucknow.

Government of Uttar Pradesh (1998), *Statistical Bulletin—Allahabad,* Department of Economics and Statistics, Uttar Pradesh.

Government of Uttar Pradesh (1999), *Memorandum to the Eleventh Finance Commission,* Vol. I, Lucknow.

Government of Uttar Pradesh, (1992 & 1996), *Statistical Abstract, Uttar Pradesh (in Hindi),* State Planning Institute, Department of Economics and Statistics, Lucknow.

Government of Uttar Pradesh, (1995), *Inter State Comparative Statistics*, State Planning Institute Department of Economics and Statistics, Lucknow.

Government of Uttar Pradesh, (1998), *Fourth Economic Census, Uttar Pradesh (in Hindi)*, State Planning Institute, Department of Economics and Statistics, Lucknow.

Government of Uttar Pradesh, (1999-2000), *Economic Review of Uttar Pradesh (in Hindi)*, State Planning Institute, Department of Economics and Statistics, Lucknow.

Government of Uttar Pradesh, *Annual Plan 2001-2002, Vols. I & II*, State Planning Commission, Lucknow.

Government of Uttar Pradesh, *Statistical Diary, Uttar Pradesh (Annual in Hindi)*, State Planning Institute, Department of Economics and Statistics, Lucknow.

Government of India, Ministry of Planning and Programme Implementation. *National Sample Survey Organization Reports, Sarvekshana*, Department of Statistics, New Delhi.

Pachayat Raj Act (1994), *Uttar Pradesh Panchayat Raj Act, 1947* as ammended upto Act 9 of 1994, Eastern Book Company, Lucknow.

Planning Commission (1998), *Draft Ninth Five Year Plan 1997-2002*, Government of India, New Delhi.

Representation of the People Act, 1951.

Newspapers and Journals:

Dainik Jagran (Allahabad) in Hindi.
Economic and Political Weekly (Bombay).
Frontline (Banglore).
Hindu (Gurgaon).
Hindustan (Lucknow) in Hindi.
Hindustan Times (Lucknow).
India Today (New Delhi).
Journal of Peasant Studies (U.K.).
Pioneer (Lucknow).
The Indian Journal of Labour Economics.
Seminar (New Delhi).
Times of India (New Delhi).
Mainstream (New Delhi).

Books and Articles:

Abraham, A.S. (1990), OBC Forces in Full Cry, Bid for Power in Perpetuity, *Times of India*, New Delhi, September 3.

Aggarwal, J. C. & Chowdhry, N.K. (1996), *Elections in India 1952-1996*, Shipra, Delhi.

Ahmed Bashiruddin (1975), Political Stratification of the Electorate in D.L. Sheth (ed.), *Citizens and Parties.*

Akinchan, S. (1995), *Caste, Class and Politics*, Gyan Publishing House, New Delhi.

Alam Javed (1999), Is Caste Appeal Casteism? Oppressed Castes in Poltics, *Economic and Political Weekly*, March 27.

Almond, Gabriel and Verba, Sidney (1965), *The Civic Culture*, Beston Little Brown.

Atal, Yogesh, (1971), *Local Communities and National Politics*, National Publishing House, Delhi.

Bagchi, Amiya, K. (1975), *Private Investment in India*, 1900-1939, Orient Longman, London.

Bava, Noorjahan (1984), *People's Participation in Development Administration in India*, Uppal Publishing House, New Delhi.

Brass Paul, R. (1997), General Elections, 1996 in Uttar Pradesh, Divisive Struggles Influence Outcome, *Economic and Political Weekly*, September 20.

Burnham, Walter Dean (1980), The Appearance and Disappearance of American Voter, in Richard Rose (ed.) *Electoral Participation.*

Butler, D., Lahiri, A. & Roy Pranay (1989), *India Decides, Elections 1952-1989*, LM Books, New Delhi.

Chandra Kanchan and Parmar Chandrika (1997), Party Strategies in the Uttar Pradesh Assembly Elections, 1996, *Economic and Political Weekly*, February 1.

Chatterjee Partha (ed.) (1998), *State and Politics in India*, OUP, Delhi.

Chaturvedi Badrinath (1990), Plausibility and Truth; Mandal's View of Social History, *Times of India*, New Delhi, September 13.

Dastur, A.J. and Mehta, U. (1963), General Elections in Greater Bombay, *Political Science Review*, 2(2).

Dastur, A.J. et.al. (1972), *Studies in the Fourth General Elections ICSSR*, New Delhi, Allied Publishers.

Deshpande Satish (1998), Counting on Caste for Social Justice, *Times of India*, New Delhi, August 18.

Desouza, Peter R. (1996), The Accountability Factor, *Seminar*, No. 440.

Dreze Jean and Gazdar, H. (1997), "Uttar Pradesh: The Burden of

Inertia", in Jean Dreze and Amartya Sen (eds.) *Indian Development: Selected Regional Perspectives.*

Dreze Jean and Sen Amartya (eds.) (1997), *Indian Development: Selected Regional Perspectives*, Oxford University Press, New Delhi.

Duncan Ian (1999), Dalits and Politics in Rural North India: The Bahujan Samaj Party in Uttar Pradesh, *The Journal of Peasent Studies*, Vol. 27, No. 1.

Editorial (1996), The Problem, *Seminar*, No. 440.

Ganguly, B. and Ganguly, M. (1982), *Dimensions of Electoral Behaviour*, Pearl Publishers, Calcutta.

Gill, S.S. (1990), Mandal: Myth of Merit and Equity, *Times of India*, New Delhi, September 5.

Hasan Zoya (1998), *Quest for Power*, OUP, New Delhi.

Hashim, S.R. (1999), Employment and Poverty: Some Emerging Policy Issues, *The Indian Journal of Labour Economics*, Vol. 42, No. 1.

Holmstrom Mark (1976), *South Indian Factory Workers: Their Life and their World Bombay*, Orient Longman, London.

Jain Meenakshi (1996), Backward Castes and Social Change in UP and Bihar, in MN Sriniwas (ed.) *Caste—Its Twentieth Century Avtaar*; Viking Penguin India, New Delhi.

Jayaram, N. (1996), Caste and Hinduism: Changing Protean Relationship, in M.N. Sriniwas (ed.) *Caste—Its Twentieth Century Avtaar*; Viking Penguin India, New Delhi.

Karanth, G.K. (1996), Caste in Cotemporary Rural India, in M.N. Sriniwas (ed.) *Caste— Its Twentieth Century Avtaar*; Viking Penguin India, New Delhi.

Karnad, Girish (1997), Citzens as Soldiers, *Economic and Political Weekly*, March 15.

Kaviraj, Sudipto (1998), A Critique of the Passive Revolution, in Partha Chatterjee (ed.) *State and Politics in India*, Oxford University Press, New Delhi.

Kini, N.G.S. (1974), *The City Voter in India*, Abhinav Publications, New Delhi.

Kothari, Rajni (1998), Rise of the Dalits and Renewed Debate on Caste, in Partha Chaterjee (ed.) *State and Politics in India*.

Kothari, Rajni (1970), 'Introduction' in Rajni Kothari (ed.) *Caste in Indian Politics*.

___________ (1975), Continuity and Change in the Party System in D.L. Sheth (ed.), *Citizens and Parties*.

___________ (1990), Caste and Politics: The Great Secular Upsurge, *Times of India*, New Delhi, September 29.

Kumar, Anand (1999), From Negative Coalitions to Dominant Caste Democracy, *Mainstream*, Oct. 16.

Kumar, Bimal and Singh, Sunit (eds.) (2000), *Economic Review Uttar Pradesh, 1999-2000*, G.B. Pant Social Science Institute, Allahabad.

Lal, A.K. (1979), Bases of Support-Recruitment in a Parliametary Constituency, *Journal of Social and Economic Studies*, VII (I).

Lal, Pradyot and Nair, Tara (1998), *Caste vs Caste: Turbulence in Indian Politics*, Ajanta, Delhi.

Lerche Jens (1999), Politics of Poor: Agricultural Labourers and Political Transformation in Uttar Pradesh, *The Journal of Peasant Studies*, Vol. 26, Number 2/3.

Lieten, G.K. and Srivastava, Ravi (1999), *Unequal Partners*, IDPAD, Sage Publishers, New Delhi.

Mehta, Usha, Billimoria, Rosebeh and Thakkar, Usha (1981), *Women and Men Voters the Election Archieves*, Department of Civics and Politics, University of Bombay.

Mishra, Amresh (1998), Kurmis and Koeris: Emerging Third Factor, *Economic and Political Weekly*.

Omvedt Gail (1999), Dalits and Elections, *Hindu*, November 5.

Pai, Sudha (1998), New Political Trends in Uttar Pradesh—The BJP and the Lok Sabha Elections, 1998, *Economic and Political Weekly*, July 11.

Pai, Sudha (1998), The BSP in Uttar Pradesh, *Seminar*, No. 471.

Panini, M. N., (1996), The Political Economy of Caste; in M.N. Sriniwas (ed.) *Caste—Its Twentieth Century Avtaar*; Viking Penguin India, New Delhi.

Powell Jr,. G. Bringham (1980), Voting Turnout in Thirty Democracies: Partisan, Legal and Socio-Economic Influences, in Richard Rose (ed.) *Electoral Participation*.

Ramaseshan Radhika (1995), Politics and Caste, *Seminar*, No. 432.

Rose, Richards (1980), *Electoral Participation*, Sage Publication, Boverly Hills, London.

Roy, Ramashray (1975), Citizen Orientation and Patterns of Political Instability in D.L. Sheth (ed.) *Citizens and Parties*.

_________ (1973), *The Uncertain Verdict*, Orient Longman, New Delhi.

Samuel, P. Huntington and Joan, M. Nelson, No Easy Choice, *Political Participation in Developing Countries*, Cambridge Mass, Harvard University Press, 1976, p. 16.

Sheth, D.L. (ed.) (1975), *Citizens and Parties*, Allied Publishers, New Delhi.

_________ (1975), Political Development of the Electorate in D.L. Sheth (ed.), *Citizens and Parties*.

_________ (1975), Partisanship and Political Development in D. L. Sheth (ed.), *Citizens and Parties*.

_________ (1975), Social Bases of Party Sopport in D.L. Sheth (ed.), *Citizens and Parties*.

Singh, Jagpal (1998), Ambedkarisation and Assertion of Dalit Identity; Socio-Cultural Protest in Meerut District of Western Uttar Pradesh, *Economic and Political Weekly*, October 3.

Singh, Rustam (1996), Reflections on a Form, *Seminar*, No. 440.

Singh, Sunit (1999), Backwardness of Eastern UP and Migration of Rural Labourers (Hindi), *Kurukshetra*, May.

__________ (2000), Poverty and Unemployment in UP: Can the Present Strategy be Successful (Hindi) in Bimal Kumar and Sunit Singh (eds.) *Economic Review Uttar Pradesh, 1999-2000*, G. B. Pant, Social Science Institute, Allahabad.

Singh, Ajit Kumar (2000), Uttar Pradesh Economy under Plans: Low Growth and Structural Stagnation, *Man and Development*, June.

Singh, L.R. (ed.) (1993), *Studies in 1991 Parliamentary Elections*, G.B. Pant, Social Science Institute, Allahabad.

Sirsikar, V.M. (1977), Caste and Politics, Romesh Thapar (ed.) *Tribe, Caste and Religion*, Macmillan.

__________ (1966), *Political Behaviour in India*, Mahaktalas, Bombay.

Sriniwas, M.N. (1990), The Mandal Formula: Backwardness-Caste vs Individual, *Times of India*, New Delhi, September 18.

Sriniwas, M.N., Shah, A.M. and Baviskar, B.S. (1990), Kothari's Illusion of Secular Upsurge, *Times of India*, New Delhi, October 15.

Srivastava, Ravi, S. (1999), Rural Labour in Uttar Pradesh: Emerging Features of Subsistence, Contradiction and Resistance, *The Journal of Peasant Studies*, Vol. 26, Number 2/3.

Tewari, G.C. (1993), Parliament Election in Nainital in L.R. Singh (ed.) *Studies in 1991 Parliamentary Elections in Uttar Pradesh* (mimeographed), GB Pant Social Science Institute, Allahabad.

Varma, S.P. and Bhambhri, C.P. (1967), *Elections and Political Consciousness in India*, Meenakshi, Meerut.

Wright, Gillian (1995), The decline of Congress: The Rise of Mulayam, The Matters of UP, *Seminar 432*, pp. 19-23.

Yadav, Yogendra (1998), Reconfiguration in Indian Politics: State Assembly Elections 1993-1995, in Partha Chaterjee (ed.) *State and Politics in India*.

Zerinini-Brotel Jasmine (1999), Options in Uttar Pradesh, *Seminar*, No. 480.

Index

Abdul Kalam, APJ 126
Achievement Status Index 13, 55, 60
— Basis of 58
— Distribution of Voters in Different Caste Groups 58
Adult Citizens 2
Age-wise Distribution of Voters 53-54
Agricultural
— and Construction Labourers 56
— Labourer Household 27
— Labour/Rural Labour 36
— State 30
Ahirs of North India 107
AIADMK 131
Allahabad District 39, 42, 44, 62
— Area and Demographic Statistics of 40
— Literary Percentage in 40
— North 118
— Parliamentary Constituency in the 62
— Scheduled Caste Population 40
Ambedkar 84
— Gram Vikas Yojna 83
— Status 82
— Installation of 81
Analysis of Electorate Attitude 73
Annual Growth Rate of Cultivators 20
Annual Plans 17
Area of Operational Holdings 29
Assembly Segments 45, 49, 51
— of Allahabad Parliamentary Constituency 104
Atal, Yogesh 9
'Ayodhya Martyrs' 137
Backbone of BSP in UP 104
Bahujan Samaj Party (BSP) 102, 171
Base of Erstwhile Bharatiya Janasangha 116
Basic Ingradient of the Democratic Process 1
Basic Value for the Success of Democratics System 194
Basis of Landholdings 35
Beginning of the Debate of Eighties 182
Bhandari, Romesh 86, 133
Bind 114, 164
BJP 101, 109, 116, 118
— Largest Single Party 124
— Lead Coalition Government 130
— Primary Worry 88
Brahmins 115, 165, 169
— Population in India 115
BSP and BJP 118
BSP-BJP Coalition 80
BSP Leaders 159

Caste
— Based Groups 178
— Mobilisation 4
— Federation 119
— Groups of Voters 43
— Politicization of 7, 178
— Wise Distribution of Electorate 113
— Wise Distribution of Voters 50-51
— Sample 92
Cauvery Water Dispute 126
Central Government 138
Chamar Community 161
Chamars 103, 105, 107, 158
Chamars and Pasi 107

Characteristics of Sample 139
Chief Justice of Tamil Nadu High Court 126
Chowdhary Charan Singh 108
Christian Missionaries—Activities of the 129
Classification of Voters by Education Levels 53
Congress 157-59, 171-72, 188
— Emergence of 142
— Leaders 128
— Party 4, 102, 105
Conversion of Hindu Poor 129
Creation of New District 83

Dastoor, Alooj and Usha Mehta 8
Demolition of Babri Masjid 92
Department of Atomic Energy 126
Description of the Questionnaire 64-67
Determinants of Votes 99
Determinants of Voting Decisions 74, 145
Different Caste and Caste Groups—Scenario Among 148
Different Size of Operational Land-holdings 35
Distribution of Voters 59
Dominant Backward Caste of the Region 110
Dominant Neo-Rich 183, 185

Effective Sample and Sample Loss 46
Election Commission 10, 61, 87, 173
Election Environment 99, 145
— Terms of 100
Electoral Exercises 1
Electroal Politics of U.P. 183
Electoral System 69-70
Emergence and Strengthening of Neo-Rich 184
Emergency Days 85
Expansion of Communication and Means of Transportation 48
Experienced Field Investigators 67
Exploited Castes 178

Features of the Rural Labour in the State 36
Five Years Plan
— V 17, 21
— VI, VII, VIII 21
Forerunners in Organizing Backward Castes 107
Forward-Backward Divide in the *BJP* 136

Gandhi, Indira 131
Gandhi, Sonia 159
Gangetic Plains and Vindhyan Plateau 39
Ganguli, Bangendu and Mira Ganguli 9
General Elections 2, 10, 131
— Fourth 5, 7, 9
Giani, Jail Singh 112
Green Revolution
— Beneficiary of 108
— Post 4
Group Theory of Politics 5
Gupta, Inderjeet 133

Harijan Act 85, 98, 137
— Misuse of 88
— Politics of 84
Hierarchy of Occupation 56
High Level of Sample Loss 47
Highest Birth Rate among All Indian States 16
Highly Educated Person in Rural Areas 36
Human Development Index 18
Hung Assembly in U.P. 79
Hung Parliament and Coalition Government 124

Impact of Liberalization and Privatization in Economic Policies 187
Important Determinant of the Campaign 100
Important Place in Indian Economic and Political System 17
Index of Democratization 1
Indian Council of Social Service Research 9
Indian Political System 4

Janata Party 101-02, 108
Jat Leadership 108
Jayalalita 126
Jayalalita's AIADMK 125
Joshi, Prof. Murli Manohar 125

Kalyan Singh 82, 84-86, 120, 132-36, 183
— Government 87
— Thakurs in the 89
Kargil War 131
Kayastha 118-19, 167-68
Key Players of Competitive Politics 194
King Shursen 112
Kol 104, 106, 161
Kothari, Rajni 5
Kurmi 110, 162
— Caste 104
Kushwahas 111-12, 163

Land Owned and Land Operated in U.P. 28
Largest Group after the Chamars 105
Largest State in India in Terms of Area Fourth 16
Leaders of Trader Community 117
Local Level Caste-Leaders 188
Local Self Government 192
Lohia, Rammanohar 82, 108
Lok Sabha Constituency of
— Allahabad 10
— Phulpur 44
— Poona 8
— West Bengal 9
Lok Sabha Elections 12, 61, 87, 134, 177
— Eleventh 78, 123
— 1977 and 1980 50
Low Growth Rate and Increasing Population Pressure 38
Low Level of Sample Loss 47

Main Contender Power 79
Main Determinant of the Nature of Voting 3
Male Agricultural Worker--Statewise Productivity 25
Mandal and Masjid Movement 116
Mandal Movement 7
Marginal Farmers 41
Mayawati 79-80, 83-84, 86, 104, 120, 137
— and BSP 81
— Government 133
— Terms 82
Mechanisation of Agriculture 34
Medium Status Category 59
Memorial of Kothari Brothers 137
Most Backward Castes 156
Muslims 103, 150
— Community 92

Nature of Castes in India 6
NDA 124
— Government 125
Neo-Rich and Rural Poor 186
Neo-Rich Yadavas of Nineties 109
Nepal and China 15
Newer Castes Combinations 88
Next Rank Brahmins in U.P. 115
Non BJP Leaders 120
Non-Yadav Backward Castes 82
Northern Parts of India 15
NSS Data 24
— on Land Ownership 27
— Statistics 30

OBCs 92, 94, 101-02, 108, 116, 155, 157, 178
Occupational Distribution of Votes 52
Oligarchic Tendency in the State 194
Organised Sector 27
ORG-MARG 127-28
Other MBCs 165

Pasi 104-05
Pasi Ruler 106
Pattern of Asset Distribution 33
Patterns of Electorates Preference 119
People of India 78, 124
Phenomenon of Caste 4
Phenomenon of Disguised Unemployment 23-24
Phoolan Devi 114
Planning Commission of India—RPC of 8-9

Planning Commission of U.P. 26
Political Participation Index 173
Political Parties 50, 70, 80-81, 182, 188
— and Candidates 3
— Policies and Programmes of the 144
— State of Disillusionment 71
Political
— Players 80
— Powers 194
— Rights of the Citizens 2
Poorest States of India—One of the 23
Populous States in India 15
Practice of Share Cropping 37
Predominance of Rural Sector 38
Principal Source of Identification 5
Purpose of Pre-Testing 45

Rate of Unemployment in U.P. 24
Reason for Increasing Unemployment 126
Regimentation Strategy 191
Relative Hierarchy of Occupation 56
Role of Castes in Indian Politics 7
Roy, Ramashray 9
Rural Areas of State 27
— of U.P. 32
Rural Leadership 4
Rural Women 47
— Voters 70

Samajvadi Party 101, 109, 113, 116, 118-19, 169
— Chief of 137
Scheduled Castes 28, 80, 84, 92, 95, 102-03, 140, 154 *et. al.*
— largest Group among the 106
— and Muslims 50
Sectoral Composition of State Income in U.P. 20
Seth, D.L. 102
Share-Croppers 38
Singh, L.R. 10
— Raj Nath 88
Siriniwas 7
Siriskar, U.M. 8
Social Scientists 2-3
— Challenge Task for 54
Social Stratification in Indian Society 54
Socio-Economic Status (SES) 54-55
Srivastava, Dr. K.P. 118, 168
Stratified Society 43
Structure of Social Networks 179
— Configuration of 180
Support Base of Congress 172

Thakur 115, 166
Three Caste Groups 92, 101
Total Population of the State 16
Traders 56
Tripathi, Kesari Nath 85
Typical Feature in the State 119

Undisputed Leaders of the Backward Castes 108
Upper Caste Electorate 103
Upper Caste Hindus 103, 156
Urban Voters 49
Urban Women 70
Use of Caste and Religion 146

Vaishya 116, 166
— Community 117
Vajpayee, Atal Behari 124, 130, 135, 138
Value of the Determinant of Votes 99
Various Forms of Political Participation 96
Vidhan Sabha of U.P. 82
Virangana, Uda Devi 106
Vishwa Hindu Parishad and Bajrang Dal 129
Vishwakarmas 111-12, 114, 163

Welfare State 192
Workforce in Manufacturing Sector 22
World Sixth Nuclear Weapon State 127

Yadav, Laloo 108
— Leadership in U.P.
— Mulayam Singh 79, 81-82, 86, 108-10, 120, 157, 159, 182
— and Kalyan Singh 83
Yadavas 107-09, 161